THE
WESLEYAN
TRADITION

THE

WESLEYAN
TRADITION

A PARADIGM FOR RENEWAL

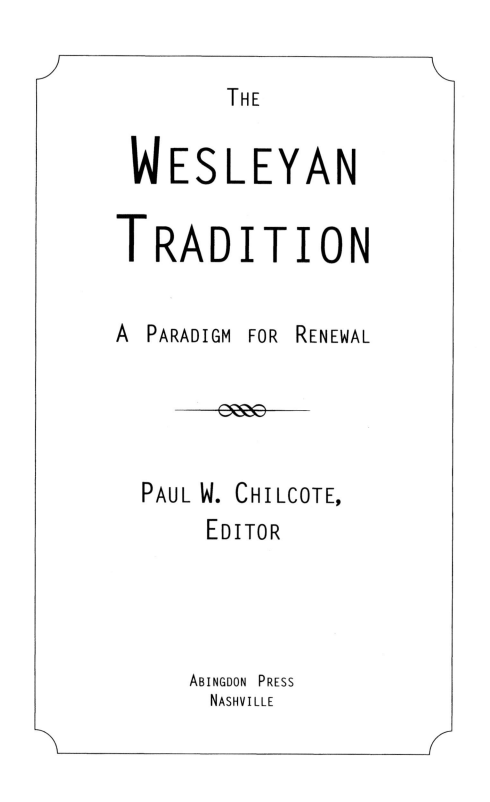

PAUL W. CHILCOTE,
EDITOR

ABINGDON PRESS
NASHVILLE

THE WESLEYAN TRADITION
A Paradigm for Renewal

Copyright © 2002 by Abingdon Press

All rights reserved.

This book is printed on acid-free paper.

Library of Congress Cataloging-in-Publication Data

The Wesleyan tradition : a paradigm for renewal / Paul W. Chilcote, editor.
  p. cm.
Includes bibliographical references.
ISBN: 978-0-687-09563-6
  1. Methodist Church—Doctrines. I. Chilcote, Paul Wesley, 1954-

BX8331.3 .W47 2002
287—dc21

2001006908

03 04 05 06 07 08 09 10 11—10 9 8 7 6 5 4 3 2

MANUFACTURED IN THE UNITED STATES OF AMERICA

For
Edmund W. Robb Jr.

And in memory of
Albert C. Outler

Both avid practitioners
of the Wesleyan Tradition

CONTENTS

PREFACE

Christians who stand in the Wesleyan tradition have an amazing history upon which to build. Our past is important to us. We know that God calls us to faithfulness now, and we move into the new millennium with hope. The future is of equal importance because the church is entering an era of grave responsibility. What does it mean to be a Christian in the Wesleyan tradition today? What are the foundations of the tradition, and how are we to rediscover these essential roots? What will our role be in a global parish that is characterized by both crisis and opportunity?

We will address these kinds of questions throughout the book. We will examine the legacy of early Methodism as a movement of Christian renewal and will project the role of the Wesleyan tradition in the future. The United Methodist Church, like the larger Church, is always in need of reform. A process of rediscovery—a reclaiming of the Wesleyan vision of Christian life—is required within our tradition if the global church community is going to chart its course successfully into the future. While building on the past, we also need to look to the future.

Christianity is essentially a religion of discovery, transformation, and liberation. The early Methodists knew this. At Christianity's core is the story of God's amazing love made visible in the person of Jesus Christ. God's unconditional love—the true and solid foundation upon which all life is built—must be discovered by individuals and communities. This is the most important discovery for anyone to make. When people anywhere encounter this amazing love, it transforms their hopes and dreams; it changes their lives. God's children begin to love because they have experienced what it means to be loved by God. Having made this discovery and having experienced this transformation, all are free to love themselves and others. All are liberated by the power of God's Spirit—by the presence of the risen Christ—in their lives.

When Christianity is understood in this way, "faith" becomes a way of life. Gratitude is faith's primary characteristic. To be a Christian means to walk in grace, to seek the fullness of God's will, and to be transformed spiritually by the love of Jesus. This also is the essence of the Wesleyan tradition. By its very nature, this tradition is bent toward renewal because renewal is making all things new—the essence of love. The keys to faithful Christian discipleship, therefore, are a willingness to change, the expectation that God's grace is always available, and a passion for God to show his love through our lives. Renewal, expectation, and compassion. Discovery, transformation, and freedom. Grace and love. This is the language of the fluent, Wesleyan Christian.

It is my conviction that this is a language we need to hear spoken more frequently in the church today. I believe that our world is yearning—even groaning—for such a language, not only for words to be heard, but also for a language to be learned and spoken and sung. All of us desperately need new ears for hearing, new eyes for seeing, and new hands for reaching out and holding on to one another. We need renewal. We need to learn how to speak in God's love again. It is in this spirit of urgency that this volume is offered for the renewal of the church. We pray that God's Spirit will revive us again.

Albert C. Outler once said that the expression "Wesleyan evangelical" is redundant. If you are a Wesleyan Christian, then you are, by definition, evangelical. The same thing could be said of the phrase "Wesleyan Revival." There is a certain redundancy here as well. If you are Wesleyan, then you are necessarily concerned about revival in the life of the church. One of the main purposes of this volume is to identify some of the primary characteristics of "renewal in the Wesleyan spirit" and offer them anew for the life of the church today. As you will discover, many aspects of this Wesleyan paradigm of renewal are shared with other reforming movements throughout the history of the church. But the way all are dynamically combined by the Wesleys makes their movement unique and offers so much to us today.

In an introductory chapter, I lay out a panoramic view of this book by describing salient aspects of Christian renewal and the Wesleyan paradigm, in particular. The primary aspects of this model are captured in the language of living Word, saving faith, holistic spirituality, accountable discipleship, formative worship, and missional vocation. The chapters that follow develop these themes and apply them to the church today.

In chapter 2, Joel B. Green explores biblical authority in the contemporary church and the way scripture informs both Christian formation and mission. Ben Witherington III, in chapter 3, carries us back to the central theme of Jesus' ministry and Paul's preaching—namely, the reign of God—and demonstrates how a renewed emphasis on God's dominion can revolutionize the church, as it did in Wesley's day. In chapter 4, Yeo Khiok-khng reassesses the principal theme of the Protestant reformations—justification by grace through faith—to help us experience and understand how Christ makes trust possible in our lives. How the evangelical conception of salvation—our inheritance from the apostle Paul through Wesley—is still a guiding force for personal and corporate renewal today is an important question that Ted A. Campbell explores in chapter 5.

Steve Harper and Rebekah Miles, in their respective chapters 6 and 7, offer insight into the renewing force of works of piety and works of mercy as spiritual formation today, drawing particular attention to the cultivation of the grace-filled life and the dangers inherent to our abandonment of the poor. In chapter 8, Gregory S. Clapper describes the transformation that takes place in people's lives when disciples are made in community. Stephen A. Seamands, in chapter 9, reminds us that the quest for holiness in the Wesleyan way will most likely lead to a form of costly discipleship that challenges the norms of our age but also opens a way to true blessedness in life.

In chapter 10, Lester Ruth revisits the "Word and Table" synthesis that affords us a balanced model for worship today, while in my own essay, "A Faith That Sings," in chapter 11, I explore the renewing influence of Christian song. In chapter 12, Laceye C. Warner provides a paradigmatic guide for the recovery and reappropriation of Wesleyan evangelism in our time that includes the central features of preaching, discipleship, and mission. Amy Laura Hall, in chapter 13, closes the volume with a description of how God has shaped love in the hearts of the Methodist people.

The principal founders of A Foundation for Theological Education (AFTE), Albert C. Outler and Edmund Robb Jr., were inspired by a vision. Their primary passion was to rediscover the Wesleyan way—the Wesleyan tradition—in order to renew the church in our time. For some twenty-five years, this organization has provided financial support to nearly one hundred evangelical scholars who have pursued doctoral studies in a wide range of theological disciplines around the world. Many of them are making profound contributions to the life of the church today. All of the contributors to this volume are John Wesley Scholars, recipients of fellowship awards from AFTE. They all speak from within the church and to the church they love, using, as Wesley himself advocated, "plain words for plain people."

In 1992, Alan G. Padgett edited a volume entitled *The Mission of the Church in Methodist Perspective: The World Is My Parish* (Lewiston, N.Y.: E. Mellen Press), the first collection of essays authored exclusively by John Wesley Scholars. The present work is the second such volume. The contribution that this new collection makes, however, is exploring the vision of renewal that gave birth to the Wesleyan tradition and articulating this vision anew for the renewal of the church today. It is a manifesto. It is the heartfelt desire of the contributors who have committed themselves through AFTE to the rediscovery of vital, scriptural Christianity. It is a memorial, moreover, to the witness of Dr. Outler and presented in honor of the life and ministry of Dr. Robb. Our hope is that we have not only caught their spirit but also preserved their vision.

I need to make several personal acknowledgments as well. First, a word of thanks to Asbury Theological Seminary for the approval of my sabbatical and the provision of a sabbatical grant for my work on this volume. I completed much of my editorial work at Duke University Divinity School where I read, studied, and ruminated in the Baker Methodist Studies Center as the first resident scholar. Because I was Frank Baker's last doctoral student, this was quite an honor and privilege for me, and not a little nostalgic! A special word of thanks to Roger Loyd who provided such wonderful assistance to me, along with Jennifer Woodruff, his assistant in the Center and another John Wesley Scholar who has devoted much energy to the Baker Collection. To colleagues and students on both the Duke and Asbury campuses, my word of thanks for kind words of encouragement, shared meals, and the potency of

Christian fellowship. I offer a special word of appreciation to Bill and Cely Chicurel who provided hospitality for me during my visits to North Carolina. Our friendship is long and deep, and I am grateful to God for them both. My gratitude as well to Beverly Schweizer for her assistance in preparing the index. My family, of course, deserves the ultimate expression of my thanks because they live with such a project as much as I do. They live out the vision of the Wesleyan tradition daily in their lives. Their simple witness to vital Christianity can quickly fan the ashes of my own faith into white heat.

Aldersgate Day, May 24, 2001
Paul W. Chilcote

CONTRIBUTORS

Ted A. Campbell is President of Garrett Evangelical Theological Seminary in Evanston, Illinois. He completed his doctoral work in Wesley studies at Southern Methodist University in Dallas. Having taught previously at the Methodist Theological School in Ohio and Duke University Divinity School, he is also an active participant in the Oxford Institute of Methodist Theological Studies and serves as President of the Charles Wesley Society. Dr. Campbell has written widely in the areas of Methodist studies and Christian doctrine. His most recent books are *Methodist Doctrine: The Essentials* (Nashville: Abingdon Press, 1999) and *Christian Confessions: A Historical Introduction* (Louisville, Ky.: Westminster John Knox Press, 1996). John Wesley Scholars Class of 1979.

Paul W. Chilcote, who was Dr. Frank Baker's final doctoral student at Duke University, is Associate Dean and Professor of Historical Theology and Wesleyan Studies at Asbury Theological Seminary and serves as Academic Dean of the Florida campus. He previously held the Nippert Chair of Church History at the Methodist Theological School in Ohio, and also taught in Zimbabwe at Africa University, in Kenya at St. Paul's United Theological College, and in Bristol, England, at Wesley College. Dr. Chilcote's most recent books include *She Offered Them Christ: The Legacy of Women Preachers in Early Methodism* (Nashville: Abingdon Press, 1993), *An African Journal of Hope* (1998), *Praying in the Wesleyan Spirit: 52 Prayers for Today* (Nashville: Upper Room Books, 2001), and *Her Own Story: Autobiographical Portraits of Early Methodist Women* (Nashville: Kingswood Books, 2001). Class of 1979.

Gregory S. Clapper is a husband, father, minister, and professor. Dr. Clapper has served as Senior Minister of Trinity United Methodist Church in Waverly, Iowa, and is presently Associate

Professor of Philosophy and Religion and Associate Director of the Lantz Center for Christian Vocations at the University of Indianapolis. His books include *John Wesley on Religious Affections: His Views on Experience and Emotion and Their Role in the Christian Life and Theology* (Metuchen, N.J.: Scarecrow Press, 1989), *As If the Heart Mattered: A Wesleyan Spirituality* (Nashville: Upper Room Books, 1997), and *When the World Breaks Your Heart: Spiritual Ways to Live with Tragedy* (Nashville: Upper Room Books, 1999). His writing also has appeared in *Quarterly Review*, *Christian Century*, *Studies in Formative Spirituality*, *Methodist History*, and *The Wesleyan Theological Journal*. Class of 1979.

Joel B. Green received his graduate theological training at Perkins School of Theology and holds the Ph.D. in New Testament studies from the University of Aberdeen, Scotland. He is currently Dean of the School of Theology and Professor of New Testament Interpretation, Asbury Theological Seminary. His research has focused above all on the Gospel of Luke and the Acts of the Apostles, as well as on theological hermeneutics. He is the author or editor of sixteen books, and his most recent publications include the major commentary *The Gospel of Luke* (Grand Rapids: William B. Eerdmans, 1997) and *Between Two Horizons: Spanning New Testament Studies and Systematic Theology* (coedited with Max Turner; Grand Rapids: William B. Eerdmans, 2000). Class of 1982.

Amy Laura Hall is Assistant Professor of Theological Ethics at Duke University Divinity School, having completed her doctoral studies at Yale University. Her primary interests include the retrieval of traditional Christian texts for moral discernment, Kierkegaard studies, and Christian bioethics. Her first book, *Kierkegaard and the Treachery of Love* (forthcoming from Cambridge University Press), examines issues related to intimacy. She is published in a wide range of scholarly journals and is currently working on a second book related to parenthood. As an ordained pastor in The United Methodist Church, she has served both inner-city and suburban parishes. Class of 1995.

Steve Harper is Vice President and Professor of Spiritual Formation at the Florida campus of Asbury Theological Seminary in Orlando. He received his Ph.D. in Historical Theology from Duke University, with a special emphasis on Wesley's spirituality. He is the author of twelve books, including *John Wesley's Message for Today* (Grand Rapids: Zondervan, 1983), *Devotional Life in the Wesleyan Tradition: A Workbook* (Nashville: Upper Room Books, 1995), his most recent book, *Prayer and Devotional Life of United Methodists* (Nashville: Abingdon Press, 1999), as well as numerous articles. He and his wife, Jeannie, have two children and two grandchildren. Class of 1977.

Yeo Khiok-khng, a Malaysian by birth, is a clergyperson, writer, and teacher in New Testament studies. Educated at Garrett-Evangelical Theological Seminary and Northwestern University and having taught previously in Hong Kong, he is currently Associate Professor of New Testament Interpretation at G.E.T.S. He has preached and lectured in major universities and seminaries throughout China and Hong Kong and serves as consultant to major Asian organizations, such as the International Bible Society Translation Committee. Having published eleven books and translated the Nag Hammadi Library into Chinese, his most recent book in English is *What Has Jerusalem to Do with Beijing?* (Harrisburg, Pa.: Trinity Press International, 1998). Class of 1990.

Rebekah Miles, Associate Professor of Ethics at Perkins School of Theology, Southern Methodist University, received her Ph.D. from the University of Chicago. She is the author of *The Pastor as Moral Guide* (Minneapolis: Fortress Press, 1999) and *The Bonds of Freedom: Feminist Theology and Christian Realism* (New York: Oxford University Press, 2001) and coauthor of *Wesley and the Quadrilateral: Renewing the Conversation* (Nashville: Abingdon Press, 1997). A native Arkansan, Miles grew up in a Methodist family and is a clergy member of the Little Rock Conference of The United Methodist Church. She and her husband, Len Delony, a spiritual director, have two daughters. Class of 1988.

Lester Ruth is Assistant Professor of Worship and Liturgy at Asbury Theological Seminary. He comes to that position from Yale University's Divinity School and Institute of Sacred Music. Prior to Yale, he served several pastoral appointments in the Texas Annual

Conference, of which he is a member. His doctorate in liturgical history is from the University of Notre Dame. Ruth is the author of *A Little Heaven Below: Worship at Early Methodist Quarterly Meetings* (Nashville: Kingswood Books, 2000) and *Accompanying the Journey: A Handbook for Sponsors*, published by Discipleship Resources as part of its Christian Initiation Series (Nashville: Discipleship Resources, 1997). Class of 1991.

Stephen A. Seamands is Professor of Christian Doctrine at Asbury Theological Seminary. Prior to his calling to theological education, he pastored United Methodist churches in southern New Jersey for eleven years. Dr. Seamands has earned degrees from Asbury College (B.A.), Asbury Theological Seminary (M.Div.), Princeton Theological Seminary (Th.M.), and Drew University (Ph.D.). He is the author of three books including *Holiness of Heart and Life* (Nashville: Abingdon Press, 1990) and *A Conversation with Jesus* (Wheaton, Ill.: Victor Books, 1994). In addition to teaching and working with seminary students, Dr. Seamands also enjoys leading retreats and seminars and conducting spiritual renewal weekends in local churches. Class of 1977.

Laceye C. Warner is the E. Stanley Jones Assistant Professor of the Practice of Evangelism and Methodist Studies at Duke Divinity School. She completed her doctoral work in Church History at Trinity College, University of Bristol in England. Having taught at Garrett-Evangelical Theological Seminary, her research interests focus on the evangelistic work of women in Wesleyan traditions, particularly in the role of the Deaconess. An ordained elder in full connection with the Texas Annual Conference, she has served in British Methodist churches and engaged in consultation with numerous churches on the theology and practice of evangelism. Class of 1996.

Ben Witherington III joined the faculty of Asbury Theological Seminary in 1995 after teaching previously at Ashland Theological Seminary, High Point College, Duke University Divinity School, and Gordon-Conwell Theological Seminary. He received his doctorate in New Testament studies from the University of Durham in England. A prolific author, he has written fifteen books and six commentaries, including *The Acts of the Apostles: A Socio-Rhetorical Commentary* (Grand Rapids: William B. Eerdmans, 1998), *Conflict and Community in Corinth: A Socio-Rhetorical Commentary on 1 and 2 Corinthians* (Grand Rapids: William B. Eerdmans, 1995), and *Grace in Galatia: A Commentary on St. Paul's Letter to the Galatians* (Grand Rapids: William B. Eerdmans, 1998). Two of his most critically acclaimed works, *The Jesus Quest: The Third Search for the Jew of Nazareth* (Downers Grove, Ill.: InterVarsity Press, 1995) and *Paul Quest: The Renewed Search for the Jew of Tarsus* (Downers Grove, Ill.: InterVarsity Press, 1998), both received coveted *Christianity Today* Book Awards in their respective years. Class of 1977.

A WORLD METHODIST
AFFIRMATON

Following the sixteenth World Methodist Conference in Singapore in 1991, the Executive Committee established a special Work Group for the task of developing a substantive theological paper on the question of diversity and pluralism, focusing in particular on the Wesleyan perspective. The consultative group met subsequently in the summer of 1995 under the leadership of Dr. Norman E. Dewire. One of the documents produced by this committee is entitled "Wesleyan Essentials of the Christian Faith." This statement, including affirmations about Wesleyan beliefs, service, common life, worship, and witness, was adopted by the World Methodist Conference meeting in Rio de Janeiro in 1996.

Since I had been involved in laying a foundation for the work of this task force at the invitation of Dr. Dewire, and since I had an intimate knowledge of the process that led to the creation of this document, he invited me to prepare a "liturgical expression" of the approved Essentials statement. An initial draft of the litany was circulated, and Schuyler Rhodes and Geoffrey Wainwright made helpful editorial comments that shaped the final product. It is appropriate to include this affirmation at the beginning of this volume on the Wesleyan Tradition.

—Dr. Paul W. Chilcote

We confess the Christian faith,
  once delivered to the saints:
  shaped by the Holy Scriptures,
  guided by the apostolic teaching,
  and rooted in the grace of God,
    which is ever transforming our lives
    and renewing our minds in the image of Christ.

SPIRIT OF FAITH, COME DOWN,
REVEAL THE THINGS OF GOD.

We worship and give our allegiance to the Triune God;
    gracious to create and mighty to redeem,
    ever ready to comfort, lead, and guide,
    ever present to us in the means of grace,
        uniting us in Baptism and nourishing us in
            the Supper of the Lord,
    who calls us in our worship to become
      sacred instruments of justice and peace,
      to love and serve others
        with a faith that makes us dance and sing.

O FOR A THOUSAND TONGUES TO SING
MY GREAT REDEEMER'S PRAISE.

We bear witness to Jesus Christ in the world
      through word, deed, and sign, earnestly seeking
        to proclaim God's will for the salvation
          of all humankind,
        to embody God's love through acts
          of justice, peace, mercy, and healing,
      and to celebrate God's reign here and now,
        even as we anticipate the time when God's rule
        will have full sway throughout the world.

JESUS, THOU ART ALL COMPASSION,
PURE, UNBOUNDED LOVE THOU ART.

We will strive with God through the power of the Holy Spirit
    for a common heart and life, binding all believers together;
      and knowing that the love we share in Christ
        is stronger than our conflicts,
        broader than our opinions,
        and deeper than the wounds
          we inflict on one another,
      we commit ourselves to the solidarity
        of nurture, outreach, and witness,
          remembering our gospel commitment to love our neighbors
            whoever and wherever they may be.

HE BIDS US BUILD EACH OTHER UP;
  AND, GATHERED INTO ONE,
TO OUR HIGH CALLING'S GLORIOUS HOPE
  WE HAND IN HAND GO ON.

We will work together in God's name,
  believing that our commitment comes to life in our actions:
    Like Christ, we seek to serve, rather than to be served,
      and to be filled with the energy of love.
    With God's help we will express this love through
      our sensitivity to context and culture,
      our compassion for the last and the least,
      and our commitment to a holiness of heart and life
        that refuses to separate conversion and justice,
        piety and mercy, faith and love.

TO SERVE THE PRESENT AGE,
  MY CALLING TO FULFILL;
O MAY IT ALL MY POWERS ENGAGE
  TO DO MY MASTER'S WILL!

1

THE WESLEYAN TRADITION

A PARADIGM OF RENEWAL FOR THE CONTEMPORARY CHURCH

Paul W. Chilcote

The Wesleyan tradition arose from within the Church of England during the eighteenth century as a movement of spiritual renewal.[1] John and Charles Wesley, who gave leadership to the Revival that bore their name, were loyal priests within the church, loved it with every fiber of their being, and above all else dedicated their lives to the rediscovery of what they called "primitive" or "scriptural Christianity." In a sermon published late in his life, John Wesley proclaimed: "How great a thing it is to be a Christian, to be a real, inward, scriptural Christian! Conformed in heart and life to the will of God!"[2] Wesley's primary concern was for the realization of God's dream in every person and in our world. He enabled his followers to discover their true identity as the children of God. He empowered them for ministry by providing means for them to uncover their giftedness and to grow in grace. Wesley's quest was for Christian wholeness, for holiness of heart and life, for faith working by love. His driving passion was to bring balance and vitality to the Christian life and to restore it to the church he loved.

The Wesleyan paradigm of renewal, while both predictable (historic) and distinctive (contextual), was also very controversial in the eighteenth century. Instead of waiting for people to come to him to hear his message of God's grace and love, he took the good news of Jesus Christ to them wherever they were. He began his so-called field preaching in 1739, and it is probably right to date the beginning of the Evangelical Revival and the birth of Methodism from the important events of that year. During the previous year, however, in 1738, both John (1703–1791) and his brother Charles (1707–1788) experienced important defining moments in their lives. While they never fixated on these spiritual breakthroughs as if they were ends in themselves, they did experience God's presence in their lives at that time in a profoundly transforming way. They had known that love was at the center—the heart—of God. Indeed, they had committed the entirety of their lives to the church that bore witness to that love. But they had never really experienced the unconditional love of God in their lives in a way that was fully transforming. These experiences—the conversions of 1738 and the mission of 1739—are important. At the core of these defining moments in their lives was God's grace offered freely to them and their reciprocal offer of the fullness of Christ to others under the guidance of the Spirit.

In their effort to live out this newfound life of grace with integrity, the Wesleys held together aspects of the Christian faith that are often torn apart. This, in fact, is one of their most profound contributions to the life of the church and to the understanding of renewal. Faith and works are presented as distinct, but not separate. Likewise, personal and social dimensions of life in Christ—the form and the power of godliness, Word and Sacrament, truth and unity, faith and love—are held together. This consistent pattern reflects the central theme of Wesley's own life and ministry, namely, "faith working by love leading to holiness of heart and life." The Wesleys not only proclaimed this message boldly in their preaching and singing but also lived it. They practiced what they preached and sang. In order to explore these issues most fruitfully, it will be necessary to examine briefly how God has renewed the church throughout its history. And then, after focusing on the Wesleyan paradigm of renewal in more detail, we can make some important observations about the applicability of this model in the life of the church today. This introductory chapter and especially the articulation of the characteristics of renewal that are part and parcel of the Wesleyan spirit will provide a panoramic view of the concerns to be explored in the chapters that follow.

Movements of Renewal
in the History of the Church

A famous Latin dictum, *ecclesia semper reformanda*, simply means "a church [is] always in need of reform." In other words, renewal is a permanent task of the community of faith. The story of God's people, of both ancient Israel and the Christian church, is a drama in which, over and over again, God has stirred the community of faith to renewal. Despite this obvious fact, it is interesting that so few studies of church history have been written from this perspective. "The most important contribution which the study of its own history can and should make to the life of the Church," the Dutch ecumenical theologian Visser 't Hooft once observed, "is to teach it how its Lord operates through judgment and renewal."[3] His primary concern was that such an exploration would demonstrate the amazing capacity for the revitalization characteristic of the church through the ages.

When we look back to extraordinary events of renewal in the life of the church, such as mendicant monasticism, the great Protestant reforming movements of the sixteenth century, Pietism, the Second Vatican Council, and the charismatic, ecumenical, and liturgical movements of our own recent past, what are the primary characteristics we can discern? Risking oversimplification, I want to look at six primary signs of renewal, which are not necessarily characteristics present in every movement but are dramatically revealing the work of the Spirit in the church.[4] The renewal of the Christian community is often characterized by the rediscovery of the *living Word*, the rekindling of *saving faith*, the promotion of *holistic spirituality*, the development of various forms of *accountable discipleship*, the community's reorientation around *formative worship*, and the affirmation of a *missional vocation* as the church's primary reasons for being. Before we see how these signs were manifest in the Wesleyan Revival, let me illustrate each from previous movements in the history of the church.

The rediscovery of the living Word and the rekindling of saving faith

I will take the first two together because they are so powerfully illustrated by the reform of the German church under the leadership of Martin Luther in the sixteenth century. The great watch cries of that age were *sola scriptura* (scripture alone) and *sola fide* (faith alone). The Protestant Reformation at its onset was characterized by its rediscovery of the Bible and its emphasis on salvation, by faith, as a gift from God. Indeed, the two were inseparably linked in the experience of Luther himself. He describes his great breakthrough in this way:

> I greatly longed to understand Paul's Epistle to the Romans and nothing stood in the way but that one expression, "the justice of God".... Night and day I pondered until I saw the connection between the justice of God and the statement that "the just shall live by his faith." Then I grasped that the justice of God is that righteousness by which through grace and sheer mercy God justifies us through faith. Thereupon I felt myself to be reborn and to have gone through open doors into paradise. The whole of Scripture took on a new meaning, and whereas before the "justice of God" had filled me with hate, now it became to me inexpressibly sweet in greater love."[5]

Faith is renewed when people encounter the living Word; scripture assumes a normative role in a Christian community that is faithful.

The promotion of holistic spirituality

The church begins to die whenever the religious practice of Christians is disengaged from the world in which they live. This, in fact, was one of the issues that gave rise to the great Mendicant Orders of the late–medieval world, primarily to the Franciscans and Dominicans. Rather than conforming to earlier patterns of withdrawal within the Western monastic tradition, both of these new religious orders took the message of God's love to the people. They modeled a life characterized by disciplined devotional practice and active social service. The Beguines lived out this same holistic rhythm of life, affording a new model of religious contemplation and service to the world and demonstrating that this was a woman's as well as man's calling in life.[6]

The development of various forms of accountable discipleship

The rise of Continental Pietism in the seventeenth century was a response to the dry, arid orthodoxy of the Protestant traditions, which had led not only to atrophy in the church but also to blood-shed among Christians as well. In their efforts to rediscover a New Testament model of the church, Pietist leaders, such as Philipp Jakob Spener put small groups at the very heart of Christian living. He called them *collegia pietatis* or "schools of piety." These *ecclesiolae in ecclesia*, "little churches within the church," to use their technical name, were concerned with not only the inner spiritual experience of believers but also the renewal of the whole church. Small groups were the key to this revitalization.

The community's reorientation around formative worship

Every age of renewal in the life of the church is characterized by liturgical revolution. Worship shapes theology, and theology shapes worship. In our memory, nothing has been more dramatic in this respect than the changes enacted in the Roman Catholic tradition by the Second Vatican Council. Ironically, many of these changes are directly parallel to the liturgical renewal that took place in the era of the Protestant Reformation. Moreover, most of these changes in worship also signaled significant new understandings related to the ministry of the laity. One important symbolic act, for example, is the movement of the communion table from the back wall of the sanctuary into the midst of the people. The reintroduction of congregational singing (not unlike Luther's use of hymns in the earlier reform) creates a participatory environment in which all are encouraged to be a part of the liturgy, rightly conceived as the word literally means the "work of the people." The use of indigenous languages in worship affirms the culture and context of peoples' daily lives. There is seldom renewal without major renovation of the way God's people worship together.

The affirmation of a missional vocation

The central question here is, What is the essential calling of the church? For the community of faith to be healthy and vital, it must be clear about its mission in the world, why it even exists. The ecumenical movement of the modern era sprang directly out of these concerns. Again, the ecumenical statesman, Visser 't Hooft, speaks a prophetic word:

> The alliance of the Church with one particular culture and its lack of evangelistic and pastoral concern for the masses of the population can lead to its annihilation. To put this in other words, it is the institutional egocentricity of a church, its unwillingness to let itself be used by the Spirit, its wrong concept of what constitutes "success," in short its rejection of the renewal which is offered to it, which may cause its sickness unto death.[7]

A church that is turned in on itself will surely die. All of the great ecumenical theologians turned their energies toward this important theme. Emil Brunner claimed that the church exists by mission as fire exists by burning. Dietrich Bonhoeffer described the community of faith as "the church for others."[8] Hendrick Kraemer said that the church, well-understood, not so much *has* a ministry or ministries, but primarily *is* a ministry. The ecumenical movement helped rediscover this central missiological identity of the church—the church *as* mission.

Here, then, is the stuff of which renewal is made. In what ways are these signs of God's reedifying presence (rebuilding the community of faith) reflected in the Wesleyan tradition? The amazing fact is that all of them are present and held together in such a dynamic way as to create a potent paradigm for Christian renewal.

The Wesleyan Paradigm of Renewal

Living Word

If we take for granted that the church is always in need of reform, we may be surprised to find that renewal often seems, or is perceived, to be radical. "Radical" literally means to go to the root of something. *Ad fontes*, "back to the fount," may have been the cry of the humanist, Erasmus, but this is precisely how the early Methodist people viewed scripture. The Wesleyan Revival was a movement back to the basics. The Wesleys rediscovered the Bible, therefore, as the ultimate place of divine encounter where the living Word can be met and known. Dead words became the Word of life for countless disciples as they read, heard, and inwardly digested the scriptures.

"I am determined to be a Bible Christian," John Wesley once claimed, "not almost but altogether."[9] In his journal, he describes in some detail an early morning exposition of 2 Timothy 3:16, in which he sought to encourage his followers to immerse themselves in the Word:

> I showed concerning the Holy Scriptures, (1) that to "search" (i.e., read and hear them) is a *command* of God; (2) that this *command* is given to *all, believers* or *unbelievers*; (3) that this is commanded or ordained as "a means of grace," a means of conveying the grace of God to all, whether *unbelievers* (such as those to whom he first gave this command, and those to whom "faith cometh by hearing"), or *believers*, who by experience know that "all Scripture is profitable," or a means to this end, "that the man of God may be perfect, thoroughly furnished to all good works."[10]

Charles, in a hymn explicitly written for use "Before Reading the Scriptures," provides a lyrical preface for the expectant seeker:

> While in thy Word we search for thee
>   (We search with trembling awe!)
> Open our eyes, and let us see
>   The wonders of thy law.
>
> Now let our darkness comprehend
>   The light that shines so clear;
> Now the revealing Spirit send,
>   And give us ears to hear.[11]

Hester Ann Rogers, one of the early Methodist women, provides her own testimony: "Reading the word of God in private this day was an unspeakable blessing. O! how precious are the promises. What a depth in these words: 'For all the promises of God in him are yea, and in him, amen, unto the glory of God.' Yes, my soul, they are so to thee!"[12] The foundation of the Wesleyan paradigm of renewal is the rediscovery of the Bible.

Saving faith

Long my imprisoned spirit lay,
   Fast bound in sin and nature's night.
Thine eye diffused a quick'ning ray;
   I woke; the dungeon flamed with light.
My chains fell off, my heart was free,
I rose, went forth, and followed thee.[13]

When Charles Wesley penned those lines, he was bearing witness to the liberating power of God's grace in human life. This was his life experience. Living faith as absolute trust in God through Christ, nurtured in fellowship, was the Methodist staff of life. Like many Christians, the Wesley brothers believed that, somehow, they first had to make themselves acceptable to God. But they ultimately came to realize that God had loved them all along. Like a spiritual sunrise, it dawned on them that God's presence and love had accompanied them each step of their journey. Like Paul, they knew that there was nothing they needed to do to win God's love; rather, God's love was always there, freely offered to them in Jesus Christ. The unconditional love of God in Christ freed them and opened up to them a whole new world of joy, peace, and inner healing. They called this "saving faith."

John Wesley drew this basic understanding of faith from the teachings of his church. In classical fashion, a distinction was often drawn between "the faith by which one believes" (the act of faith or subjective, living faith) and "the faith in which one believes" (the substance of faith or objective, propositional faith).[14] While Wesley felt very strongly about the necessity of holding both forms of faith together, there is no question that it was the act of faith he sought to elicit in the lives of his followers. This living faith was a " 'true trust and confidence of the mercy of God through our Lord Jesus Christ and a steadfast hope of all good things at God's hand'. . . . This is the true, [living] Christian faith, [which] is not in the mouth and outward profession only, but it liveth and stirreth inwardly in the heart."[15]

The Methodist movement, then, revolved around this shared experience of faith-as-trust and salvation by grace. The more John preached and the more Charles sang this gospel through his hymns, the more people experienced spiritual liberation in their lives. The Spirit of God was alive and at work in the hearts and minds of many people, especially in the poor people, who before had never experienced God as someone real in their lives. Many encountered the faithfulness of God for the first time in Methodist Society meetings. This was the solid foundation upon which many Christians like Grace Bennet built their lives. She left this dying testimony:

> I would have no encomiums passed on me; I AM A SINNER, SAVED FREELY BY GRACE: Grace, divine grace, is worthy to have all the glory. . . . Some people, she said, I have heard speak much of our being faithful to the grace of God; as if they rested much on their *own* faithfulness: I never could bear this; it is *GOD'S FAITHFULNESS to his own word of promise,* that is my only security for salvation.[16]

Resting is the faithfulness of God and trusting in Christ restores life to broken people.

Holistic spirituality

John Wesley's primary vision of the Christian life was that of wholeness. One of the means to this spiritual health was the dynamic interrelation of "works of piety" and "works of mercy." The works of piety are simply what we would call classic spiritual disciplines today, including prayer, Bible study, Christian fellowship, and participation in the sacrament of Holy Communion. Works of mercy consist essentially in serving God and one's neighbor in the world. These Christian practices, held together, reshape or conform the lives of devoted Christians to the image of Christ. By immersing themselves in these disciplines, people become truly Christlike in their attitudes, actions, and words. The Wesleys realized that works of piety devoid of compassion are simply pharisaical. They also knew that works of mercy that are not rooted in a grace-filled relationship with God are ultimately bankrupt.

John discussed the importance of both disciplines and made their connection abundantly clear in his sermon "The Important Question":

As the love of God naturally leads to works of piety, so the love of our neighbour naturally leads all that feel it to works of mercy. It inclines us to feed the hungry; to clothe the naked; to visit them that are sick or in prison; to be as eyes to the blind and feet to the lame; an husband to the widow, a father to the fatherless. But can you suppose that the doing this will prevent or lessen your happiness? Yea, though you did so much as to be like a guardian angel to all that are round about you? On the contrary, it is an infallible truth that

All worldly joys are less
Than that one joy of doing kindnesses.[17]

The primary insight of the brothers was that no act of worship or devotion was complete in its fullest sense until God's love was carried into the world in concrete acts of compassion and justice. To engage in these disciplines renews the soul and reenergizes the church.

Accountable discipleship[18]

In the "Preface to *Hymns and Sacred Poems*" of 1739, John Wesley unleashed his fury against those who would take religion in an individualistic, privatistic direction: " 'Holy solitaries' is a phrase no more consistent with the gospel than holy adulterers. The gospel of Christ knows of no religion, but social; no holiness but social holiness."[19] In defense of his expanding network of Methodist Societies, he identifies the rediscovery of mutual accountability in fellowship as the critical and distinguishing mark of the movement. Wesley's followers were encouraged to "watch over one another in love." They shared their pilgrimages of faith. To be mutually accountable in the fellowship of the community meant very simply to help each other along the way toward holiness of heart and life. Sarah Crosby, the first woman preacher of early Methodism, noted how important these small groups were to her in her journey toward love. In a letter to John Wesley, she explained that the greatest means of increasing Christian love in her life was the conversation she had shared with others about her trials and temptations, her preaching and practice of God's love.

Mutual encouragement and genuine care for one another were

the hallmarks of the early Methodist people, who sang with Charles:

> Help us to help each other, Lord,
>   Each other's cross to bear;
> Let each his friendly aid afford,
>   And feel his brother's care.
>
> Help us to build each other up,
>   Our little stock improve;
> Increase our faith, confirm our hope,
>   And perfect us in love.[20]

The purpose of this accountable lifestyle was the cultivation of truly holy lives; and the Wesleys knew that holy people were truly happy people.

Formative worship

Most Methodists do not realize that the Wesleyan Revival was both "evangelical" (a rediscovery of God's word of grace) and "eucharistic" (a rediscovery of the sacrament of Holy Communion as a way to experience that grace). The Wesleys believed that sacramental grace and evangelical experience are necessary counterparts of a balanced Christian life. In an age when both preaching and sacrament were at low ebb in the life of the church, the Wesleyan emphasis on pulpit and table was like a two-edged sword; this conjunction was a potent agent in the spread of the revival. And when Charles Wesley's hymns were added, the Wesleys revolutionized worship.

In the Wesleys' view there could be no suggestion of setting the preaching of the gospel over against the celebration of the sacrament. It was impossible to think about the spoken word (preaching) apart from the word made visible (Eucharist). Hardly a new discovery in the life of the church, this essential connection of word and sacrament has been the hallmark of virtually every movement of Christian renewal. Therefore, it is not a surprise to find the frequent mention of word and sacrament together in the journals of both Wesley brothers. "The Lord gave us, under the word, to know the power of His resurrection," Charles wrote on Easter in 1747, "but in the sacrament he carried us quite above ourselves and all earthly things."[21] The point is that the Wesleys nourished their flock spiritually by both preaching the gospel and celebrating the gospel enacted in the sacrament.

Perhaps nothing is more important to the renewal of the spirit in worship than music. "The eighteenth-century revival," Richard P. Heitzenrater observes, "was to a great extent borne on the wings of Charles's poetry. Charles's hymns not only helped form the texture of the Methodist mind but also, perhaps more importantly, set the temper of the Methodist spirit."[22] Of the many things that could be said of Wesley's hymns at this juncture, perhaps the most important observation for our immediate purposes is that the hymns often functioned as catalysts of renewal and rebirth in the lives of the Methodist people. In other words, the hymns themselves were a powerful tool in the Spirit's work of revival. This was the experience of Sarah Colston who linked the singing of a Charles Wesley hymn with a critical turning point in her own spiritual journey. "After you had prayed and were singing [the] words of the hymn," she recalled, "...I felt such a power and love of God in my soul that I did not know how to live. When I came home I was praying and singing all day long."[23] Worship that involves the whole person—head, heart, and hands—through Word, sacrament, and song, uplifts God's people.

Missional vocation

Much like the Pietists, the Wesleys attempted to replicate the model of the church they discovered in the pages of the New Testament. But their understanding of the Methodist Societies within the Church of England was more complex than that of the Pietists.[24] The Church of England in the Wesleys' day was an institution in need of repair. It had exchanged its true mission for maintenance. It had become distant from and irrelevant to the world it was called to serve during a time of tremendous change. Its forms and its structures had become so inflexible and devoid of life that the weight of its "institutionalism" was quenching the Spirit, suffocating the life of God's people. It needed healing. It needed to rediscover itself and reclaim its identity as God's agent of love in the world. The Wesleys believed that God raised them up to resuscitate the church.

They were not only called into mission themselves but also were equally committed to helping the church rediscover its true vocation by means of their examples. Their ecclesiology (understanding of the church), therefore, was essentially missiological (formed around mission). Charles expressed it so potently in a well-known couplet, "To serve the present age,/My calling to fulfil."[25] All of their energy was directed toward the empowerment of Christ's faithful disciples in ministry to God's world. Indeed, they all viewed evangelism and mission—the proclamation of God's love in word and deed, in witness and service—as the reason for their existence. They gathered together to learn how to love and were then sent out to share that love with others, singing their faith along the way.

In fact, Charles gave the church some amazing hymns to remind the members of their proper calling in life. One hymn that expresses this missiological concern is worth quoting at length:

> Happy soul, whose active love
> emulates the Blessed above,
> in thy every action seen,
> sparkling from the soul within:
>
> Thou to every sufferer nigh,
> hearest, not in vain, the cry
> of widow in distress,
> of the poor, the shelterless:
>
> Raiment thou to all that need,
> to the hungry dealest bread,
> to the sick givest relief,
> soothest hapless prisoner's grief:
>
> Love, which willest all should live,
> Love, which all to all would give,
> Love, that over all prevails,
> Love, that never, never fails.
> Love immense, and unconfined,
> Love to all of humankind.[26]

The movement in this hymn is unmistakable. It is a movement from contemplation to action that connects evangelism and mission. It is a movement that both puts worship at the center of a life of devotion to God and offers justice and mercy and compassion to all the children of God, whether they have found their way back to their true home or not. A disciple who has embraced a Wesleyan vision of life is the one whose whole heart has been renewed, who longs to radiate the whole image of God in his or her life and therefore hears the cry of the poor and wills, with God, that all should truly live! The Wesleyan way is one of incarnational ministry that empties itself of all but love and finds its greatest reward in the realization of God's dream of shalom for all.

The Wesleyan Paradigm Today

This dynamic model of renewal in the life of the church—combining the rediscovery of the Word and faith with an holistic spirituality oriented around accountable discipleship and lived out in a balance of doxology and mission—has much to offer the church today. Indeed, it is exciting to be able to point to its signs in our midst. Several movements within the life of the church are helping us reclaim our roots and project a healthy future. Disciple Bible Study (and now its spin-off, Christian Disciple), perhaps more than any other programmatic aspect of the church's life, has helped countless Methodists rediscover the Word. Covenant Discipleship Groups have spread across the country and the world, introducing nominal Christian folk to an exciting form of accountable discipleship and combining works of mercy and piety in an intentional way. The Emmaus Walk has renewed individuals and congregations as they seek to become more faithful in their discipleship in explicitly Wesleyan ways.

One innovative ministry, among many, illustrates the new wind of the Spirit that is blowing across the church, namely, the Ginghamsburg Church in Ohio.[27] The vision of renewal that has emerged in the experience of this congregation and of its leaders is a manifestation of the Wesleyan paradigm and is outlined in six basic principles. It advocates a clear focus on Jesus Christ as the starting point for renewal in the life of the church. This vision orients belief and action around scriptural truth as the ultimate source of authentic Christian existence. It presses for the discovery of new forms of worship. It recognizes that commitment to the integrity of membership is the foundation of accountable discipleship. It empowers people through a priesthood principle that seeks to equip all baptized Christians for ministry. It calls for the discernment of spiritual entrepreneurs who can articulate the why (mission), the what (goal), and the how (strategy) of the community of faith.

Our present time and circumstances are not dissimilar to the transitional age in which Methodism was born, which gives me tremendous hope for the future of the Wesleyan tradition. Certainly, sustained renewal among God's people will be dependent upon the rediscovery of the Bible. It will not be enduring unless we are willing to repent, to face our failure to be an obedient church, to love our neighbors, and to hear the cry of the needy. It will be enriched as we walk hand in hand and in fellowship with believers, not only of the Methodist fold but also of all who proclaim with eagerness of heart that Jesus is Lord. Our church will find itself anew as it rediscovers its reason for being in God's mission in the world. But more important than anything else is our openness to the work of the Spirit of God. Without the Spirit, there is no life; rooted and grounded in a Christlike spirit of love, our lives are complete. We move forward with confidence that the God who began a good work among us nearly three centuries ago will bring it to completion in the fullness of Christ's love.

2

SCRIPTURE IN THE CHURCH

RECONSTRUCTING THE AUTHORITY OF SCRIPTURE FOR CHRISTIAN FORMATION AND MISSION

Joel B. Green

> I want to know one thing, . . . the way to heaven; how to land safe on that happy shore. God himself has condescended to teach the way: For this very end he came from heaven. He hath written it down in a book. O give me that book! At any price, give me the book of God![1]

This justly famous passage from John Wesley's preface to his *Sermons on Several Occasions* is but one of almost countless references in Wesley's writings to his belief in the centrality of Scripture in all matters of faith and life. Though tossed at him as words of slander, such epithets as "Bible bigot," "Bible moth," and "Bible Christian" he wore as badges of honor and insisted that the same was true of all Methodists. As Scott J. Jones observes in his study of *John Wesley's Conception and Use of Scripture*, Wesley's own view of Scripture underscored its authority and inspiration.[2] In an earlier, more popular examination of *The Bible in the Wesleyan Heritage*, former United Methodist bishop Mack B. Stokes insists, "Among 'the people called Methodists' there has never been any doubt that the Bible is the basis of Christian belief and practice."[3]

It is easy to affirm the centrality of Scripture within the Wesleyan tradition. However, this does not mean it is a simple thing to articulate how Scripture is central. This is partially because Wesley's own remarks and assertions about Scripture do not lend themselves to systematizing, and his own explicit statements concerning Scripture are not always on full display in his actual use of Scripture.[4] Within The United Methodist Church, our difficulties are exacerbated by the ambiguities revolving around statements on theological method concerning the so-called "Wesleyan Quadrilateral." Introduced into the vocabulary of Methodists some thirty years ago, this fourfold conjunction of authorities—Scripture, Tradition, Reason, and Experience—is widely reputed to represent both Wesley and Wesleyan Methodism.[5] This is true in spite of widespread uneasiness with what most regard as an artificial formulation that represents neither Wesley's position and practice nor the Wesleyan tradition.[6] Not only can a theological emphasis on the conjunction of Scripture, Tradition, Reason, and Experience not be traced back to Wesley's own theological method, but also it has never been clear among modern-day Methodists how these four authorities might be correlated and especially whether or how differences among them on a given topic (say, homosexual unions) might be adjudicated. And many of us believe that the ascent of Reason, Tradition, and Experience as theological benchmarks has resulted in the further marginalization of the Bible from the center of the church's struggle for faithfulness in belief and practice.

This is not to say, however, that questions concerning the place of the Bible in the church are the consequence of such squabbles. The roots of our dilemma run deeper in the cultural soil of the Enlightenment and, more recently, have found their way into the cracks and crevices of postmodernity. In this chapter, I will devote some energy to the historical considerations of the situation we now face with regard to the crisis of biblical authority. With this orientation, we will explore how the authority of Scripture might be construed for the church today and the implications of this authority for those who daily engage with the Scriptures to find and shape their identities and to form their practices as Christian communities.

A Tale of Three Crises

The loss of the Bible from both our public and ecclesial lives in the last half of the twentieth century is not difficult to document.

In a recent analysis of altruism and acts of compassion in the United States, Robert Wuthnow discovered a positive relationship between charitable behavior and widespread familiarity with Jesus' parable of the good Samaritan.[7] What is interesting about this "good Samaritan effect" is that Wuthnow found few people who could recite the parable in a recognizable form and no one who actually grasped the arresting point of the story. According to Wuthnow, the grand narrative of Scripture—including Creation and Fall, Exile and Restoration, and moving on toward New Creation—no longer shapes our collective identity. The situation is hardly any better in the church, where sermon illustrations are more likely to engage and influence if derived from Academy Award–winning movies than taken from the stories of Sarah and Abraham, much less Euodia and Syntyche. At the turn of the twenty-first century, the dominant idiom of our Western lives is that of the therapeutic society; we speak easily of addiction and recovery.[8]

This malaise regarding the place of Scripture in the church eludes easy analysis. Risking oversimplification, I want to describe the malaise in three ways—in terms of a crisis of function, a crisis of relevance, and a crisis of authority.

Crisis of function

Huge numbers of persons explicitly embrace the authority of Scripture. However, our situation has not been greatly helped by developments within the evangelical arm of the church in the nineteenth and twentieth centuries. In these communities of believers, biblical authority has come to reside especially in the propositional content of the Bible and in affirmations concerning its trustworthiness. In the past century, American evangelicals have developed a well-nuanced vocabulary for speaking of Scripture—especially "infallibility" ("the full trustworthiness of a guide that is not deceived and does not deceive") and "inerrancy" ("the total trustworthiness of a source of information that contains no mistakes").[9] Such formulations as these are not easily harmonized with Wesley and, indeed, with the nature of Scripture itself and have proved unhelpful in the use of Scripture in the life of the church. The basis for these claims is threefold: Affirmations of the trustworthiness of

Scripture incorporate no guarantees regarding the faithful interpretation of Scripture. They extract no commitments from persons
regarding fidelity to the witness of Scripture. Moreover, such affirmations tend to reduce the Word to its propositional content and
adjudicate scriptural "truth" in questionable ways.

The first two of these claims can be discussed together. If, as
evangelicals and many others are right to affirm, the authority of
Scripture is best discerned in the lives (and not only the assertions)
of those communities oriented around Scripture, then it is evident
that affirmations regarding Scripture are never enough. This tru-
ism is on display in the Gospels themselves and in Acts, where
"the battle for the Bible" focuses not on *whether* the Scriptures of
Israel are to be taken seriously, but on *how* those Scriptures are to
be understood within the framework of God's purpose and appro-
priated within the lives of God's people. Pharisees have one view,
the Jewish elite residing in Jerusalem have another view, and Jesus
has still another—each view with regard to the same authoritative
Scriptures. This is not a struggle over how best to construe biblical
authority; rather, it is a hermeneutical quandary—one with such
high stakes that differences of viewpoint surrounding the message
of the Scriptures eventually would lead to the execution of one of
its interpreters, Jesus. That evangelicals today can agree on affirming the authority of Scripture and yet fail to agree on numerous
issues regarding its message (on any number of questions, theological and ethical) is testimony enough that we can never be sat-
isfied with affirmations alone.

What of my third concern, namely, the reduction of the Scriptural
witness to propositions and the questionable understanding of
"truth" as it relates to Scripture? The difficulties here are several.
For example, the biblical witness to God embraces a complex and
dynamic interaction of different sorts of language and modes of
expression, including poetry, parable, narrative, and law, among
many others. What definition of "truth" can be used to deduce
whether this variety of linguistic expressions is "true"? True
according to what? What is more, claims to truth and trustworthiness in reference to Scripture are never made by persons occupy-
ing a neutral ledge on which to adjudicate such matters; these
claims are, rather, theological judgments. Whether one believes
that Jesus Christ is (or is not) the self-communication of God has a

determinative role in the credence one allows the biblical witness to Jesus and to the God who raised him from the dead. Whether we see the truth depends on our commitments and on whether we do the truth, on whether we present ourselves to God in willingness to be transformed (cf. John 7:17 and Rom. 12:1-2).[10] In fact, arguments in favor of the special status of the Scriptures tend to be convincing only to those who are already inclined to grant them this status. This is not surprising, given that theological arguments are best characterized as "faith seeking understanding."

The difficulty here is that modern persons who think of themselves as Christians and who identify themselves with the Christian church have often been enculturated to imagine not only that they *can* but also that they *must* approach the Scriptures objectively. This is an issue to which we will turn momentarily. At present, it is enough to celebrate the growing sense—characteristic of the times in which we live—that neutrality is not an option, that as human beings we are deeply implicated in our own practices and commitments, and that, whether we want to admit it or not, we have already embraced a grand story by which we order our lives. The pressing question is whether this grand story is in fact the story of Scripture or some other. Competitors include such life-forming, grand narratives as "The little engine that could" (if only it worked hard enough and kept pushing and kept pushing, it could conquer that mountain), the promise of "unrelenting progress" (a kind of social and religious and political Darwinism that has long been integral to our self-consciousness), and "I did it my way" or "Be all that you can be" or "We give you what you want when you want it" (a portrait of life expressed in search for selfhood that, almost invariably, leads to radical individuation, as if to say that maturation comes as we learn "to give birth to ourselves"). Have we deliberately involved ourselves in a community oriented around the Triune God—Father, Son, and Holy Spirit—a community that takes its fundamental identity from the witness of divine-human relations in the Bible; a community that sees the story of Scripture as its story and writes itself into the ongoing narrative of the people of God; a community that is formed by practices as worship, hospitality, repentance, and gathering around Scripture to discern together the shape of faithful life and witness?

Crisis of relevance

I need to return to the concern, characteristic of the modern period, to approach the Bible objectively. To the rank and file of the church, one of the most puzzling aspects of the modern study of the Bible is the high degree to which academic biblical studies have been segregated from the proclamation of the Word. Since the eighteenth century, the reigning paradigm in biblical studies has been focused on isolating matters of description (What does the Bible say?) from matters of prescription (What should we believe and do in light of the biblical witness?). Thus, biblical study has been developed into a specialization open only to those capable of working with scholarly procedures. Issues of religious life and practice have been marginalized far from the center of the concerns of biblical interpretation. Biblical scholarship, identified above all as historical study of the Bible, has defined the truth of the biblical material primarily in terms of historical veracity and has repeatedly answered with profound skepticism. Historical study of the Bible has emphasized the altogether alien character of the world of the Bible, digging more deeply and widely the chasm separating us from the biblical message. As a consequence, many graduates from our theological institutions (across the theological spectrum) must look elsewhere for a word to proclaim. That is, faced with the task of preparing a sermon on a passage from Daniel or Matthew, the preacher dutifully consults the major critical commentaries and discovers plentiful historical and philological data and assessment of scholarly views but is given little help for the risky business of speaking of God here and now on the basis of the Scripture.[11] Robert Morgan helpfully summarizes our dilemma when he notes that, for one kind of reader, Scripture refers to the texts by which we contemplate the history of Israelite and Christian religion, while the other kind of reader is concerned with the texts by which we orient the meaning of our lives.[12]

In short, the practical effect of widespread and long-held commitments in the area of biblical interpretation has been to undermine the centrality and authority of the Bible. This is the consequence whenever we promote approaches to Bible reading that have to do with mastering its data rather than grasping its message. Biblical authority is also compromised when we pit one part of the canon of Scripture against another, turning a blind eye to the theological claim of Scripture to narrate one story.

Crisis of authority

The impediments we face when fashioning a coherent and useful understanding of the role of Scripture in the church are tied to more pervasive cultural movements represented succinctly in the famous bumper sticker, "Question Authority!" That is, the difficulty we face today when speaking of biblical authority is intimately related to a more overarching aversion to authority as such. In a penetrating exploration of how we view the human person, Charles Taylor finds that personal identity has come to be based on presumed affirmations of the human subject as autonomous, disengaged, self-sufficient, and self-engaged. Modern identity is thus shaped by assumptions such as the following: Human dignity lies in self-sufficiency and self-determination; identity is grasped in self-referential terms: I am who I am; and basic to authentic personhood are self-autonomy and self-legislation.[13] If we in the West have found it increasingly difficult to posit as an authority anything external to ourselves (my own conscience, my own experience, my own desires), and if in the late–twentieth century "growing up" has conventionally been tied to achieving independence and autonomy, then we may not be surprised to discover that attempts to express the authority of the Bible largely have fallen on hard times. The church may not be "of the world," but its contemporary views of and practices with reference to the Bible have very much been shaped on the potter's wheel of the modern world.

Reconstructing Biblical Authority

Nevertheless, that we should speak of the need and possibility of the renewal of the place of Scripture in the life of the church is also a sign of the times, just as it was in Wesley's transitional age. I have suggested thus far that the roots of much of our current dilemma have drawn their nourishment from assumptions and commitments characteristic of the Modern Age. Today, many people believe that modernity is being eclipsed by the Postmodern

Age, or postmodernity, and this opens new possibilities for thinking about the role of Scripture in faith and life. One of the primary characteristics of modernity has been its view of history as problematic. If all knowledge is historically grounded, as people in the West have understood in the last three centuries, then we moderns should not be governed by someone else's history—not by the history of the Christian tradition and not by the history of God's people related in the Bible. Moreover, the Bible has its own history, and it is only within the horizons of its history that the Bible has meaning; hence, the Bible has no particular relevance for people in other times and places. Meaning belongs "back there—that was then, this is now." Those who rejected this view, however, did not necessarily escape the manacles of modernity. More conservative students of Scripture have worked "back there" at locating the text's "original meaning" and in doing so, ignored the perspectives of contemporary interpreters, neglected the theological claim that the history of these biblical texts is, in a profound sense, our history, and disregarded the traditions of the church informing (in countless ways, both formally and informally) our readings of the texts. Modernity has nurtured practices of biblical interpretation oriented toward pinning down the meaning of a biblical text, deciphering it once and for all, mastering it, and controlling it.

Postmodernity has the propensity to discard history altogether and with history, all notions of authoritative history. Postmodernity also opens up new possibilities for thinking not *against* history (as in the Modern Age) but *with* history. That is, postmodernity brings with it a freedom to engage with ancient texts with respect and with the expectancy that we have much to learn from them. On other related fronts, postmodern thinkers are suspicious of modernism's foundation stones, including the claim that change means progress or the imposition of what is true or real on others by those in power. Postmodernity exposes our tendency to confuse God's word with our own words, unmasks our idolatrous preoccupation with "what is new," and denies pretentious and self-serving assertions of "what is true." Although we may grant that postmodern thinking, taken to its extremes, has little to offer us (and much to harm us), we also may see that postmodernity cultivates fertile soil for reevaluating biblical authority and for nourishing humility before the biblical witness.

What fresh visions of biblical authority are open to us today? Risking sounding old-fashioned, I want to suggest that the era into which we are moving actually allows us to take more seriously than before the character of the Bible's authority on the Bible's own terms. If we are allowed to shed the concerns of a modernist approach to biblical authority, we may think of biblical authority in such ways as the four I want to sketch: the Bible's intrinsic authority, the authority of the biblical narrative, biblical authority as invitation, and biblical authority as grace.

The intrinsic authority of the Bible

One of the hallmarks of talk about scriptural authority in the past two centuries has been the degree to which it has been given over to making truth-claims on the Bible's behalf. Unfortunately, it has done so, typically, in idiom that is foreign to the biblical witness itself. How does the Bible assert its own authority? Actually, it does so only rarely, and this presses us to make a key distinction between two sorts of authority, extrinsic and intrinsic. The first authoritative statement—the extrinsic one—we accept as true not because the statement itself is compelling but because we grant the speaker the authoritative status necessary to make that statement. But if the statement itself is convincing or compelling, irrespective of who said it, then we might say that we recognize its intrinsic authority. Most Christians relate to the Bible by granting it some combination of both intrinsic and extrinsic authority. Scripture itself presents its appeal in a variety of ways—calling upon our imaginations, reminding us of our commitments, asking us to consider reasoned arguments, urging us to engage in self-reflection on our experience as God's people—persuading and convincing, but rarely demanding. Given the citation from Wesley's preface to his *Sermons on Several Occasions* that opened this essay, we might insist that Wesley's own view of the Bible's truthfulness rests here—in the question of whether Scripture does indeed allow one "to know one thing—the way to heaven; how to land safe on that happy shore." As John Goldingay helpfully summarizes, "Scripture as a whole is more inclined to seek to persuade us of the truth of things than to expect us to 'believe seven impossible things before breakfast.' "[14]

In the end, that famous example of deduction—"God says it;

I believe it; That settles it"—does not represent very well the Bible's own way of speaking. Instead, we find that, as we give ourselves to the life of the Spirit and engagement with Scripture, God so works in our lives and imaginations that we are led further into the biblical narrative, so that we find the Bible to be true more and more. As will be suggested more fully below, this means that those of us who seek after methods for reading and interpreting the Bible correctly are usually looking for the wrong thing. Needed most are not good methods for reading the Bible, but good people reading the Bible— that is, people deeply embedded in faithful communities of discipleship, people in whom the Spirit is actualizing the Word of God and, thus, for whom the Word of God is authenticated.

The authority of the biblical narrative

One of the problems with the way biblical authority has been articulated in the past has been the focus on the truth of Scripture's propositions. This is problematic because the majority of Scripture does not assert in prose but narrates. Because the bulk of Scripture is narrative, it is worth inquiring into the sort of truth-claims made by biblical narrative. Does biblical narrative promise to tell us "what actually happened," so that we may measure its truthfulness by its verisimilitude and arbitrate its authority by proving that "things happened precisely as the Bible reports them"? Three responses are important.

First, in reality, an agenda such as I have proposed is alien to every culture except to the culture spawned by Enlightenment rationalism, the vestiges of which continue to influence. Reporting of historical events is never as neutral as required of this way of measuring the "truth" of a narrative; "history" is always "partial"—in the sense of being both incomplete and committed to a perspective. Events are selected and narratives spun in light of the interests of the communities that formulate their own histories. On the one hand, it would be reprehensible to subject biblical narrative to this sort of modernist test of historical truthfulness, when the test itself is deeply flawed.

Second, on the other hand, this is not to deny the need for historical investigation. If Scripture purports to narrate human-divine relations, then Scripture itself invites historical questions, not the least of such key events as God's deliverance of Israel from Egypt and the incarnation. Having said this, however, it is important to realize that historical study can never *prove* the incarnation, in the sense of demonstrating beyond doubt that Jesus was God-in-the-flesh. Historical study can and should explore the evidence for Jesus, together with the cultural conditions within which he lived, conducted his ministry, and was executed. Historical study can and should explore the evidence for the Christian claim that Jesus was raised from the dead. But historical study alone cannot answer such questions as whether Jesus is God's Son, whether Jesus was the long-awaited Messiah, whether Jesus died for our sins, or whether Jesus' resurrection signaled the restoration of God's people and the ushering in of the new age.

We have yet to address the question of the authority of narrative, except to say that this authority is not focused particularly on modern notions of history. Our third response, then, is to note that the truth-claim made by biblical narrative resides above all in the authority of narrative to speak on God's behalf. The claim's truth-fulness rests in its ability to interpret reality in light of God's self-disclosure of God's own character and will working itself out in the cosmos and on the plain of human events. In this sense, the Bible's authority as Scripture rests in its status as revealed history.

Having said this, it is important also to realize that the particular narratives related in the biblical books—together with the non-narrative portions of Scripture—participate in a more extensive, overarching narrative. This is the story of God's purpose coming to fruition in the whole of God's history with us, from the creation of the world and humanity's falling away from God through God's repeated attempts to restore his people, culminating in the coming of Jesus of Nazareth and reaching its full crescendo in the final revelation of Christ and the new creation. The Bible is nothing less than testimony to the actualization (and ongoing promise) of the purpose of God in human history. The Bible's authority thus rests, ultimately, in this divine purpose.

Biblical authority as invitation

It is never enough to make such affirmations about the authority of Scripture. This is because what it means to refer to the Bible as Scripture is to declare its role in shaping a people, transforming their most basic commitments, their dispositions, their identities. The *narrative of Scripture* is a unitary story about the world—not only the world of the past but also the world we inhabit. Hence, "to be a Christian is in some sense to have one's own story shaped in a decisive way by and taken up into this other larger story of God's redemptive action in the world."[15]

> It is precisely here that moral conviction of the truth of this story, and hence its authority, is rooted. God speaks. He convinces us that things between himself and the human race are in reality much as they are in the story. We are drawn into the world of the text precisely as we are drawn into a relationship with its central character [that is, with God]. As this happens, we find ourselves confronted by many of the same realities and experiences as are narrated in the text. Suddenly sin, guilt, grace, reconciliation, the power of God's Spirit, the risen Christ and so on are not mere elements in a narrative world, but constituent part of our own world, players and factors to be taken into consideration in our daily living and our attempts to make sense of our own situation.[16]

In short, the authority of Scripture is less demand and more invitation to come and live this story, to inhabit the narrative of God's ongoing and gracious purpose for his people. The authority of Scripture is an invitation to resist attempts to revise the words of Scripture so as to make them match our reality and to make sense of our reality and our lives, within its pages and within its story. To embrace the Bible as Scripture is not to accept it as one narrative among others but to accord it a privilege above all others and to allow ourselves to be shaped by it ultimately.

Biblical authority as grace

The narrative that is Scripture does not first require assent but invites and, indeed, draws us into its world. It engages us imaginatively as we follow its path through the lives of our traveling companions, Seth and Enoch, Joseph and Ruth, Sarah and Daniel, Martha and Priscilla. Precisely because Scripture is first and foremost about God, it draws its chief character from God. How, then, could the authority of Scripture be anything but a gracious gift, an expression of divine care? If the gracious character of God grounds divine-human relations in God's generous initiative and sustaining faithfulness, culminating in the powerful, restorative activity of God on behalf of humanity, then the claims of Scripture on our lives could never be mistaken for expressions of coercive power or for a kind of divine "trump card" held by God (or by God's agents) to be played when we are backed into a corner. On the night of Jesus' betrayal, he submits to God's will, not as one lacking backbone kneeling before an authoritarian command, but as one who discerns God's purpose and embraces it as his own (Luke 22:39-46). This is not to deny that obedience sometimes comes before understanding; the story of Abraham, whether one thinks of his initial call from God to "go...to the land that I will show you" (Gen. 12:1) or to offer his own son as sacrifice (Gen. 22:1-14), is evidence enough of the priority of faith. Even these events must be located within the wider narrative of Scripture and thus set within the wider self-disclosure of God, for whom outward appearances are hardly the measure of reality (see Hab. 3:17-18).

Conclusion

To read the Bible as revealed history entails asking how these events, these stories, fit within the grand story of God's creation and redemption. It means taking seriously the implicit claim of historical narratives within the Bible to provide God's perspective on what historical events are most important and why they are important. This does not entail our reading the Bible in ways that open a great chasm between biblical times and our own. We participate in the grand story of God's work, too. As we read the Bible as revealed history, we come to better understand that this story is our story. We come to understand the events and progress of our own lives within the narrative of Scripture.

To read the Bible as Christian Scripture entails an explicitly Christian position—one that affirms that the Old and New Testaments are inseparable in their witness to God the Savior and affirms that the coming of Christ is the point of orientation that gives all biblical books their meaning as Scripture. Even if Christians have long pushed the Old Testament aside, the reality is that we cannot genuinely know Jesus Christ apart from the God of

Jesus Christ revealed first in the Scriptures of Israel. The Old Testament is thus more than a preface to the good news of Jesus Christ; it is the revelatory narrative of God's dealings with Israel, the story of God's saving purpose which culminates in the advent of Jesus. The Old Testament prepares the way of the Lord, and the New Testament proclaims that the Word became flesh and dwelt among us.

Even though we recognize that each book of the Bible was written to people and in places far removed from us in time and culture, when we approach the Bible as Scripture, we take seriously the faith statement that this book is our Book, these scriptures our Scripture. We are not reading someone else's mail—as though reading the Bible is recovering an ancient meaning intended for someone else and then translating its principles for use in our own lives. When we recall that *we* are the people of God to whom the Bible is addressed as Scripture, we realize that the fundamental transformation that must take place is not the transformation of an ancient message into a contemporary meaning, but rather the transformation of our lives by means of God's Word. This means that reading the Bible as Scripture has less to do with what tools we bring to the task, however important these may be, and more to do with our own dispositions as we come to our engagement with Scripture. We come not to retrieve facts or to gain information, but to be formed. Scripture does not present us with texts to be mastered but with a Word—God's Word—intent of mastering us and shaping our lives.

3

LIVING IN THE REIGN

THE DOMINION OF GOD IN THE WESLEYAN TRADITION

Ben Witherington III

The "Kingdom of God" is unquestionably the major theme of Jesus' and Paul's teaching and preaching. We should not be surprised, therefore, to discover that the image of the kingdom figures quite prominently in the theology of the Wesleys and functions as an important foundation for their movement of renewal. After examining the meaning and significance of this theme in the New Testament in a summary fashion and discussing its importance in the preaching of John Wesley, I will offer some reflections on the significance of the Dominion of God in the life of a church renewed today.

Jesus, Paul, and the Dominion of God

Perhaps the first thing to be said about the Dominion of God is that the phrase *basileia tou theou* is not best rendered Kingdom of God for the reason that the phrase often does not refer to a place, but rather to an event, to the result of an event, or to a state of being. I choose the phrase "Dominion of God" to translate the underlying Greek concept for the reason that it can convey both a verbal and a noun sense. One can have dominion over something or someone, but a dominion also can be a place one enters. We find this dynamism in both Jesus' and Paul's uses of the term. For example, both refer to the Dominion as something that exists in the future and that can be inherited, entered, or obtained. But just as often, they refer to God's Dominion as something already realized, primarily as God's present saving activity breaking into human history. To put it quite simply, there is an "already" and a "not yet" quality to God's reign.[1] But in either case, the focus of this dynamic image is the ongoing nature of God's divine saving activity in relation to the world created by God's grace.

Jesus indicates in numerous ways that the Dominion of God is breaking into history in his own time and through his own ministry. His response to the persistent questions of the Pharisees concerning the kingdom is particularly revealing. In saying that *"the Dominion is in your midst"* (Luke 17:21, author's translation), he declared the present reality of God's inbreaking reign and the dawn of a new age that would be characterized by overwhelming spiritual power. But Jesus also refers to God's Dominion as a future reality. Obviously, a central petition in the Lord's Prayer speaks of a Dominion for which the community of faith must still pray, as something that will come in the future. Of particular interest is Jesus' saying (Matt. 8:11-12) that speaks of dining in the Dominion with a wide variety of interesting dinner guests. The implication is that the future Dominion of God, in which one participates following Jesus' resurrection, will be much like the practices of Jesus' own ministry, in which he dined with all sorts of unexpected folk, including the least, the last, and the lost. The note of celebration and koinonia is hard to miss in such sayings. The coming of the Dominion is something to celebrate, and it is also the place where the celebration will begin.

Paul's letters, the earliest New Testament sources, reveal an equally dynamic concept. In at least eight instances, Paul uses the phrase "Dominion of God" to say something about God's salvific work.[2] A number of conclusions can be drawn from these texts concerning the "not yet" nature of God's reign. Whenever Paul speaks of entering or inheriting the Dominion, he refers to something that is yet to come. Even though he clearly affirms that salvation is by grace through faith—indeed, this is a hallmark of his vision of salvation—he is equally emphatic about the way in which certain behaviors among the believers potentially will disqualify them from God's Dominion. John Wesley reiterates this same concern in his own republication of the theme. Moreover,

Paul implies consistently that this inheritance is only available to us in its fullness after Christ returns and the dead in Christ are raised. Despite the pervasiveness of this future point of reference, when Paul says the Dominion doesn't consist in talk but in power (1 Cor. 4:20-21), it seems clear that he is talking about something present and active in the world. In a similar vein, when Paul says that the Dominion does not consist in food and drink, but in righteousness, peace, and joy in the Holy Spirit (Rom. 14:17), he provides a terse definition of the *effects* of the Dominion in the lives of real people here and now. This particular Dominion text was one that John Wesley turned to frequently, not surprisingly because of his preoccupation with the doctrine of salvation and the effects of God's saving activity among believers.

It seems to be clear that Dominion as a realm is for Paul, as is for Jesus, only a future reality. To put it another way, for both Paul and Jesus, the Dominion in the present is seen in a primarily spiritual way, focusing on God's transforming power in the lives of God's people. By contrast, when they refer to the Dominion in the future, the image is that of a place where we go, of a community explicitly involved in eating and drinking together. Just as a purely material view of the present Dominion of God is inadequate, so, too, a purely spiritual conception of the future Dominion falls short of the reality. It is also important to point out that neither Jesus nor Paul equate this Dominion with the church. Rather, the Dominion is quite simply God's saving activity, which redeems people and then reigns in their lives. For this very reason, one may also see the Dominion happening outside the church whenever someone is rescued or saved by the power of God. Similarly, neither Jesus nor Paul equate the Dominion of God with the world as it is now. The fact is that the kingdoms of this world have not yet completely become "the kingdoms of our Lord and of his Christ" (Rev. 11:15, author's translation). This is why the church's reason for being is mission—carrying the divine saving activity of God (albeit in earthen vessels) to places where God is not yet recognized as ruler of the earth.

John Wesley and the Dominion of God

In biblical theology, the concept of God's Dominion and the doctrine of eschatology (last things) are closely connected. I have had occasion to discuss Wesley's view of eschatology elsewhere at some length, so here I wish to make only a few relevant points on this related topic before turning to the specific issue of Wesley's treatment of the Dominion theme.[3] A careful study of Wesley's eschatology shows an increasing interest in the future dimensions of Dominion in his later and more mature years. More specifically, during the last third of Wesley's life, he began to preach regularly on subjects like the coming final judgment. Perhaps age brought an increasing level of inquisitiveness in these directions. Wesley's "optimism of grace" propelled him to a postmillennial theology in his sermon "The General Spread of the Gospel,"[4] in which he envisages the current revival continuing and thriving and leading to a worldwide spiritual renewal, the fruition of which would be the culmination of human history. Wesley concludes that sermon with these words:

> All unprejudiced persons may see with their eyes that he is already renewing the face of the earth. And we have strong reason to hope that the work he hath begun he will carry on unto the day of his Lord Jesus; that he will never intermit this blessed work of his Spirit until he hath fulfilled all his promises; until he has put a period to sin and misery, and infirmity, and death; and re-established universal holiness and happiness, and caused all the inhabitants of the earth to sing together, "Hallelujah!"[5]

We may say then that Wesley had an increasing interest in the future of God's Dominion on earth the longer his life lasted.[6] And this is the context in which one must exegete his remarks about the present Dominion, which are much more pervasive in his earlier sermons known as the Standard Sermons. The second sermon that Wesley wrote or preached was on Matthew 6:33 with the title "Seek First the Kingdom."[7] This sermon begins much like his later Standard Sermon, "The Way to the Kingdom," based upon Romans 14:17. Wesley contrasts worldly concerns of eating and drinking with seeking the Dominion of God. The difference in this sermon is that it suggests the earthly things will be added after one gets one's Kingdom priorities straight, whereas the later sermon remains almost exclusively spiritual in its orientation.

Wesley insists that the Dominion Christ bids his audience to seek is "not of this world."[8] He equates this kingdom with the heavenly mansions that await the believer beyond the grave. He associates the kingdom with the dwelling place of God and true believers, namely, with heaven. This characteristic emphasis is also found in Wesley's *Notes on the New Testament* in a revealing comment on Matthew 6:10. After encouraging his followers to pray for the heavenly kingdom to come, Wesley again encourages them by adding that if the kingdom of glory tarries, they can look forward to entering it at death.

Throughout, Wesley stresses that Christ does not merely command us to seek the Dominion of God first, but he connects this rule in an intimate way with the righteousness of God. Here, as in "The Way to the Kingdom,"[9] Wesley provides his most basic and characteristic description of this righteousness, namely, the love of God and neighbor. The importance of this association of righteousness with the kingdom rests in the connection between works of piety and works of mercy, which are seen to be part and parcel of what it means to seek God's Dominion. Seeking the Dominion, in his view, therefore, is not something merely theological or internal. It is most fully realized in ethics and especially in the keeping of the greatest commandment about loving God and loving neighbor.[10] The implications in this regard are immense.

Romans 14:17 was one of the major texts for Wesley during the earliest years of the Revival. He preached on this text some seventeen times between 1739 and 1743, but the evidence suggests he proclaimed this text only twelve times thereafter between 1744 and 1791. In the Standard Sermon, "The Way to the Kingdom," he couples this text with a treatment of Mark 1:15, which was in fact another of Wesley's favorite preaching texts. Wesley defines the Dominion of God at the very outset of this sermon as "the nature of true religion." Like Paul, Wesley introduces the theme of the Dominion of God by explaining what it is not. It is not "meat and drink," which Wesley interprets as a reference to all the food laws and related conventions in the Old Testament, or more broadly, as "any ritual observances."[11] Wesley stresses that the kingdom does not consist in "any outward thing whatever, in anything exterior to the heart; the whole substance thereof lying in 'righteousness, peace, and joy in the Holy Ghost.'"[12] In this regard, Wesley, like many of his religious contemporaries, distinguishes between the heart and the mind. In this sermon, he stresses the interiority of "true religion," contrasting correct opinions or orthodox beliefs (Christianity improperly understood) with qualities of the heart, namely, righteousness, peace, and joy (true religion). Wesley says that when the believer is truly righteous, the heartfelt love of God and self-effacing love of neighbor is the fulfilling of the Law. It is clear that his focus is on the effects of God's divine saving activity in people's lives; for Wesley, this was the heart of the matter.

For Wesley, peace is the quintessential effect of the Dominion in the heart of the believer. Anyone who has studied Wesley knows that, for him, peace hardly could be reduced to the absence of activity. Rather, the peace he speaks of is nothing other than the presence of God: "It is a peace that banishes all doubt, all painful uncertainty, the Spirit of God 'bearing witness with the spirit' of a Christian that he is 'a child of God.'" Note here the important role played by the Holy Spirit in the realization of God's Dominion in the human heart. It is the Spirit that actualizes the reign of God and produces its fruitful effects, not the least of which is rejoicing in the Lord as a true child of God. Wesley recapitulates his theme:

> This holiness and happiness, joined in one, are sometimes styled in the inspired writings, "the kingdom of God"...and sometimes, "the kingdom of heaven." It is termed "the kingdom of God" because it is the immediate fruit of God's reigning in the soul. So soon as ever he takes unto himself his mighty power, and sets up his throne in our hearts, they are instantly filled with this "righteousness, and peace, and joy in the Holy Ghost." It is called "the kingdom of heaven" because it is (in a degree) heaven opened in the soul.[13]

In the climactic appeal that concludes his sermon, Wesley returns to the central themes of intimacy and immediacy: "Now cast thyself on the Lamb of God, with all thy sins, how many soever they be; and 'an entrance shall *now* be ministered unto *thee* into the kingdom of our Lord and Savior Jesus Christ!'"[14]

There is no question that the focus of Wesley's early theological reflection on the Dominion was the present nature and internal effects of the rule of God in the life of the believer. The context of the Revival nearly demanded an emphasis in this direction. In Wesley's preaching, so, too, in his understanding of the Dominion of God, the defining word is "now." The "nowness" of God's reign and love and grace was the message that masses longed to hear and to which they responded with enthusiasm and zeal. And so, there was a particularly existential power in Wesley's statement about the kingdom in the *Notes on the New Testament* (Luke 17:20-21): "It is now in the midst of you: it is come: it is present in the soul of every true believer: it is a spiritual kingdom, an internal principle. Wherever it exists, it exists in the heart."[15] Yet we must not forget that in later years Wesley turns his attention to the future Dominion of God and its fullest manifestation in the consummation of all things. In the same *Notes,* Wesley articulates the dynamic tension between the already and the not yet of God's rule in a potent reflection on Paul's great resurrection chapter (1 Cor. 15:24): "For the divine reign both of the Father and the Son is from everlasting to everlasting. But this is spoken of the Son's mediatorial kingdom, which will then be delivered up, and of the immediate kingdom or reign of the Father which will then commence."[16]

Implications for a Renewed Wesleyan Tradition

In this all too cursory survey of the Dominion theme in the New Testament and in the preaching of John Wesley, we have noticed certain themes in regard to the present and future Dominion. It is no surprise that for Wesley, a dutiful exegete of the scriptural witness, the "already" and "not yet" character of the Dominion is republished in its dynamic form, albeit with an emphasis in the early years of the Methodist Revival on the interior nature of God's rule. What remains for us to explore are the implications of the teachings of Jesus, Paul, and John Wesley on the Dominion for a Wesleyan theology about the future and God's will for that future.[17]

Though it could be said from a Wesleyan point of view that in the present, the Dominion of God exists on earth only in the lives of those who acknowledge God's saving reign in their lives, with regard to the future, the Dominion is regularly described in the New Testament as a place that can be entered or inherited. The vision of the future includes a time when God's saving reign will spread throughout the earth, when the "kingdoms of this world become the kingdoms of our God and of his Christ" (Rev. 11:15, author's translation). To state the obvious, if the Dominion of God is going to be on earth and if God is going to dwell here below, then necessarily there will have to be some changes in our world. God in Christ is light, and in him there is no darkness at all. God in Christ is life, and in him there is no disease or decay or death at all. God in Christ is holy, and in him there is no impurity at all. If God is going to dwell with us, not only must we totally be transformed into a truly holy people full of the likeness of Christ, but also our surrounding supporting environment will likewise need to change. What would such a renewal of the earth entail? And what is the role of the Christian community, or more specifically, of the Wesleyan family, in relation to this inbreaking of God's Dominion.

The Old Testament prophets often conjured up images of the end time being like the beginning of time in the garden of Eden. Consider the following extended quote from Isaiah 65:17-25:

> For I am about to create new heavens and a new earth; the former things shall not be remembered or come to mind. But be glad and rejoice forever in what I am creating; for I am about to create Jerusalem as a joy, and its people as a delight. I will rejoice in Jerusalem, and delight in my people; no more shall the sound of weeping be heard in it, or the cry of distress. No more shall there be in it an infant that lives but a few days, or an old person who does not live out a lifetime; for one who dies at a hundred years will be considered a youth, and one who falls short of a hundred will be considered accursed. They shall build houses and inhabit them; they shall plant vineyards and eat their fruit. They shall not build and another inhabit; they shall not plant and another eat; for like the days of a tree shall the days of my people be, and my chosen shall long enjoy the work of their hands. They shall not labor in vain, or bear children for calamity; for they shall be offspring blessed by the LORD—and their descendants as well. Before they call I will answer, while they are yet speaking I will hear. The wolf and the lamb shall feed together, the lion shall eat straw like the ox; but the serpent—its food shall be dust! They shall not hurt or destroy on all my holy mountain, says the LORD.

Likewise, the familiar testimony of Isaiah 2:4 speaks of the time of final judgment upon the earth when God will judge between the nations and when "they shall beat their swords into plowshares, and their spears into pruning hooks; nation shall not lift up sword against nation, neither shall they learn war any more." What is striking about both these passages is that they envisage a perfectly good but also perfectly natural new heaven and new earth. Eden, not eternal life, is the benchmark or desideratum here. The first passage speaks of people living a lengthy blessed life and then dying. Though there is no premature death of young or old, nothing is said about living forever. What is suggested, however, is that the surrounding animal and human world will be at peace, which will facilitate a normal lengthy and healthy human life. Human strife will no longer dominate life; no more predatory behavior in the animal world will transpire. "Shalom," or peace, justice, and wholeness in their full senses will have descended upon the world.

As beautiful as this picture is, the descriptions in the New Testament go even further to suggest the elimination of death altogether by means of resurrection (cf. 1 Cor. 15). Furthermore, some New Testament passages suggest the renewal of the earth, so the raised may live in an environment suitable to their new holy and blessed condition. For example, consider the testimony of Romans 8:19-24:

> For the creation waits with eager longing for the revealing of the children of God; for the creation was subjected to futility, not of its own will but by the will of the one who subjected it, in hope that the creation itself will be set free from its bondage to decay and will obtain the freedom of the glory of the children of God. We know that the whole creation has been groaning in labor pains until now; and not only the creation but we ourselves, who have the first fruits of the Spirit, groan inwardly while we wait for adoption, the redemption of our bodies. For in hope we were saved.

The fate of creation and of creatures is bound together. Since the effects of the Fall on the world were extensive by the biblical account, we would expect the effects of redemption to be equally expansive in nature. Paul goes so far as to talk about a promise that the creation will one day be set free from its bondage of decay and will obtain the freedom as God's children will at the resurrection. New persons, made like the risen Christ, will live in a brand new world. And it will not be just a matter of Eden revisited. It will be

Eden as it should have become if Adam and Eve had eaten of the tree of eternal life, not of the tree of the experience of evil and good, including the evils of disease, decay, and death.

Often at funerals, we have heard the stirring words of Revelation 21 about the descent of the new Jerusalem and then the voice from the throne saying: "See, the home of God is among mortals. He will dwell with them; they will be his peoples, and God himself will be with them; he will wipe away every tear from their eyes. Death will be no more; mourning and crying and pain will be no more, for the first things have passed away" (vv. 3-4). If this promise were to come true, it would necessitate, not just new persons, but also a new environment—one free from disease and decay, one free from struggle and strife. Of course, God's permanent residence with God's people would also necessitate such changes, for God is holy and purely good. If we were to ask why and how this transformation will take place, the short answer would be because of and by means of God's very presence. For example, notice that in Revelation 22:1-5, the water of life flows directly from the presence of God, alluded to by reference to the throne, and this river enlivens and heals all that it touches. It has the opposite effect of a polluted and disease-filled river, which defiles all that it touches and all that touch it.

The upshot of this is that God is the ultimate conservationist or ecologist. This should not surprise us since the God of the Bible is the same God who made all that is and then, when that work was finished, reveled in all that had been made. When the Bible refers to redemption, it is creation that is being redeemed, and this entails not just human beings but all of creation. The visions of Revelation 21–22 are not about a new humanity only, but about a new creation, a new world, also. A moment's reflection will show the wisdom of God's plan. Imagine perfected human beings with eternal life and resurrected bodies who live in a world full of imperfections and disease and decay. Imagine perfected human beings who would have to spend eternity watching all things bright and beautiful and all other creatures great and small continuing to decay and die. This scenario would lead only to eternal frustration and sorrow. It would be somewhat more preferable to the condition of the man in a famous story by Jonathan Swift. He asked for eternal life but failed to ask for eternal youth, thereby condemning himself to getting older and older and more feeble and yet being unable to die. There is good reason that the new creation is depicted in the Bible as one where God will be wiping away the tears from every eye, and where there will be no more sorrow or suffering. Eternal life without eternal joy and love and peace would not be the best of all possible worlds. Eternal life, without the companionship of the rest of God's creation, would not be life in its fullest form. The Bible does not encourage us to have an egocentric view of salvation, as if it were only about saving human souls and letting the material world go to blazes. To the contrary, God has much bigger plans for creation.

The transcending beauty of this vision of the future can be seen also in some of Jesus' brief remarks concerning the ultimate fellowship meal—the messianic banquet in the Dominion of God when it is fully established on earth. Notice that Jesus speaks of his disciples as sitting down with the great saints of the Old Testament, such as Abraham or the prophets, at the table in the Dominion of God (Matt. 8:11-12). In fact, Jesus himself said he was looking forward to a day after his death when he would once again drink the fruit of the vine anew in the Dominion of God (Mark 14:25). The parable of the wedding feast involving the wise and foolish virgins (Matt. 25) and the parable of the king's wedding feast (Matt. 22) also reinforce the image of celebration at the consummation of the ultimate union, namely, the marriage of God to the people of God. Now if there are to be such fellowship gatherings, there must also be food that requires the good earth as well, unless the menu always included manna from heaven. All things considered, most of the descriptions of the afterlife strongly favor a less ethereal and more concrete vision of what the final future will be for the world and its inhabitants than what is sometimes described from our pulpits.

Much of what I have been dealing with above comes in parables or apocalyptic literature. It is more a form of poetry than prose. The temptation, therefore, is not to take these images very seriously. This would be a significant mistake, for in Romans 8, we find the same ideas about the renewal of creation and creature as in the great Old Testament narratives as well. I take it then that we are meant to think that God does indeed have a plan for the future of this material world as well as for his people, even if some of the images used to convey this fact are poetic and not meant to be taken literally. The fact remains that all of this biblical material is meant to describe a hoped for, and believed in, future reality that will appear when Christ returns and when the Dominion of God comes in full measure on earth.

What then are the implications of such a worldview, or better said Dominionview? For one thing, the Dominionview suggests that if we wish to be harbingers to the world of the afterlife, we would do well to tend to, and care for, the garden God has given us called the earth. The doctrine of the resurrection is the ultimate statement indicating God's concern for the conservation of matter and energy. Nothing wasted, nothing for nought would be God's motto. All of creation has a purpose, and all of it has a future. Thus, we must treat that creation with care and respect.

Caring for the earth is not merely sensible for the short term, so our children and grandchildren will have a decent place to live as they grow. We understand that the earth and all that is in it belongs to God (see Psalm 8). We are not owners of this world; we are only stewards and caretakers of it, for God's sake. The Bible supports neither a godless communistic philosophy of property and the use of the world's resources, nor a godless capitalistic vision that privatizes the wealth of resources that surrounds us at all times. The Bible suggests there is neither private nor public property, only God's property of which we are all stewards. The whole modern theory of ownership is faulty, for we brought nothing with us into this world and will take none of it with us. Following this theology of stewardship is that since the earth belongs to God, we have an obligation to use it and dispose of it in a way that glorifies God and helps humankind. The theory of charity too often has as its essential premise "what's mine is mine, but I may choose to share it with you." The problem with this thesis is that the earth and all that is therein belongs to the Lord. We simply have been entrusted with a small portion of it to tend and use for the good of God's Dominion while we are here.

This theological perspective is taking seriously the future reign of God upon the earth, because most assuredly God will hold us accountable for our stewardship. This may not prove a very pleasurable experience for those of us who are terribly wasteful. What shall we answer when God asks why Americans throw away enough food every day to feed the world's starving and still have leftovers? What shall we say when God asks why we support industries that heedlessly pollute our rivers and destroy our air, simply in the name of profits? How shall we answer when God asks us why we persist in mistreating our bodies by eating things that hasten disease, decay, and death in our bodies? If we are supposed to treat our bodies like temples where God dwells, there are many of us that need to reconstruct our bodies and our chosen lifestyles.

The function of this discussion is not merely theological (to heighten our awareness of what the Bible says about the future of God's Dominion) but also ethical (to heighten our sense of responsibility as those who are to mirror the values of God). John Wesley suggested a threefold dictum about the matter of good stewardship of the earth and its resources: (1) make all you can by working hard at an honest and honorable trade; (2) save all you can, never squandering money; and (3) give all you can by supporting your immediate family, the household of faith; and then to all who are needy. Wesley says in the sermon "The Use of Money" (the sermon that he preached more frequently than any other sermons except "Justification by Faith") that if you make all you can and save all you can but do not give all you can, you may be a living person but you will be a dead Christian. Lest we arrive at the door of God's Dominion spiritually "dead on arrival," it would be wise of us to reflect on our spending habits and our stewardship of the resources we have in this world.

One of the lessons to learn from our reflection on the image of God's Dominion is that we often settle for a purely "spiritual" gospel—a purely spiritual Dominion of God—so we don't have to deal with the implications of God's Word in relation to our material realities. But if God's reign is a reign over both human body and human spirit, over both the invisible and visible realms, over both heaven and earth, then the spiritual/material divisions of life are not only unjustified but also dangerous. If we examine the gospel closely, God's Word to us is about the salvation of the whole person, both body (at the resurrection) and spirit, heart, mind, and will (beginning now). If the Dominion of God is indeed coming to earth in the future and if there will be an accounting for what we have done on this planet, it behooves us to recognize the implications of the whole gospel for every aspect of life. The Dominion has a claim on it all. Both the biblical and Wesleyan witness insist upon these claims. We would do well to recover such an emphasis in our teaching and preaching today. A church without a vision of the Dominion of God—the dynamic "already" and "not yet" of God's divine saving activity—is a church without a future.

4

SALVATION BY GRACE THROUGH FAITH

A REASSESSMENT AND ITS IMPLICATIONS

Yeo Khiok-khng

The spirit of the Wesleyan tradition can be characterized as biblical, evangelical, reformational, and missional. It is biblically grounded because of its convictions about the centrality and authority of Scripture for the theology and practice of the Christian faith. It is evangelically focused because of its belief that the gospel of Jesus Christ is salvific and transformative for individuals and for the world. It is reformational in the sense that the gospel messenger must perennially engage the context in which the Word is proclaimed and that the interpretation of Scripture, therefore, needs to be informed by a renewing and reforming spirit.[1] It is missional in its vocation and worship because of its essential commitment to a spirituality that is both compassionate and relevant. Since Methodists identify themselves as a Christian tradition within the Protestant heritage, it is important for us to pay tribute to the honored doctrine of justification by grace through faith, a doctrine consistently preached and lived by the Wesley brothers. At the same time, it is in the spirit of the Wesleyan tradition to critically assess this Pauline concept, which remains foundational to contemporary Christian praxis, and to apply it to changing contexts.[2] I will approach this topic by summarizing the understanding of the doctrine within the Evangelical Revival under the Wesleys' direction, by reinterpreting the doctrine of justification by

grace through faith in the light of critical contemporary scholarship, and by identifying crucial implications of this central doctrine for our Wesleyan praxis today.

The Doctrine of Justification by Grace
Through Faith in the Wesleyan Revival

There is no question that the Wesleys' rediscovery of the doctrine of justification by grace through faith was a powerful force in
the renewal of the church in their day.[3] Not only was this a theological concept, to which the Methodist people gave assent, it was
also a living experience that reoriented their lives and drew them
into a different relationship with God than was generally expected
in their day. It should be no surprise that the Wesleys, in this
regard, stand in the "evangelical succession" that traces its roots
distinctively back to Paul. According to the Apostle, the gospel of
Jesus Christ is a message of the power of God to bring salvation to
those who believe (or trust) in the faithfulness of Christ. Properly
understood, then, our faith is not the foundation of redemption,
but Christ's faith is. Faith—in the sense of putting our trust in
Christ—is the means for us to participate in the faithfulness and
salvation of Christ. The foundation of salvation is the faithfulness
of Christ, that is, the death and resurrection of Christ.[4]

The verb "justify" means "to make righteous" (being transformed as righteous) or "to reckon as righteous" (given the status
of righteous). The righteousness of God can be either the
essence/action of God (subjective genitive) or the gift of God
(objective genitive). The righteousness of God can refer to: (a) a
divine attribute; God's moral character of being the Righteous or
the Just One, thus the justified ones are those transformed and
sanctified by God's grace as the holy ones (saints); (b) a forensic
reality; the righteousness in which God is the Just One in the legal
sense; therefore, anyone who is righteous must meet the standard
of God's law (righteousness), otherwise we who are being justified
(made right) are imputed the legal status of righteousness without
the requirement of moral perfection; and (c) a covenantal status;
that righteousness, in which the elect are being initiated as the people of God by grace and, therefore, seek themselves to maintain the
covenant by upholding certain services.[5]

The Wesleyan tradition teaches that the righteousness of God comes through faith in Jesus Christ to all who believe. The word "believe" here can mean faith, trust, and faithfulness. Faith, as described by Paul in his letters, is not a qualification that some people possess in themselves, so that the gospel finds them eligible to receive its benefits. Faith arises only through an encounter with the gospel of Jesus Christ. In other words, saving faith is elicited only as a response to the proclamation of the gospel. Otherwise, faith implies a meritorious human work, which contributes in some way to the gospel. For Paul, the essence of faith is its opposition to all human merit and all human boasting. Faith signals an openness to the gospel. It is this understanding of the doctrine of justification by grace through faith that fueled the Wesleyan Revival. Faith, in essence, is the expression of freedom, which God, through the gospel, creates—a freedom of acknowledgment, obedience, and commitment. And this is what I mean by the word *trust* throughout this chapter.

John Wesley drew his conception of faith as trust straight out of the doctrinal heritage of his beloved Church of England. The *Homilies* of his church, which he republished for the benefit of his followers who were poor, contain a definition of faith that would shape his ministry and movement throughout his lifetime: "The right and true Christian faith is not only to believe that Holy Scripture and the articles of our faith are true, but also to have a sure trust and confidence to be saved from everlasting damnation by Christ."[6] Obviously drawing from Hebrews 11:1, as well as from classic Pauline texts, he echoes this definition in a profoundly biographical way in his formative sermon "Justification by Faith," where he writes: "Justifying faith implies, not only a divine evidence or conviction that 'God was in Christ, reconciling the world unto himself', but a sure trust and confidence that Christ died for *my* sins, that he loved *me*, and gave himself for *me*."[7]

In all of his sermons that touch upon faith in one way or another (and the list is long), Wesley's objective is always to help move people beyond simply knowing about Christ to having a vital relationship with God based upon trust. One of his early followers, Grace Murray, apparently learned the lesson well (better put, accepted the gift gratefully) and penned one of the most succinct statements of "faith as trust" as her epitaph:

I would have no encomiums passed on me; I AM A SINNER, SAVED FREELY BY GRACE: Grace, divine grace, is worthy to have all the glory. Some people I have heard speak much of our being faithful to the grace of God; as if they rested much on their *own* faithfulness: I never could bear this; it is *GOD'S FAITHFULNESS to his own word of promise*, that is my only security for salvation.[8]

Salvation by Trusting (Believing) in God's Grace and the Faithfulness of Christ

The doctrine of justification by grace through faith is confusing to many because the word "faith" can simultaneously refer to Jesus' work and to the human response. I use the word "faithfulness" to speak of Christ's saving work (his faithfulness to God even unto death, and his trust in God that salvation and resurrection is the *telos* of history rather than death) and the word "trust" to speak of the human response to Christ's gospel. Our faith has an instrumental or mediating function in that faith is a mode of receiving and participating in, not creating, the gospel of Jesus Christ. The faithfulness of Christ is the fountainhead of the doctrine of justification by grace because righteousness has its foundation in the redemption that comes by Jesus Christ (Rom. 3:24, 25).[9] This righteousness has its source, in other words, in the grace of God.[10] The action of God in redemption vindicates the righteousness of God both in nature and in God's promise (3:25b-26). Thus, the nature of this righteousness by faith precludes all boasting (3:27). Boasting is eliminated because of the principle of faith. Faith is a gift, not something in which anyone can boast.

There is no better place to engage a discussion of these issues than in Paul's Letter to the Galatians because the "gospel of grace" is one of its distinctive themes. I have found it especially helpful to reexamine the doctrine of justification by grace through faith by contextually interpreting the Galatian case. Paul warned the Galatians that they were turning away "from the one who called you by grace" (1:6, author's translation). "The one who called" was God whose will was to appoint believers to salvation and responsibility.[11] Paul preaches the *en chariti* (in grace) gospel of Jesus Christ and is astonished that the Galatians are turning away from that message of good news. So he offers a theological response to the Galatian community concerning the "works[12] of the law[13]" and the "faith[14] of Jesus Christ." The salvific event of Christ's faithfulness signified the covenantal love of God, which is the basis for Jews and Gentiles alike (i.e., all people) to be full members of God's household.[15]

Given this larger context, the doctrine of justification by grace through faith is expounded most clearly in the following ways.

First, faith means trust in Christ. In response to the exclusive mind-set of the Jewish Christians, Paul appeals to the Jewish concept of being justified/made righteous[16] (2:16). The difficulty he encounters, however, is the fact that justification through faith in Christ is unprecedented in the Jewish believers' assumptions. He explains to Jewish Christians that, by their own theological acknowledgment, "a person is not made righteous by works of the law but through the faith in/of Jesus Christ" (2:16). And so, "faith" in Galatians 2:16 does not denote just any trust. T. D. Gordon demonstrates that "faith" here always refers to faith in Christ, so much so that Paul uses the two terms "faith" and "Christ" interchangeably to mean the same thing.[17] Cosgrove also notes:

> There is no reason to interpret the polarization of works and faith in terms of antithetical principles of existence before God. The contrast is between the works of the law and the faith of Jesus Christ as soteriological instruments of justification. . . . In the context of Gal. 2:16 this interpretation finds an immediate confirmation in verse 17, where Paul speaks of justification en Christo. And the expression in 2:16a has its restatement in Gal. 3:11 where the apostle formulates.[18]

Second, trusting in Christ who "sets us right" is the new identity symbol of the people of God. The expressions "works of the Law" and "faith of Jesus Christ" create a parallelism between Law and Christ as the principle identity markers for God's people; only secondarily do they contrast the *works* of the Law with the *faith* of Jesus Christ. Paul dismisses the idea of being justified "by works of the law" (appears three times in Gal. 2:16; cf. 3:2, 5, 10). He is not placing a proper understanding of the law in an antithetical relationship with a perverted view of the law or to the Mosaic or Abrahamic covenant, which the law represents. Such an interpretation tends to see Judaism as a sort of perverted religion. It also ignores the Jewish context and the situational character of the Galatian epistle. It assumes too quickly that the guilty conscience of individuals leads to the quest for salvation through a legalistic life. The Galatian debate is concerned not with individuals but with the people of God; more precisely, it is concerned, not with the legalistic life of the individual, but with the identity symbol of the people of God: justification through faith in/of Christ or by works of the Law.

Given an audience of Jewish and Gentile Christians (not Jews and Gentiles), and given the context of the need to clarify symbols of identity in order to maintain one's covenanted status as God's people, the word "justified" cannot mean entering the covenant of grace, obtaining salvation in its beginning point, or receiving the imputed righteousness of Christ. The word probably is better translated as "set right" in the sense that a person or group is keeping the covenant that defines their restored relationship with God. The word "justified" (*dikaioun*), as a matter of fact, can have several meanings: to show justice, to vindicate someone as just, or to acquit someone.[19] The word's emphasis is not on the sinlessness of the just, rather it is on the one (in this case, God) who graciously vindicates or acquits others. The emphasis is not on acquittal from guilt and wrongdoing. The word *dikaioun* denotes a relationship that is set right by God from shame and curse to propriety, honor, and freedom.

Third, the doctrine of justification by grace through faith includes the foundation of Christ's faithfulness in which our faith dwells. The primary issue here is how to understand the phrase "faith in/of Jesus Christ." Is the more proper understanding rooted in the genitive subjective ("faithfulness of Jesus") or objective ("believe/trust in Jesus")? We have already seen how the principle of faith/trust is required on the part of believers in the old covenant maintained by moral legislation and in the new covenant oriented around Christ. Therefore, believing in Jesus Christ is part of the meaning of the phrase "faith of Jesus Christ." Certainly, the phrase "faith in/of Christ" has its unique connotative meaning in Galatians. Christ is the object of faith and not the subject of faith. But note it is not just "faith" that matters here. It is "Jesus Christ" that matters. Though justification through faith is a Jewish concept, justification in Christ Jesus is not. Given that in Jewish understanding, covenantal adherence to the law (nomism) is not antithetical to faith, then at this point, the only change or extension that the new movement, namely Christianity, asks for is that the traditional conservative Jewish faith be more precisely defined by faith in Jesus the Messiah.[20]

Perhaps Paul is intentional in keeping the ambiguity of the phrase "faith of/in Jesus Christ," using it sometimes to stress Christ's faith, sometimes to stress believers' faith in Christ, and sometimes to highlight the interplay of subjective and objective genitive (e.g., I have been crucified with Christ, and Christ lives in me). Whatever the case may be, Paul responds to the fear of the Jewish Christians about the old and the new identity symbols (Law and Christ) by summarizing his *faithing* (bonding trust) in the faith of Christ: "I am crucified with Christ. . . . Christ lives in me. . . . I live by the faith of the Son of God,[21] who loved me and gave himself over for me" (3:20, author's translation). While the Law may be misused to differentiate human beings into Jews and Gentiles, Christ by means of his death offers equality, identity, and new life to all people. So Paul's participating in the Christ event is a universal paradigm, into which all people in all times can find a place.

Fourth, faith in Christ is closely related to our identification with the faithfulness of Jesus, particularly to his absolute obedience and utter trust of God. Within the early Christian community, rituals such as baptism and eucharist were symbols pointing, at least in part, to Jesus' crucifixion. Romans 6:6 is the most transparent text in this regard: "We know that our old self was crucified with him." Again, the identification process of the self with Christ is in the imitative ritual; that is, the self lets go of self and allows the cruci-fied Christ to live in its place (Rom. 2:20). Yet, this form of "partic-ipation in Christ" is not so much a passive letting go of the self. It is the self actively living by the faith of the Son of God (Rom. 2:20). In other words, despite the constraining and negative influence of cosmic forces on the flesh *(sarx)*—or maybe because of these forces—the self has to actively live by identifying with and imitat-ing the faith of God's Son.

Since the process of identifying with Christ already assumes the need of faith on the part of believers, the phrase "I live by faith of the Son of God" most probably has the meaning of the subjective genitive—the faith of God's Son. The title Son of God, used frequently by Paul,[22] connotes the absolute obedience and utter trust of Jesus in the Father. This obedience and trust constitute the faithfulness of Christ, which becomes the paradigm and object of the believers' living force. Of most critical import, therefore, is the fact that Christ's faithful obedience—Christ's absolute trust in God—is the only sufficient symbol to grant both Jews and Gentiles rightful relationship with God. Christ is able to grant righteousness to both Jews and Gentiles!

Fifth, falling from grace has serious consequences. Paul explains the serious consequence of falling from grace, which he equates with retaining the works of the Law as a primary identity symbol to supplement the work of Christ: "You are cut off from Christ, you who would be justified in the law; you have fallen from grace" (5:4, author's translation). "Justified in the law," as a powerful symbol of the old covenant, means being set right to be God's people.[23] In the new age, however, "justified in the law," is not principally a matter of ethnic or national identity (to be a Jew); rather, for Paul, it symbolizes falling back to the old age, placing oneself essentially into bondage to the custody of the law. Since Paul has already explained that the Age of the Law and the Age of Christ cannot overlap each other, to revert to the Age of the Law, then, is to cut oneself off from Christ, from all his works and benefits. The Galatian Christians, however, have not yet been cut off from Christ.[24] Paul's concern is that the experience of justification by grace through faith leads humanity from bondage into freedom, from curse to blessing, from death to life. It is God's grace that sets them right as God's people, not the works of the law.

Sixth, the life of faith is essentially the acknowledgment of God's grace. Not only is Galatians 5:5-6 a classical locus for Wesley's definition of Christianity, namely, "faith working by love," but it also is the apex of Paul's argument: "For by the Spirit in faith, we await the hope of righteousness. For in Christ Jesus neither circumcision nor uncircumcision is of any worth, but faith working itself through love" (author's translation). Through the works of the Spirit and Christ, believers in Christ "await the hope of righteousness." The solidarity of the new community in Christ is even highlighted with the emphatic *hemeis* ("we") before the verb *apekdexometha* ("we await"). Human existence, lived out within the context of this new community of God's people, is a constant acknowledgment of the grace of God working out salvation through the past, the present, and the future. The grace of God functioned in the past as a promise of a greater reality that was to come (e.g., the Abrahamic covenant). The grace of God reaches out to us in the present to redeem us from the evil age through Christ's crucifixion, transferring those who believe from the old age into the new. The grace of God will continue to work in the future to draw us in union and obedience to God through the Holy Spirit. Freedom, understood in terms of living toward a greater reality, experiencing emancipation from powers of bondage in our lives, and faithing (living out of a bonding trust) that renews and re-creates through the power of the Spirit is the spiritual liberation of the Pauline theology.

To be God's people is to imitate Christ's faith and to live in this new age of freedom. To be God's people is to look forward to walking in the Spirit and living into that righteousness that God has promised as the hallmark of God's children.

Some Implications of "Justification by Grace Through Faith" for the Wesleyan Tradition Today

What wisdom can we garner from the two great mentors, Paul and John Wesley, that will reinvigorate the life of our Christian communities today? Several principles are clear in terms of finding our way forward into a renewed vision of our faith in Christ.

First, a properly understood doctrine of justification by grace through faith locates the individual identity of the Christian within the larger reality of the People of God. Faith is not simply the right or choice of an individual, a mistaken attitude so prevalent in, particularly, North American culture today. This misconception of faith as individual practice has resulted in spiritual bankruptcy for many because isolationism and competition segregate the believer from the strength and support of the community of faith. This is by no means to say that faith is not personal. The personal nature of Paul's own faith is profoundly affirmed in his words to the Galatian community: "*I* have been crucified with Christ; and it is no longer *I* who live, but it is Christ who lives in *me*... who loved *me* and gave himself for *me*" (Gal. 2:19-20, emphasis added). Here is the same "enpersonalization" of faith, characteristic of Wesley's "Aldersgate Experience," an essential understanding of faith in relationship that shaped his ministry from beginning to end. Yet, for the most part, Paul talks about the *social* dimension of the "in Christ" reality (Gal. 1:4)—the social dimension of children of Abraham (3:29), the children of God (3:26; 4:5, 6), and the fellowship meal shared among Jewish and Gentile Christians (2:9, 12). In faith, as in life, there is no such thing as a solitary Christian.

Second, the faithfulness of Jesus Christ is the basis of our faith in Christ. This understanding of Christ's faithfulness and its relation to our faith, which may be a new concept to many, refuses to make a new legalism of one's faith. It is important to remember that the primary reality that Paul was seeking to uphold by means of this doctrine was the grace of Jesus' salvific work. Many individuals (I should really say all Christians) have discovered repeatedly that their own faith is inadequate, weak, fragile, and thus they fail time and time again to be the true people of God. This is often the case because their individual faith has no object (Jesus Christ). A faith that has no Jesus Christ as its object essentially has no foundation. It is Christ the solid rock on which we stand. Any other self-oriented understanding of faith can only lead to a form of Christian legalism with all of its devastating effects.

A proper understanding of justification by grace through faith, however, holds our faith/trust and the faithfulness of Jesus Christ in a creative and dynamic tension. In Galatians, Paul is talking not only about our trusting response to the covenanted grace and love of God, but also about the covenanted grace and love of God as explicitly expressed by the faithfulness of Jesus Christ. In the critical verse that we have studied at length, Paul claims that "a person is not set right (in the sense of realizing membership in the covenanted community of God) by doing 'works of the law,' but through the faithfulness of Jesus Christ, even *we have believed in Christ Jesus*, in order to be set right by faithfulness in Christ, and not by 'works of the law,' because by 'works of the law' shall no one be set right" (2:16, author's translation). The phrase "we have believed in Christ Jesus" means our trusting response to the faithfulness of Christ's salvific work.

Third, the faithfulness of Christ and our faith in Christ help us better understand the useful role of the Law and the freedom found in the Spirit. The forensic (or legal) language of Paul, and understandings of justification that revolve primarily around these images, do not help us resolve the problem of guilt. The declaration of acquittal might temporarily suspend and cocoon the conscience from the attachments of guilt as grace and faith are "injected" as spiritual antidotes, but the declarative language of legally pardoned sinners, who continue to sin, only tears the guilty conscience apart into a sinner-righteous spiritual schizophrenia. The result, especially in cultures and among people that are deeply self-reliant, is the compulsive need to boost one's faith. The inadequacy of *my* faith is ever before *me*. Furthermore, within this paradigm of understanding, the Law appears as a judge that constantly convicts us of our guilt, rather than as a guidance mechanism that directs both individuals and communities to be faithful members of the covenant of grace.

Paul's language of justification was never intended to mean "legally pardoned and declared righteous exclusively" in the sense of sinlessness. His language is couched in a social interaction between Jews and Gentiles who shared the promise, salvation, and freedom of God. The concept of the Law and the full reality of Christ both assume grace and point to a love of God's covenanted bonds that potentially embrace all of God's children. The crux of the matter is not how an individual stands righteous before God; rather, the issue for Paul is how humanity is to be emancipated "from the present evil age" (1:4), "from the curse of the law" (3:13), from "the weak and beggarly elemental spirits" of the enslaving cosmos (4:9), and from bondage "to beings that by nature are not gods" (4:8).

Paul's understanding of the gospel of grace argues for a life of freedom for both Jew and Gentile. The goal is new creation (6:15) and liberation (1:4-6; 3:13; 4:31), for we are called by God to freedom (5:13). In other words, salvation is not concerned primarily with finding ways of being righteous before God. Salvation is living in the freedom of the covenanted love of God and under the guidance of the Spirit of Christ. More specifically, in the Galatian polemic, salvation is granting freedom to Jews and Gentiles so that as full members of the people of God, they *all* can live freely in Christ. The question is not whether the guilty conscience can be salved. It is our authenticity before God that defines who we are and that potentially leads to the freedom of others. The gospel of grace proclaims the triumph of the cross and resurrection of Jesus Christ so that all members of God's covenanted community are honored as heirs of God, children of the promise, people of freedom. The Wesleys made these same discoveries in eighteenth-century England, and these discoveries transformed their rugged band of followers into a chorus of "singing Christians."

5

THE WAY OF SALVATION

THE WESLEYAN TRADITION
AND THE RELIGION OF THE HEART

Ted A. Campbell

John Wesley once wrote to his sophisticated contemporaries—
"men of reason and religion," as he called them—and pleaded
with them to realize that true religion is "the religion of the heart."[1]
A consistent hallmark of the Wesleyan tradition has been the conviction that true religion not only consists of correct beliefs and
correct actions, but also involves a heart that is purified by genuine
repentance and by true love for God and for one's neighbor. True
religion fulfills the Great Commandment, "You shall love the Lord
your God with all your heart, and with all your soul, and with all
your mind," as well as the commandment "You shall love your
neighbor as yourself" (Matt. 22:37, 39).

The Religion of the Heart in Wesley's Age

In John Wesley's time, the spirit of the early Methodist movement emphasized a religion of the heart. For a hundred years
before Wesley's birth, European nations had been torn apart by
struggles over religion, with Protestants killing Catholics,
Catholics killing Protestants, and members of the same churches in
deadly military struggles for the reform of their nations and
churches. Christian theologians and pastors did their part to support these interreligious wars by producing elaborate systematic
theological treatises and sermons that justified their parties'

involvement in the wars of religion. Reacting against this religious bloodbath, many Europeans gave up on traditional religion. And the modern European remains haunted by the specter of religious coercion and religious bigotry. Other Europeans began to see that the essence of religion did not lie in correct beliefs or correct practices, but was a deeper matter of the heart.

The outlook on religion that stressed the role of the heart affected Catholics as well as Protestants in the 1600s. The Jansenist movement, for example, was a Catholic spiritual movement that emphasized the priority of God's grace and the need for genuine affections (repentance and love for God) in receiving the sacraments. The Quietist movement taught traditional meditative techniques that had been utilized by Catholic monks and nuns but tried to make these techniques and the deeper religious experiences that they involved part of the life of lay Catholics. Although Jansenism and Quietism were eventually condemned by Catholic authorities, the movement for devotion to the Sacred Heart of Jesus also came to widespread popularity in the late 1600s and remains one of the most important expressions of heartfelt religious piety in popular Catholic religious life.

The emphasis on the heart and the affections can be seen in a variety of Protestant movements in this period. English Puritanism, for example, began as an attempt to bring about more formal changes in the English Church, such as changes in the Church's ritual and its forms of government. By the early 1600s, though, Puritanism had begun to develop a concern for heartfelt religious piety. Puritan teachers, elaborating on a pattern they saw in Romans 8:30, saw the Christian life as following distinct stages: (a) effectual calling or vocation, associated with repentance prior to conversion, (b) justification, usually associated with a supernatural sense that one's sins had been forgiven, (c) sanctification, the process of growth in holiness following conversion, and (d) glorification, when a believer was joined to Christ after death. Puritan spiritual writers used this pattern to describe the lives of Christian believers or "saints," and they encouraged individual believers to write accounts of their conversion experiences and to keep a diary or journal recounting their spiritual struggles.

By the middle of the 1600s, the Puritan way of thinking about the religious life had begun to affect Protestant churches on the

European continent. A powerful religious movement that we call Pietism emphasized the importance of heartfelt repentance and faith as the Puritans had emphasized. Pietist leaders such as Philipp Jakob Spener and August Hermann Francke organized believers into small groups, or "conventicles," often meeting in believers' homes, where the scriptures were studied and personal religious experiences were recounted. Francke was influential in the development of Halle University, where he built a number of charitable institutions and tried to make religious experience a part of the normal curriculum for the students.

One very particular expression of Pietism was the renewal of the Moravian Church under Nikolaus Ludwig, the Count von Zinzendorf. Zinzendorf, who was almost exactly John Wesley's age, had been baptized by Spener and grew up in a household infused with Pietism. When the remnants of the medieval Moravian brethren fled from religious persecution to Germany, Zinzendorf allowed them to settle on his country estate at Herrnhut. He was quickly acknowledged as the leader (and was ordained as bishop) of the renewed Moravian community and vigorously supported its ministries, including its expansion into Britain and its missionary enterprise to the British colonies in North America.

Wesley's Encounter with the Religion of the Heart

John Wesley encountered almost all of the expressions of the religion of the heart mentioned above. He was a voracious reader and had studied works by the Jansenist author, the Abbé de Saint-Cyran, and by the famous Quietist teacher, Madame Guyon. He was deeply influenced by Puritan literature and had studied Pietist works as well, including August Hermann Francke's account of his charitable institutions in Halle. But until he left England for Georgia in October 1735, Wesley had never encountered these various strands of the religion of the heart as a living, contemporary religious movement.

On board the *Simmonds,* bound for his missionary service in the Georgia colony, Wesley encountered two groups representing Pietism. He met a group of Moravian missionaries, under the leadership of August Gottlieb Spangenberg, on its way to establishing a subcolony of its own in Georgia. He also met Lutheran pastors trained at Halle University, also involved in settling a group of colonists. Throughout his stay in the infant colony, which took all of the years 1736 and 1737, John Wesley continued to meet with the Moravian and Austrian Pietists, and he became deeply impressed with their sense of a personal experience of divine grace.

It was under the influence of these Pietists, especially the Moravians, that John Wesley had his well-known Aldersgate Street experience of May 24, 1738. Having returned from America earlier in the year, he continued to meet with a joint Moravian-Anglican society that met in Fetter Lane in the London borough of Chelsea. The Moravian leader Peter Böhler was particularly influential in helping Wesley believe that Christ would give him a supernatural assurance that his sins had been forgiven. John Wesley experienced this assurance at a meeting in Aldersgate Street on Wednesday evening, 24 May. Following this experience, he traveled in the summer of 1738 to Germany, visiting the Moravian settlement at Herrnhut and also visiting the son of Pietist leader August Hermann Francke at Halle University.

It is clear that these varied movements for a religion of the heart continued to affect Wesley throughout his life. Although the relationship was strained, he remained in contact with Moravians for several decades, holding a lengthy dialogue with Moravian leader Zinzendorf at London's Grays Inn in 1740. When Wesley published his *Christian Library*, a remarkable and eclectic series of editions of Christian authors, he included substantial works by English Puritans as well as by German Pietists. From the other side, the Methodist movement was understood to be part of a broader spiritual movement that included Pietism and Moravianism. A Moravian synod meeting in 1740, at precisely the time when Moravians had come into conflict with the early Methodist movement in England, explicitly linked all of these religious movements throughout Europe, specifically naming "those zealous servants of God, who, in Germany, by some were called Pietists, in England, Methodists, in France, Jansenists, in Italy and Spain, Quietists, in the Roman Church in general often known by the character of preacher of repentance and ascetics, but in the Protestant Church generally thought Mystics."[2]

It should be clear, then, that the Wesleyan movement was part of this broad trend toward heartfelt religious experience that John Wesley had encountered.[3] As we shall see in the next section, the most distinctive notes of the Wesleyan movement reflected this trend towards a "religion of the heart."

The Religion of the Heart and the Wesleyan Movement

If we look even briefly at the substance of the Wesleyan movement—the sermons, hymns, tracts, even the consistent manners of speaking that characterized the movement—we can see the emphasis on heartfelt religious faith through and through. One of the most characteristic notes of the Wesleyan movement, for example, was preaching on "the way of salvation." John Wesley believed that he could identify a general pattern to the religious life and encouraged his preachers to recognize the stages or progress of the spiritual life, so that they, in turn, could guide followers into the next appropriate stages of spiritual development.

In many ways, Wesley's understanding of the "way of salvation" reflected the Puritan delineation of the "order of salvation" proceeding from "effectual calling," or vocation, through justification, and then through the process of sanctification. But Wesley stressed the universal availability of grace in contrast to the Puritans' insistence on election and predestination, and he consistently maintained that the goal of sanctification is complete love for God, or "entire sanctification," which he believed to be available by divine grace in this life. The characteristically Wesleyan pattern, then, is sometimes described using the three categories of prevenient, justifying, and sanctifying grace, although Wesley himself could give more elaborate and nuanced understandings of the stages in the way of salvation.

Moreover, the categories of prevenient, justifying, and sanctifying grace describe what we might call the divine side of the process of salvation. What is equally distinctive of the Wesleyan movement is that at each step or stage, Wesley's sermons not only describe but also elicit the affections or emotions appropriate to that stage. We might say that this affective or emotional response represents the human side of the divine-human encounter in sal-

vation. At least, it represents the way in which the process of salvation appears to the human participant.

For example, in preaching to unrepentant sinners, John Wesley
spoke of the claims of the divine Law and the certainty of judgment, eliciting reverence for the Law and appropriate fear of
divine judgment. In preaching to sinners who had repented but
were yet unconverted, Wesley spoke of the promises of the gospel,
including the promise of the "assurance" of pardon, eliciting faith
and confidence in the promises of God and joy in the thought of
forgiveness. To believers, Wesley spoke of the need for purity of
heart, of appropriate moral action, and of the quest for sanctification, eliciting a wide variety of affective responses: fear of backsliding, continuing reverence for the claims of God in scripture,
constancy and fervency in prayer, compassion for the poor and the
suffering, present joy in Christian fellowship, and the even greater
joy of contemplating eternal fellowship with Christ and the saints
in heaven.

Often at the conclusion of sermons, Wesley most explicitly elicited
these emotional responses to the work of God. Consider, for example, the way in which Wesley elicits fear of sin and of backsliding
in the conclusion to his sermon "The Great Privilege of Those that
are Born of God":

> Let us fear sin more than death or hell. Let us have a jealous
> (though not painful) fear, lest we should lean to our own deceit-
> ful hearts. "Let him that standeth take heed lest he fall." Even he
> who now standeth fast in the grace of God, in the faith that
> "overcometh the world", may nevertheless fall into inward sin,
> and thereby "make shipwreck of his faith." And how easily then
> will outward sin regain its dominion over him! Thou, therefore,
> O man of God, watch always, that thou mayest always hear the
> voice of God. Watch that thou mayest pray without ceasing, at all
> times and in all places pouring out thy heart before him.[4]

This is in many ways characteristic of Wesley's sermon conclusions. But the range of emotions elicited in his sermons is huge,
and Wesley developed an elaborate vocabulary—a specialized tax-
onomy—to describe this range of affective responses to the gospel.

One of John Wesley's lesser known works, his "Directions
Concerning Pronunciation and Gesture," offers a concrete image

of what it might have been like to hear Wesley or one of the early Methodist preachers as he delivered a message such as this. Wesley gives elaborate instructions following the traditions of classical rhetoric and speech, concerning ways to vary the voice, ways to speak, and even directions on how to utilize the hands in gesturing during a sermon. He drives home the point that the preacher's whole mannerism, especially the preacher's own affective stance, must echo the substance of the sermon. In other words, if a preacher were to deliver the conclusion given above without displaying genuine fear, the preacher's mannerism would contradict the message of the sermon itself. Wesley envisioned a symphony of emotional or affective display and response in preaching, with the preacher's message and mannerism uniting to elicit the appropriate emotional response to the message of the gospel.

As John Wesley's sermons elicited this range of heartfelt responses, his brother Charles Wesley's hymns did also. The hymns reinforced the same range of affective or emotive responses as the sermon corpus. In Methodist preaching and worship, the combination of hymns and sermons (preached in the manner described above) produced remarkable emotional force. Consider, just as a single example, the following lines from Charles Wesley, which elicit the same affective response of fear of sin as the sermon excerpt from John Wesley given above. Note that the word "want," as Charles Wesley used it, has both the sense of "desire" and "need" (or even "lack"):

> I want a principle within
> Of jealous godly fear,
> A sensibility of sin,
> A pain to feel it near.
> I want the first approach to feel
> Of pride or wrong desire,
> To catch the wandering of my will,
> And quench the kindling fire.[5]

John Wesley collected Charles Wesley's hymns in 1780 under the title *A Collection of Hymns for the Use of the People Called Methodists*. This became the first Methodist hymnal in widespread use, and

John arranged the hymns in a careful topical arrangement that displayed the range of religious affections, following his understanding of the "way of salvation." In this way, the systematic arrangement of the hymnal itself reinforced the distinctly Wesleyan emphasis on "the religion of the heart."

What Happened to the Religion of the Heart?

As Methodism spread following the course of the Industrial Revolution in eighteenth-century England and the frontier expansion of nineteenth-century America, the emphasis on heartfelt religious faith was understood to be a hallmark of the Wesleyan movement. Accounts of Methodist meetings frequently refer to the fervor of preaching and hymn-singing among the people, who in some places were known as "Shouting Methodists."

Although fervor and emotion may persist in some Methodist quarters today, Methodists often express nostalgia for the emotionalism of their past. It is not easy to blame any one person or group for this loss of emotive potency. Victorian Methodism (on both sides of the Atlantic) developed a formality, to which earlier Methodist "enthusiasm" seemed alien. Although some forms of theological Liberalism (e.g., that of Schleiermacher) emphasized religious experience, its religious experience tended to be a generic sort of experience than the fervent religious experiences of earlier Pietists or Methodists. Moreover, the powerful movement to Neo-Orthodoxy in the past century had its own reasons to disparage or at least to de-emphasize claims of personal religious experience in its stress on the objective reality of divine grace. Perhaps the overriding truth is that it is difficult to sustain religious fervor and enthusiasm over a period of two centuries and through several generations of religious leadership.

But the historic Wesleyan tradition was so much a "religion of the heart" that there can be no adequate understanding of that tradition without explicitly understanding its emphasis on the role of the heart and the affections in Christian life. And moreover, there surely can be no genuine renewal of the Wesleyan tradition today without a renewal of the sense of personal encounter and affective response that has so distinctively marked our tradition.

Like the Methodists of earlier generations, we cannot program God to revive the Church in a particular way, but we can pray (fervently!) that God's grace will enable us to reclaim this unique and distinctive sense of the Wesleyan tradition as a religion of the heart.

6

WORKS OF PIETY AS SPIRITUAL FORMATION

CULTIVATING THE GRACE-FILLED LIFE

Steve Harper

We live the Christian life by grace. Prevenient grace precedes our first conscious desire to please God. Converting grace provides both justification and regeneration. Sanctifying grace enables us to mature in Christ. And glorifying grace leads us from this world into the next. Before we take our first breath and after we have drawn our last one, grace awakens, guides, sustains, and protects us. God's unmerited favor attends us all our days. Grace is the keynote of the Wesleyan salvation song.

But having said that, we must ask, "How does grace operate?" It does not dangle in our lives as an abstract concept or influence us as a magical element. To be sure, the grace of God has more than enough mystery in it to keep us exploring its nature and manifestations all our days. But its operation is not beyond our ability to describe the fundamental ways in which it comes to us and operates in us. Closely connected to a theology of grace are the means of grace, which Wesley defined as "the ordinary channels of conveying [God's] grace into the souls of men."[1] The means of grace become the way we describe our appropriation of grace day by day.

Wesley divided the means of grace into two categories—works of piety (the instituted means) and works of mercy (the prudential means). In doing so, he was connecting the early Methodist movement with the larger Christian tradition, in general, and with the Anglo-Catholic tradition, in particular. He did this as an expression of a larger theology of grace, in which God works in the believer to promote both inward and outward holiness. In this chapter, I will concentrate upon the works of piety. In the next chapter, Rebekah Miles will explore issues related to the works of mercy. Taken together, the instituted and prudential means of grace form the basic structure for spiritual formation in the Wesleyan tradition.[2] The works of piety in particular are those means of grace that contribute to the development of Christlike character—the shaping and strengthening of the inner life of the believer.

This chapter does not presuppose any previous knowledge of the topic, so a brief review of the works of piety is in order. Albert C. Outler maintained that the phrase "means of grace" probably appeared for the first time in "The General Thanksgiving" in the 1662 edition of the *Book of Common Prayer*.[3] Wesley himself says that the term "has been generally used in the Christian church for many ages," but he does not elaborate on its genesis or major manifestations.[4] Within the larger concept, he enumerated five works of piety: prayer, searching the scriptures, the Lord's Supper, fasting, and Christian conference.[5]

A study of these means reveals quickly and clearly that they were practiced personally and corporately, privately and collectively. No charge of "privatized spirituality" can be laid at Wesley's feet. As an inheritor and advocate of the holy living tradition, Wesley could not be troubled more than to see the way some contemporary interpretations of the means of grace have made them too personal and private—divorced from the Christian community and the world for whom Christ died. Consequently, as we study them in this chapter, we must keep the personal and the communal dimensions together, and we must remember (as the next chapter will show) that all the means of grace are for the purpose of enabling believers to live as representatives of Christ in the world.

The Works of Piety for Wesley

At the center of Wesley's concept of spiritual formation was his desire for the establishment and maintenance of Christlikeness.

But like all genuine spiritual guides, he knew that the promotion of such character is not automatic or accidental. Rather, it is the fruit of a devoted response on the part of believers to the prior and primary workings of God. Even the response is not haphazard; it is the conscious and conscientious practice of key disciplines that God has chosen to effect the formation of the life of God in the human soul. These actions he called "the means of grace."

An examination of his views reveals that he placed the means of grace at the center of Methodist devotional life for reasons that enabled him to set forth key elements of genuine Christianity and also to stand against some of the prevailing notions of his day, which eroded a life of dedicated discipleship. A brief review of these reasons will help set the means of grace in their proper context.[6]

Wesley believed that, within the aspects of genuine Christianity, the means of grace helped establish the proper identity and activity of God—that is, God as essentially a God of grace, who acts relationally and redemptively in the person of Jesus Christ. He also saw the means of grace essential to promoting "religion of the heart," which he summarized as love of God and neighbor through a life expressive of the fruit of the Spirit. The means of grace likewise contributed to his concern for "perfection in love" as believers sought to grow in the grace and knowledge of Jesus Christ over the course of their lifetimes. Connected to these ideas of growth and maturation was the role of the means of grace in helping Christians remain connected to one another and to the church. In short, the means of grace made real the presence of God in the Christian life.[7]

With regard to the use of the means of grace as protection against eroding notions of his day, Wesley saw them as particularly suited to guard against formalism, on the one hand, and enthusiasm, on the other. The former was an expression of a cold (indifferent) practice of one's religion, while the latter was an emotional superficiality that lacked the substance of true Christian faith. Practicing the means of grace enabled believers to hold the cognitive and affective dimensions of faith together and to experience a depth of maturity, which either extreme failed to produce.

In a similar fashion, the means of grace stood against the antinomianism of the eighteenth century. Wesley was deeply troubled at those who held the false notion that God's grace operates irresistibly and infallibly and therefore neglected the personal and corporate spiritual disciplines that shaped the church. At the same time, the use of the means of grace also canceled out any notions of "perfectionism" by keeping believers radically dependent upon the grace of God all the days of their lives. And thus, even this brief survey of the context in which Wesley placed the means of grace is sufficient to show their essential role in authentic spiritual formation.

With respect to the instituted means of grace, we focus upon the character formation necessary for the Christlikeness to which we have already pointed. Believers must "be" persons of piety even as they seek to "do" acts of mercy in the name of Jesus. The instituted means of grace are the usual channels God uses to form people into the image of Christ.

Prayer is the first work of piety. Wesley did not go out of his way to prioritize the instituted means of grace. In fact, he most often showed them to be in a dynamic relationship with each other in their actual practice. For example, he put the use of prayer alongside searching the scriptures while reading the Bible devotionally. But he did refer to prayer as the chief means of grace—"the grand means of drawing near to God."[8] This is most likely due to his understanding of the Christian life as a relationship between ourselves and God. Relationships are established and maintained on the basis of good communication. Prayer is the means of grace by which we commune with God, the means that creates and promotes the essence of the Christian relationship.

An examination of Wesley's works reveals that he used all types of prayer: adoration, confession, thanksgiving, supplication, and intercession. He followed the basic pattern of the Daily Office as provided in the *Book of Common Prayer*, but he also interspersed extemporaneous praying into his devotions. He prayed for the same kinds of things we pray for, and he did so even when his emotions were dry and his confidence was lacking.[9] Wesley lived to pray and prayed to live. And that which he practiced, he commended to others through his personal counsel and his published works.

Searching the Scriptures followed closely in the works of piety. The higher critical study of scripture was not foreign to Wesley, but the ancient practice of *lectio divina* ("divine reading") was still his favored way of approaching the Bible. In fact, it can be argued that searching the scriptures was another form of prayer, as it had been for his predecessors in the faith. Through a careful and prayerful exploration of the text, he was enabled to "read, mark, and inwardly digest" the Word of God.[10]

We must not fail to note that Wesley's phrase "searching the scriptures" was an intentional way of defining this work of piety. He meant more than merely reading the Bible. Rather, he saw it as a deep contemplation upon the text using all his faculties and senses. He described it this way: "I meditate thereon, with all the attention and earnestness of which my mind is capable."[11] His stated goal was to know "the way to heaven" not only for himself, but also for others to whom he would teach what he was learning.

Searching the scriptures was also a phrase that had method and purpose attached to it. Whether he was using the lectionary readings in the *Book of Common Prayer* or exploring the Bible in some other fashion, the following items were always included in his reading:

1. Dailiness—morning and evening;
2. Singleness of purpose—to know God's will;
3. Correlation—to compare scripture with scripture;
4. Inspiration—to receive instruction from the Holy Spirit;
5. Resolution—to put into practice what is learned.[12]

Through searching the scriptures, Wesley was enabled to encounter the whole counsel of God and to be shaped by the formative influence of the Bible's normative revelation. Throughout his lifetime, he did not hesitate to describe himself as *homo unius libri* — "a man of one book." Scripture was both the source of light and life and the soul's "supreme court" in matters of faith and practice.[13]

The Lord's Supper is the third work of piety. Wesley inherited a sacramental spirituality from both the Puritan and Anglican traditions of his parents, but his promotion of Holy Communion was far more than an extension of his family and faith heritages. It was a deep belief that participation in the sacrament was a God-ordained means of experiencing the spiritual presence of Christ. He lamented the fact that the Lord's Supper had been grossly neglected in the Church of England, and he called the early

Methodists to a principle of "constant communion," which included partaking of the sacrament as often as possible. Wesley's own words say it best: "Let every one, therefore, who has either any desire to please God, or any love of his own soul, obey God, and consult the good of his own soul, by communicating every time he can."[14] It has been estimated that Wesley lived up to his own exhortation by receiving the Lord's Supper once every four or five days.

He felt that, as with prayer and searching the scriptures, Holy Communion would most benefit believers, but he also believed the means of grace (including the Lord's Supper) could convey God's prevenient and converting grace as well. Consequently, all persons were cordially invited to the table if they "truly and earnestly repented of their sins" and sought to lead a new life made possible to them by God through Jesus Christ.[15] Celebration of the Lord's Supper became the high point in early Methodist worship.

Fasting is the fourth work of piety. After a flirtation with a more ascetic understanding of fasting, Wesley settled into a healthy and sustained practice of it. Rather than viewing it as a protracted time of abstinence from food, he saw it as an ongoing discipline intended to wean the soul from an attachment to earthly things and to keep the priority on our spiritual destiny.[16] For a time, he fasted on Wednesdays and Fridays, but later, he dropped Wednesday. Friday remained a prescribed day of fasting for the people called Methodists.

Wesley's approach to fasting is as incisive as his weekly practice of it. He would begin to fast after the evening meal on Thursday. From then until midafternoon on Friday, he abstained from food, committing the time he would normally spend eating to an extended time of devotion. Around 3:00 P.M. on Friday, Wesley would break the fast with tea. From this process, we can see not only a patterning after the passion of Christ from Thursday evening until Friday afternoon, but also a realistic denial of food that did not place his health in jeopardy. In fact, if he was sick, he would include liquids (such as tea and soup) during the period. The purpose of fasting was not to mortify the flesh, but to elevate the soul.

Christian conference is the fifth work of piety. As with his predecessors in the faith, Wesley believed that God conveyed grace when two or more Christians gathered to "confer" on matters of faith and practice. Consequently, he intentionally functioned as a spiritual guide for people (through personal counsel and correspondence), and he set out to structure the early Methodist movement as a "conferring" connection of believers. Methodist bands, classes, societies, and annual conferences illustrate his commitment to community and the grace that comes through sacred fellowship.

The importance that Wesley placed on Christian conference can be seen in an oft-quoted statement he made after visiting Pembrokeshire and finding no regular society meeting there. He commented bluntly that "preaching like an Apostle, without joining together those that are awakened, and training them up in the ways of God, is only begetting children for the murderer."[17] He concluded that nine out of ten of the once-awakened ended up more asleep than ever. As Methodism grew, he maintained his belief that the movement would cease to be vital if Christian conference were lost.

These are the works of piety commended by Wesley both through his personal practice of them and by his continuous counsel to the early Methodists to make them central in their spiritual formation. Before we turn to the significance of these means of grace for today, we must emphasize one point. Wesley was clear and adamant in his belief that in and of themselves, the means of grace were impotent to produce the life of God in the human soul.

Again, his own words say it best: "*Before* you use any means let it be deeply impressed on your soul: There is no *power* in this. It is in itself a poor, dead, empty thing: separate from God, it is a dry leaf, a shadow. Neither is there any *merit* in my using this, nothing intrinsically pleasing to God, nothing whereby I deserve any favour at his hands, no, not a drop of water to cool my tongue."[18] He had seen too much of dead orthodoxy, the mere superficial use of disciplines divorced from the devoted spirit that practices works of piety properly. Even the means of grace are gifts given to believers by the God of grace. But when rightly viewed and used, they formed the essence of spiritual formation in the early Methodist movement.

Works of Piety Today

The past two decades have shown a marked increase of interest in Wesley studies. Thanks to the efforts of persons like Albert C.

Outler and Frank Baker (and a host of their colleagues), almost every aspect of Wesleyan history, theology, and ministry has received fresh attention. Spiritual formation in the Wesleyan tradition is no exception, and all the more so given the renewal of interest in the spiritual life throughout Christendom.[19]

At the same time, a resurgence of interest in character development and ethics has been seen in areas such as leadership and management, both in the church and in the business community. All of this makes a discussion of the means of grace more natural and valuable than might otherwise be the case. When we look at the works of piety today, we can see that they play a vital role in relation to contemporary spiritual formation.

First, they help recapture "religion of the heart." Such religion is more than either the cognitive or the affective dimensions of life. Rather, it is a reference to the center of a human being, the core of who we are. John Wesley used the term to describe a Christian faith larger than either orthodoxy (right belief) or orthopraxy (right actions). He used it to portray a faith that Gregory S. Clapper has called "orthokardia."[20] When "orthokardia" is applied to the works of piety, we can see how those works predispose us toward love of God and neighbor, which Wesley often defined as the essence of the Christian life. The works of piety are essential precisely because they create the desire to behave in certain ways.

We need a recovery of "heart religion" in our time. The Body of Christ has been too fragmented between those who prefer a personal gospel and those who lean toward a social gospel. In more recent times, a large portion of the church has become enamored by "signs and wonders" and a very emotional practice of faith, while yet another segment has continued to promote a very rationalistic view. A "religion of the heart" challenges the whole church to integrate faith. Far from being touchy-feely practices, the works of piety dispose us to deep levels of devotion, into which God speaks not only a formational word, but also a missional word. We need that level of devotion today.

Second, the works of piety root us in biblical Christianity. We have already noted Wesley's own propensity to call himself a "Bible Christian" and his desire to establish the early Methodist movement firmly on the foundation of scriptural Christianity. In the same way that "religion of the heart" is neither exclusively personal nor social, so also scriptural Christianity cannot be captured by words such as "fundamentalist" or "liberal." Instead, biblical Christianity is a vantage point, from which to understand that all of life is lived in relation to divine revelation. We are not the masters of our fate and the captains of our souls; we are the children of God. As such, we consciously and conscientiously place ourselves under the guidance of scripture.

Biblical Christianity is encountered directly through the activity of searching the scriptures, but it remains an active and objective presence in the other means of grace as well. When we ask about prayer, the Lord's Supper, fasting, and Christian conference, we root our inquiry in the question, "What does scripture say?" We do this not because of an aberrant bibliolatry, but rather because we know that there must be some normative source for the arrangement of faith and life. Otherwise, we are left to the whims of a contemporary subjectivism that grows increasingly relative and transient.[21]

Third, the works of piety resource us in classical Christianity. They set us free from the various "cults of the contemporary." Rooted in scripture, each of the works of piety is enriched by the example of people and faith traditions spanning two millennia. The works of piety call us to be dissatisfied with spiritual food drawn from any single source. The Body of Christ is rich in its Roman Catholic, Orthodox, Protestant, Nondenominational, and Parachurch components. We have much to learn.

Classical Christianity is yet another transcending term, not defined by either "ancient" or "modern," but more nearly akin to those streams of faith that have stood the test of time and have been represented by the unquestioned leaders of Christianity. We may be benefiting from Julian of Norwich one moment and E. Stanley Jones the next. In either case we are within the bounds of classical faith. A look at Wesley's personal reading lists gives quick and deep evidence to the benefits of this kind of spiritual formation. Conversation with those whom we most admire today likewise confirms the role of that which is "classical" in their formation.[22]

Fourth, the works of piety relate us to ecumenical Christianity. This is closely connected to the previous point, but it bears specific mention. Spiritual formation in the Wesleyan tradition is not about "making Methodists" but about "forming people into the image of Christ." The Christ-image has not ever been and never will be captured by a single stream or tradition of faith. The works of piety inevitably call us to drink from wells all along our journey. Sometimes, those wells will not be the ones our accustomed tradition has dug.

We are living in a time when a growing number of persons believe we are headed for something akin to another Reformation. I happen to be among them. And like them, I believe that one of the hallmarks of this new movement of God will be a reconnecting of parts of the Body of Christ, which have previously been separated by doctrinal, liturgical, or institutional differences. One of the things the Holy Spirit seems to be doing today is "lowering the walls" just enough so that we can peer into one another's territory and smile at each other. The differences are not eliminated or obliterated, just reduced enough so that a new mutual appreciation and cooperation can emerge. The works of piety bring us into all segments of the church.

Finally, the works of piety renew us in authentic Christianity. By that, I mean that they do, in fact, enable us to respond to God's grace so that "the mind that was in Christ" is increasingly formed in us. There is a genuine impartation of Christlikeness in our lives instead of limited effects of righteousness. Wesley put it this way: "And what is righteousness but the life of God in the soul, the mind which was in Christ Jesus, the image of God stamped upon the heart, now renewed after the likeness of him that created it?"[23]

Unfortunately, the recent history of the faith has had more than its fair share of defections of faith by noted leaders. Perhaps these have been no more severe or numerous than in times past, but we are close enough to them to see the damage they have done to both believers and nonbelievers. They are far from what God intends the witness of the people of God to be. A deeper work is needed—something that grounds our witness in the depths of character. The works of piety are given to us by God specifically for that purpose. A devoted use of them personally and corporately will not guarantee immunity from a fall, but it will surely function as a "watchman on the walls" for our lives.

After you have read the next chapter related to the works of mercy, you will have your basic primer in Wesleyan spiritual formation. But like so many other aspects of genuine Christianity, an introduction will also be an invitation to spend the rest of your life exploring all the avenues of faith development that the means of grace provide. We have the weight of Christian history (in both scripture and tradition) moving to this kind of discipleship. We have the reasonable and experiential witness of Wesley and of those who preceded and followed him to know we are on the right track. Through the works of piety, we are invited by the living God to have our hearts warmed at the fires of gracious love.

7

WORKS OF MERCY AS SPIRITUAL FORMATION

WHY WESLEY FEARED FOR THE SOULS OF THE RICH

Rebekah Miles

Wesley's vision of the moral life challenges a common assumption of many today—that morality, good works, and social justice are distinct from a spiritual life of holiness.[1] You cannot understand John Wesley's ethics without grasping this one point: *For Wesley, moral living is absolutely necessary to a life of holiness*. It is not just a fruit or an evidence of a holy life; it is a means of grace necessary to nourish the holy life. Moral living is crucial for our holiness and happiness in this life and in the next.

One of the clearest examples of this intimate link between moral living and holiness is seen in Wesley's passionate preaching on wealth.[2] In sermon after sermon, Wesley argued that the rich person's failure to give to the poor endangers the rich person's very soul. He insisted that for the wealthy, holiness, spiritual vitality, love of God, and even faith are directly linked to generosity to the poor. This example is important in an immediate, personal way because by Wesley's standards, most of us reading this chapter are rich. And as we will see, this example is important for my larger point also. Wesley's admonitions to the rich illuminate his understanding of the link between moral living and holiness.

But why did Wesley believe that giving was so crucial? For Wesley, charity to the poor is one example of what he calls "works of mercy." These works of mercy are important means of grace in the Christian life. To understand his vision of the moral life, then, we must answer several questions about these works. What are works of mercy, and how are they means of grace for the Christian? What are the specific works of mercy that Wesley recommended to others and practiced himself? What role do these works of mercy play in the Christian life? Drawing on one example of these works of mercy—giving to the poor—we ask what role charitable giving, as well as the larger issue of the proper use of money, plays in the holy life. Finally, what does this eighteenth-century vision of the moral life have to do with our lives in the twenty-first century?

Wesley's Understanding of Works of Mercy

First, what are works of mercy, and how are they means of grace for the Christian?

For Wesley, a means of grace, as Steve Harper has shown, is a regular channel by which God offers us grace. Wesley notes that though "works of piety" tend to come to mind when we think of the means of grace, there is surely more to it than that. He writes:

> We usually mean by [means of grace] those that are usually termed "works of piety", namely, hearing and reading the Scripture, receiving the Lord's Supper, public and private prayer, and fasting.... But are they the only means of grace? Are there no other means than these whereby God is pleased, frequently, yea, ordinarily to convey his grace to them that either love or fear him? Surely there are works of mercy, as well as works of piety, which are real means of grace.[3]

Second, what does Wesley mean by "works of mercy"?

Doing works of mercy means doing good to one's neighbor. Wesley notes that although works of mercy are most commonly associated with almsgiving, they cover a much broader scope.[4] He devotes considerable energy to a description of such works in his sixth discourse of "Upon our Lord's Sermon on the Mount." Among these merciful works, we must certainly include "everything which we give, or speak, or do, whereby our neighbour may be profited, whereby another man may receive any advantage, either in his body or soul."[5] Though these works of charity could include innumerable activities on behalf of others, Wesley emphasized a few central works of mercy in his preaching and practice, those in fact that reflect the mandate of scripture. They include "the feeding the hungry, the clothing the naked, the entertaining or assisting the stranger, the visiting those that are sick or in prison, the comforting the afflicted, the instructing the ignorant, the reproving the wicked, the exhorting and encouraging the well-doer."[6]

These specific works of mercy were central not only to Wesley's teachings about Christian faith but also to his living of faith. He and the early Methodists visited the sick and the imprisoned. They set up schools and offered basic medical care. They gave generously to the poor and helped them secure loans and jobs.[7] Wesley exhorted members of his Methodist Societies to engage in works of mercy not only because it was a command of Scripture and benefited the recipients. He encouraged them to do good also because they could neglect works of mercy only at the peril of their growth in holiness.

Third, what role do these works of mercy play then in the Christian life?

Works of mercy are expressions of our love for God and for neighbor as well as a way of practicing and even feeding our love. As a means of grace, works of mercy are a channel of God's grace to us as we offer ourselves in caring for others. Practicing these works is a way of strengthening the Christian virtues or "holy tempers," such as meekness and humility. Just as physical exercise promotes the growth of our bodies, works of mercy can promote the growth of our souls. As we practice these virtues, they become more fully developed in our lives. They are, ultimately, both an expression of, and tinder for, the love of God that centers our life. For Wesley, love of God and neighbor, the holy tempers, and works of mercy are all organically and intimately related, as he sought to demonstrate in his sermon "On Zeal":

> In a Christian believer *love* sits upon the throne, which is erected in the inmost soul; namely, love of God and man, which fills the whole heart, and reigns without a rival. In a circle near the throne are all *holy tempers:* long-suffering, gentleness, meekness, goodness, fidelity, temperance—and if any other is comprised in "the mind which was in Christ Jesus." In an exterior circle are all the

works of mercy, whether to the souls or bodies of men. By these we exercise all holy tempers; by these we continually improve them, so that all these are real *means of grace.*[8]

Why does Wesley consider these works of mercy to be necessary?

Do they earn us salvation? Wesley is adamant throughout his writings that no works, whether works of piety or works of mercy, merit justification. We are justified or pardoned by God's mercy as we trust in Christ. But for the followers of Christ, good works are a means of grace for a life of holiness and even for eternal salvation. In the sermon "On Visiting the Sick," Wesley writes: "The walking herein is essentially necessary, as to the continuance of that faith whereby we 'are' already 'saved by grace,' so to the attainment of everlasting salvation."[9] These works are not optional, then, but necessary for the Christian life and the Christian hope for eternity. On the one hand, when Christians practice works of mercy in love, their love increases, their holy tempers (patience, gentleness, etc.) are exercised and improved, and they grow in grace. On the other hand, when they fail to practice them, they "do not receive the grace which otherwise they might. Yea, and they lose, by a continued neglect, the grace which they had received."[10]

Wesleyan Solidarity with the Poor

A primary example of the link between moral living and holiness is evident in Wesley's many exhortations to the prosperous on the dangers of riches and the benefits of giving.[11] Over time, Wesley came to preach more often as well as more passionately about money—specifically, the horrible dangers of riches. This is hardly surprising. Wesley's people, following his injunctions to work hard, gaining all they could by honest, healthy industry, wasting no time but being serious and diligent at their work and, saving all they could by avoiding luxurious spending, had naturally become quite prosperous.[12] Wesley was anxious because many were not giving away all they could and in some cases, not even saving all they could but living in luxury and excess. The tendency for his people to gain without giving all left Wesley fearful because it would surely have disastrous consequences not only for the bodies of the poor but also for the souls of the rich.

When Wesley preached the sermon "Causes of the Inefficacy of Christianity," his diagnosis of the spiritual illness of the Methodists was that they grow wealthy but do not give. He writes of his Methodist people:

> You may find many that observe the first rule, namely, "Gain all you can." You may find a few that observe the second, "Save all you can." But how many have you found that observe the third rule, "Give all you can"? Have you reason to believe that five hundred of these are to be found among fifty thousand Methodists? And yet nothing can be more plain than that all who observe the two first rules without the third will be twofold more the children of hell than ever they were before.[13]

Wesley was not afraid for only the extremely or ostentatiously rich. For Wesley, the rich are simply those who have enough to supply themselves and their households (and where applicable, their businesses) with the "necessaries" and "conveniences" and still have a little left over. This fairly low threshold for wealth meant that by Wesley's estimation, many of the Methodists, especially in the later years of his life, were rich. Wesley was increasingly desperate to encourage these ordinary Methodists to use their prosperity wisely and generously, not only for the sake of the poor but also for their own souls' sake. One finds in his sermons on money repeated warnings about the hazards of riches. In the continual refrain, Wesley reminds his listeners that he has warned them about riches for all of his ministry, that they have paid little attention, and that the time is short for them to take heed. The day of judgment is coming. For example, in "The Danger of Riches," he exclaims:

> O ye Methodists, hear the word of the Lord! I have a message from God to all men, but to *you* above all. For above forty years...I have not varied in my testimony....I fear there is need to apply to some of *you* those terrible words of the Apostle: Go to, now, ye rich men! Weep and howl for the miseries which shall come upon you. Your gold and silver is cankered, and the rust of them shall witness against you, and shall eat your flesh, as it were fire." Certainly it will, unless ye both save all you can and give all you can....By the grace of God begin today![14]

This pattern is repeated again and again as Wesley ages. Preaching on frivolous spending in the sermon "On Dress," Wesley complains that "for near fifty years," he has given a "clear and faithful testimony." He continues, "I have not shunned to declare the whole counsel of God. I am therefore clear of the blood of those that will not hear. It lies upon their own head."[15] Likewise, in "The Danger of Increasing Riches," he reminds a complacent flock, "For considerably above half a century I have spoken on this head, with all the plainness that was in my power. But with how little effect!"[16] In 1789, just two years before his death, he continues the lament concerning the "Causes of the Inefficacy of Christianity":

> O that God would enable me once more, before I go hence and am no more seen, to lift up my voice like a trumpet to those who *gain* and *save* all they can, but do not *give* all they can. Ye are the men, some of the chief men, who continually grieve the Holy Spirit of God, and in a great measure stop his gracious influence from descending on our assemblies.[17]

And, finally, from his sermon "The Danger of Increasing Riches," written in 1790, the year before his death, a final reproof and plea:

> After having served you between sixty and seventy years; with dim eyes, shaking hands, and tottering feet, I give you one more advice before I sink into the dust. Mark those words of Saint Paul: "Those that desire" or endeavor "to be rich", that moment "fall into temptation"...."They fall into a snare"..."and into divers foolish and hurtful desires, which plunge men into destruction and perdition." You, above all men, who now prosper in the world, never forget these awful words! How unspeakably slippery is your path! How dangerous every step![18]

Wesley not only admonished others to give of their wealth and tried to set a good example by giving, but he also was keen that it be known he did not keep money. When he mistakenly thought he was dying in 1753, he wrote his own short epitaph, which included the important point that he died "not leaving, after his Debts are paid, Ten Pounds behind him."[19] Several years before, he had written, "If I leave behind me ten pounds (above my debts and the little arrears of my fellowship) you and all mankind bear witness against me that 'I lived and died a thief and a robber.' "[20]

Clearly, the issue of wealth was a point of monumental concern for Wesley that struck at the heart of his understanding of the Christian faith. What teaching on wealth is he so desperate to convey in these sermons, written across his ministry? Wesley's writings on riches illustrate the crucial link in his theology between holiness and the moral life. For Wesley, giving to the poor—providing clothing, food, and other necessities—is a chief work of mercy. Money is not an evil but is, instead, a primary vehicle by which people help one another and thereby grow in faith and love. Money is unspeakably precious and an excellent gift of God precisely because of the good it can do. According to his famous sermon "The Use of Money":

> In the hands of his children it is food for the hungry, drink for the thirsty, raiment for the naked. It gives to the traveller and the stranger where to lay his head. By it we may supply the place of an husband to the widow, and of a father to the fatherless; we may be a defence for the oppressed, a means of health to the sick, of ease to them that are in pain. It may be as eyes to the blind, as feet to the lame; yea, a lifter up from the gates of death.[21]

Money well used, then, is a great blessing. But when money is ill used, the blessing becomes a curse. And because riches are so often ill used, they pose a great danger. "It is no more sinful to be rich than to be poor," claims Wesley in his sermon "Dives and Lazarus." "But it is dangerous beyond expression. Therefore I remind all of you that are of this number, that have the conveniences of life, and something over, that ye walk upon slippery ground. Ye continually tread on snares and deaths. Ye are every moment on the verge of hell."[22] Very few people, Wesley claims, can hope to escape the temptations and snare inherent to wealth. For those who by grace are able to make their escape, the wounds inflicted are often deep and longlasting. It is because of this grave danger inherent to the possession of riches that Wesley expends so much time and passion preaching about wealth.

Central to Wesley's simultaneous optimism and pessimism about riches is his model of the good steward.[23] All that people possess, including all money, belongs to God. God is the proprietor, and the goods that people think of as their own are actually God's property temporarily given into their hands. Chief among the goods given to human stewards is money. "Above all," says Wesley in his sermon "The Good Steward," and drawing on Luke 12:42, "he has committed to our charge that precious talent which contains all the rest, *money*. Indeed, it is unspeakably precious if we are 'wise and faithful stewards' of it; if we employ every part of it for such purposes as our blessed Lord has commanded us to do."[24] The proper stewardship of this resource is one of the most important works of mercy.

The witness of the good steward is important and beneficial not only for this life but also for the next life. In the sermon "On Riches," Wesley underscores the urgency of his words about riches by pointing first to his own coming death and then to the death and judgment of his hearers:

> But now the time of our parting is at hand: my feet are just stumbling upon the dark mountains. I would leave one word with you before I go hence; and you may remember it when I am no more seen. O let your heart be whole with God!...Sit as loose to all things here below, as if you was a poor beggar. Be a good steward of the manifold gifts of God, that when you are called to give an account of your stewardship, he may say, "Well done, good and faithful servant: enter thou into the joy of thy Lord"![25]

When Christians use their money properly to serve God and neighbor, they are acting as God's faithful stewards. But when Christians use money improperly, by hoarding it or using it for their own luxury, they are robbing God as well as the poor for whom any excess wealth is intended. Wesley repeatedly warns that wasting money on luxuries is a double theft—from both the poor and God.[26] In his sermon "On Dress" he pleads:

> When you are laying out that money in costly apparel which you could have otherwise spared for the poor, you thereby deprive them of what God, the Proprietor of all, had lodged in your hands for their use. If so, what you put upon yourself you are, in effect, tearing from the back of the naked; as the costly and delicate food which you eat you are snatching from the mouth of the hungry. For mercy, for pity, for Christ's sake, for the honour of his gospel, stay your hand. Do not throw this money away. Do not lay out on nothing, yea, worse than nothing, what may clothe your poor, naked, shivering fellow-creature![27]

Failure to be a good steward is of consequence not only for the bodies of the poor as they continue in hunger and nakedness, but also for the souls of the prosperous. By desiring and using more than is necessary to support one's household and business, one endangers one's soul. This is one of the central themes of Wesley's sermon "The Danger of Riches." By continually living in wealth without care for the poor, one turns away from the desire for the love of God and neighbor and toward the desires that are " 'hurtful', both to body and soul, tending to weaken, yea, destroy every gracious and heavenly temper; destructive of that faith which is of the operation of God; of that hope which is full of immortality; of love to God and to our neighbour, and of every good word and work."[28]

Much is at risk, then, for the prosperous. By seeking to increase their wealth and by purchasing fashionable clothing, jewelry, fine furniture, paintings, and other things that please the eye, the rich feed within their own souls unholy tempers, such as vanity, pride, envy, and sloth. At the same time, riches improperly used destroy the holy tempers—humility, meekness, and patience. In the same sermon, Wesley enumerates the vices spawned by wealth:

> Riches, either desired or possessed, naturally lead to some or other of these foolish and hurtful desires; and by affording the means of gratifying them all, naturally tend to increase them. And there is a near connection between unholy desires and every other unholy passion and temper. We easily pass from these to pride, anger, bitterness, envy, malice, revengefulness; to an headstrong, unadvisable, unreprovable spirit—indeed to every temper that is earthly, sensual, or devilish. All these the desire or possession of riches naturally tends to create, strengthen, and increase.[29]

Such vices multiply because these unholy tempers infect not only the ungiving rich, but also others, by their poor example. Nothing was more insidious in this regard in Wesley's day than the matter of dress (How does this differ from our own age?), and in his sermon on that subject he draws a clear conclusion:

> It is giving so much money to poison both yourself and others, as far as your example spreads, with pride, vanity, anger, lust, love of the world, and a thousand "foolish and hurtful desires", which tend to "pierce" them "through with many sorrows". And is

there no harm in all this? O God, arise, and maintain thy own cause! Let not men or devils any longer put out our eyes, and lead us blindfold into the pit of destruction.[30]

Because of the devastation to the soul brought about by the desire for and accumulation of riches, one often loses one's desire entirely to do works of mercy. In this circular process, failure to give promotes a further callousness of the soul toward the poor, which hinders later giving. This is a critical point because failure to give is actually an antithetical action in relation to the means of grace for Wesley. It is a powerful counterforce to the upbuilding of the soul provided through merciful action. While the means of grace build faith, hope, and love in the believer, the failure to practice works of mercy does not simply leave the Christian in a neutral state; rather, such abstinence exerts an equal and opposite force, which can lead to a spiritual downward spiral of serious proportion.

The failure of the wealthy to do works of mercy is bad news not just for the poor, then, but also for the rich. By not availing themselves of the benefits of works of mercy on their souls, they gradually weaken in faith. Speaking about the Christian obligation to visit the sick, Wesley wrote:

> And those that neglect them [i.e., works of mercy] do not receive the grace which otherwise they might. Yea, and they lose, by a continued neglect, the grace which they had received. Is it not hence that many who were once strong in faith are now weak and feeble-minded? And yet they are not sensible whence that weakness comes, as they neglect none of the ordinances of God.[31]

The weakness comes, Wesley insists, from neglecting the works of mercy. And here is the obverse, then, of an aphorism Wesley laid down in his sermon "On Working Out Our Own Salvation," namely, "stir up the spark of grace which is now in you and God will give you more grace."[32]

By spurning works of mercy and desiring riches, Christians lose many things. By desiring riches, their "thirst after righteousness" slackens. Over time, their "longing" for God, their "desire" for perfection, and even their faith is weakened.[33] Again, from his sermon "The Danger of Riches," Wesley's plea is filled with pathos: "Have [riches] not so hurt you as to stab your religion to the heart? Have they not cooled (if not quenched) your *love of God*? ... And if your love of God is in any wise decayed, so is also your love of your neighbour. You are then hurt in the very life and spirit of your religion! If you lose love, you lose all."[34]

In the end, the weakening of faith and of the holy tempers and the growth of pride and vanity are significant developments. Over time, they lessen our love for God and neighbor, ultimately putting our faith at risk. This loss endangers our happiness not only in this life but also in the next life. Again and again, Wesley warns of the eternal consequences of failing to share one's excess wealth. By hoarding wealth, one risks eternal damnation. Those desiring riches " 'drown' the body in pain, disease, 'destruction', and the soul in everlasting 'perdition.' "[35] Wealthy Christians are at "every moment on the verge of hell."[36]

The news is not all bad for the rich. Wesley is clear, indeed, that there is good news. There is always good news for those who will heed. We have a ready remedy to the hazards of wealth, and in his sermon "The Danger of Increasing Riches," Wesley clearly prescribes the antidote for this disease:

> There is one preventative of it, which is also a remedy for it—and I believe there is no other under heaven. It is this. After you have "gained" (with the cautions above given) "all you can", and "saved all you can", wanting for nothing: spend not one pound, one shilling, or one penny, to gratify either the desire of the flesh, the desire of the eyes, or the pride of life; or indeed, for any other end than to please and glorify God. Having avoided this rock on the right hand, beware of that on the left. Secondly *hoard nothing*. Lay up no treasure on earth, but "give all you can", that is, all you have. I defy all the men upon earth, yea, all the angels in heaven, to find any other way of extracting the poison from riches.[37]

Throughout Wesley's many admonitions about riches, we see that he is not concerned that his hearers give simply because it is the right thing to do, because it is a command of Scripture, because it is an expression of their faith, or because the poor need their help. Wesley instructs them to give both because giving will be a means of grace, strengthening their love and, just as important, because failure to give is a means of diminishment, weakening their love and endangering their very souls.

This one example—giving to the poor—illustrates a larger point of Wesley's work. Christian moral action is a crucial component of our growth in holiness or, in contemporary language, of our spiritual formation. Like prayer, moral living feeds our love for God and neighbor, while its absence leads to the deterioration of that love and the erosion of our faith.

Rich Christians in an Age of Affluence and Deprivation

Wesley's word to his eighteenth-century hearers rings true in our twenty-first century ears. What can we learn from Wesley?

First, the tendency among many to separate spirituality and morality is clearly "unWesleyan." When many Christians today talk about spiritual formation, they emphasize private prayer, Scripture reading, and worship (those aspects of Christian practice that Wesley described and that Steve Harper has discussed as works of piety), while saying little about the moral life and, more specifically, the practice of works of mercy. For Wesley, moral action, like giving to the poor or visiting the sick, is not just related to spiritual formation; it is at the heart of spiritual formation. At the same time, other Christians talk about the necessity of social justice while saying little about spiritual formation or piety. Wesley's insistence that the privileged help the poor stems from his concern not only for the bodies of the poor but also for the souls of the rich. For Wesley, spiritual formation—holistically understood as works of piety and works of mercy held together—is at the heart of Christian social justice.

Second, Wesley's specific admonitions about the spiritual benefits of saving and giving and about the spiritual hazards of frivolous spending are prophetic to the affluent, consumerist cultures, in which many of us live. For American families, just to illustrate, debt is at an all-time high. Credit card debt doubled from 1990 to 1996 and has continued to rise. Household savings rates have plummeted and are lower than in any of the other developed nations. Giving to the poor, to the church, and to other charities is also down. At the same time, consumer spending has skyrocketed along with our desires and our expectations for more and more material goods.[38] Clearly, our culture, every bit as much as, or even more than, Wesley's, could use some advice on earning, saving, spending, and giving.

On many matters, twenty-first century Wesleyans cannot know with any certainty the answer to the question, "What would Wesley do?" In this case, however, it is not hard to imagine. Surely, he would still be impatient with the Methodists and other Christians and would continue to preach his old, familiar refrain, drawn here once again from "The Danger of Riches":

> For above [two hundred and seventy] years...I have not varied in my testimony....I fear there is need to apply to some of *you* those terrible words of the Apostle: "Go to, now, ye rich men! Weep and howl for the miseries which shall come upon you. Your gold and silver is cankered, and the rust of them shall witness against you, and shall eat your flesh, as it were fire." Certainly it will, unless ye both save all you can and give all you can....By the grace of God begin today![39]

The good news, of course, for the privileged of Wesley's time and of ours, is that the grace of God *is* available to help us begin today. As we live well, giving our money and doing good to our neighbor in many other ways, we will be opened to even more grace as we faithfully practice works of mercy. Truly, for Wesleyan Christians, moral living, including charity to our neighbor, is at the heart of spiritual formation and growth in Christ.

8

MAKING DISCIPLES IN COMMUNITY

GUIDANCE AND TRANSFORMATION IN THE LIVING BODY OF BELIEVERS

Gregory S. Clapper

When offered the chance to take a flight in the backseat of an Air Force A-7 two-seat jet, I jumped at it. I served as chaplain in an Air National Guard unit that had gone through some rough experiences, and this ride was offered as a kind of special reward. Since I am a big fan of roller coasters, I received the invitation with relish. It was a bit unsettling to have to go through a briefing on what to do should it be necessary to eject. But undaunted by that sobering rehearsal, I donned the flight gear and climbed into the backseat.

It is hard to explain the exhilaration one feels when rocketing down the runway, lifting off, and then, at the height of about 100 feet, zooming over the plains of South Dakota while cows, cars, and trees flip by in an intoxicating blur. After a few minutes of this low-altitude flying, the pilot pulled back on the stick and we went up to about 10,000 feet. He asked me if I would like to do an aileron roll, and I asked him, "What's that?" He said, "Just grab hold of the stick and move it to the right." So I did, and before I knew it, we had rolled completely around—360 degrees. Then he said, "Now push it to the left." I did, and we did the same maneuver in the opposite direction.

While I was still waiting for my stomach to settle down, the pilot asked if I would like to try a loop. I hesitated, and he said, "Great! Let's go!" At that point, he started diving and then pulled back on the stick. I watched the horizon go beneath the vision of the cockpit, then my horizon became the sun, and then as we turned completely around, the horizon came up to the cockpit again until it assumed the position I was longing to see it in—straight ahead of me. We did not do a lot more acrobatics after that, but I am happy to say that I did not have to use the green garbage bag that the crew chief had handed me—with a smile—as I had taken my seat in the cockpit.

As we were once again flying straight and level and as I was greedily sucking all of the oxygen I could from my mask, the pilot was talking to me in a reassuring and friendly manner in an attempt to help me regain my normal consciousness. Part of our discussion during that time was about the functions of the instruments on the panel that faces the pilot of a modern airplane. As the pilot explained, there are instruments that tell if the plane is flying flat and level or if it is climbing or diving. There are instruments that tell if the nose of the plane is up or if the nose is down. There are instruments that tell what the compass heading is, what the flight speed is, how much fuel is left, and virtually every other thing that a pilot would want to know.

The pilot explained that it is necessary for pilots to become habituated to trusting what their instruments tell them. It is entirely possible, he said, and in fact is not uncommon for a pilot's internal feeling and sense of spatial orientation to be completely out of relationship with where he or she is heading. In those situations, the best pilots trust their instruments.

When flying at night or in clouds or in bad weather, many pilots feel their insides telling them that they are flying straight and true, when in fact they are flying right into the ground. Apparently, this is what happened in John F. Kennedy Jr.'s plane crash. He was not "instrument rating," or being guided by his instruments, and he thought he was flying straight to his destination when in fact he was flying right into the ocean, which killed him and his passengers.

The Christian life is a lot like piloting a plane. Christians are presented with their own instrument panel, but they must learn how to read it and when it is important to take directions from the instruments. Christians have to learn to trust the instruments that the tradition has provided and not to rely solely on what their feelings are telling them about their relationship with God and with others.

A fair moniker for John Wesley's theology is "heart religion." The problem is that people have often misinterpreted what Wesley meant by "heart religion" and, subsequently, have gotten themselves in trouble because of it. In the name of following Wesley's heart religion, people have metaphorically flown into the face of the earth, or crashed, because they thought that embracing "heart religion" meant ignoring anything other than the inner impulses of the individual heart. Wesley, though, knew that we have to learn to trust all of the instruments that God provided for our journeys.[1]

What are these "instruments" that Christians need to check, especially in the rough weather of the "dark night of the soul"? Certainly, scripture is key, especially as interpreted by the tradition and summarized in creeds and classical liturgical formulations. But it was one of the peculiar geniuses of John Wesley's appropriation of the Christian tradition to see that the living community of fellow believers is among the key "instruments"—to which Christians need to pay attention in order to grow spiritually. If our only "community" consists of the saints of the past, we will miss a great deal of the formative possibilities that God has made available to us in the living present.

This is why Wesley, whenever he went around on his circuit riding ventures, would not just preach and then leave. Instead, he would take pains to organize those people who responded to his preaching into small groups, mini-communities of seekers and believers. These groups would meet with each other to grow together in heart holiness and in the disciplined life of loving service.[2] There is no question that these "little churches within the church" were the secret of early Methodism. Wesley knew that our past spiritual malformation and our own pride-based ignorance could best be revealed to us through the honest, but loving, reflections of those who know us well. It is only with such "self-knowledge" (a term that Wesley used as an equivalent for true repentance[3]) that we can break out of our egoistic apprehension of the gospel and grow in grace and love. Before we explore in greater depth how this might work, and in order to help us appreciate how important the community can be in forming heart religion, perhaps it will be helpful to be reminded of how important community life has been throughout the history of the Christian tradition.

The Pervasiveness of Community in Christianity

Scholars have long studied the process of canon formation. Just how did the book we know as the Bible come to be compiled? What factors shaped the final form? One thing that scholars agree on is that the texts that were widely accepted and used by the Christian communities were those that came to be accepted into the canon. The people recognized authority in certain texts—an authority that shaped their worship and their lives—and this led to the formation of the canon. In short, there was a community of believers before there was a New Testament canon.[4]

Many of the doctrines that the early church fathers and mothers saw to be illustrative summaries of biblical truth also came out of the life of the community. For instance, when the Christological controversies arose, one of the main pieces of evidence that was raised regarding the necessity of honoring Jesus as God was that the people were in fact already praising and worshiping him as divinity. The simple deduction was: Since Jesus is praised by the community as God, our doctrine will be that Jesus is God.[5] This traditional emphasis on the interplay between worship and belief is known as *lex orandi, lex credendi,* or the order of prayer is the order of belief.[6]

One might think that the stereotypical "pietist" approach to the Christian life (a stereotype into which Wesley is often shoehorned), an approach that emphasizes the personal relationship between self and God, is an exception to the communal vision of Christianity. But we must see by reference to contemporary under-standings of language that the community is key even for this seemingly "private" relationship.

The twentieth-century philosopher Ludwig Wittgenstein has shown that there is no such thing as private language. Language itself is a social reality, and the language we use to interpret our experiences has been formed by a society.[7] Given this, if we use that language in ungrammatical ways, as we often do if we are not guided by the truths of the tradition (or at least guided by those who know the correct grammar), we become delusional and lost in our failed attempts to have an unmediated and "private" apprehension of, and communication with, God.

Aside from these larger theoretical concerns, however, we can see the important role of the community in the Christian life when we look at Wesley's famous doctrine of "assurance," a doctrine that seemingly calls the believers to an especially private, inner, and individualistic experience.

The Wesleyan Emphasis on Assurance in Community

Wesley's heart religion is the result of a specific and contingent pattern of formation, or "grammar," that relies on the doctrinal truth of the Christian tradition as seen in the classical creeds and articles of religion that Wesley adapted from the Church of England's *Articles of Religion*. Wesley saw these articles as based on the truths of Scripture as interpreted by the Christian community over time. To be a disciple in the Christian tradition, one is first a disciple of Jesus Christ as described in the scripture and interpreted through the tradition, with that tradition issuing summaries and snapshot visions of God and the Christian life in the form of creeds and doctrines. It is this formation in the tradition that makes certain experiences possible, and not some universal religious experience, that makes the tradition possible.[8]

Wesley neither assumed a universally present "religious experience," which could provide all necessary religious guidance through introspection, nor assumed that any particular living community necessarily exemplified Christian truth. Wesley instead emphasized the role of community in discipleship-making through the formation of the virtues of humility, honesty, and faithfulness to the truths of the tradition. In the community of small groups, members are expected to lift each other up in truth and honesty and to accept the correction of their brothers and sisters. It is by the witness of others that we can come to know how often we hide behind our delusional self-images, how often we rationalize our behavior, and how short we can fall from our ideals. We can also see, conversely, the strengths and giftedness that humility has prevented us from naming and claiming as an important part of our reality.

Wesley preached, and wrote, at some length about what it meant to have Christian "assurance." Especially in three sermons—"The Witness of the Spirit, I," "The Witness of the Spirit, II," and "The Witness of Our Own Spirit"—Wesley makes clear that Christians are to live out the truth of Romans 8:16, which speaks of the "Spirit bearing witness with our spirit that we are children of God." The point he makes in this series of sermons that is most relevant to our current concerns is that it is impossible to conceive of any witness of the Spirit not accompanied by the "fruit of the Spirit." As he puts it in his second sermon on the witness of the Spirit, "To secure us from all delusion, God gives us two witnesses that we are his children. And this they testify conjointly. Therefore, 'what God hath joined together, let not man put asunder.' "[9]

What this means is that while the "witness of the Spirit" itself may be an ineffable, incommunicable experience, if it is genuinely present, then "love, joy, peace, patience, kindness, generosity, faithfulness, gentleness, and self-control" (Gal. 5:22) will also be present. While the community may not be able to look inside a believer to see if the "witness of the Spirit" is in his or her heart, the community *is* uniquely privileged to judge whether or not one is living out the "fruit of the Spirit." One common misunderstanding of sanctification in the Christian life and of Wesley's emphasis on "experience" is that the fruit of the Spirit is primarily inner feelings or experiences. But in fact, when one thinks about the very nature of the terms "experience" and "sanctification," one sees very clearly that all of these are *relationship* terms. One cannot love without loving a *particular object*, one cannot have joy without being joyful *about* something, and one cannot have peace except *in relationship* to potential sources of unease and unsettlement. This is true for all nine fruit of the Spirit, and John Wesley knew that to grow these fruit, one had to be in relationship with both God and fellow human beings. That perhaps is the clearest implication of Wesley's often-quoted statement that there is no such thing as holiness other than social holiness.[10]

Wesley believed that if you meet regularly with someone who has come to know what it is you truly love, what it is you truly fear, what it is you truly find peace and hope in, you will have a hard time fooling yourself about your own relationship with God. This mutually accountable community is one of the instruments of grace that God has given the Christian church, that John Wesley emphasized, and that we too often ignore.

Being Real

I often teach some of the theological components of the "parish nursing" curriculum in the university where I work. This program is designed to train nurses to embody Christ's call to healing and wholeness in the local church. After talking about the holistic understanding conveyed by the New Testament Greek word *"sodzo"* (which, in different parts of the Bible, is translated as both "salvation" and "healing"), I spend a lot of the time speaking, not about scripture or theology, but about "being real." Only when we are real about who we are—and about who others are—can the truths of the Christian gospel have a chance to shine in our lives, form our perceptions and our actions, and bring about healing and, finally, salvation.

The gospel tells us that we are all created in the image of God (Gen. 1:26). The gospel tells us that we are all sinners (Rom. 3:23). The gospel tells us that we are all precious creatures for whom Christ died (John 3:16). When we are true to all of this gospel reality, we cannot help being humble about who we are and being compassionate toward the realities of others. It is this kind of humility and compassion that living in community can engender when that community is truly working under the power of the Holy Spirit.

The power of community to bring about change when people are real with one another—"speaking the truth in love" (Eph. 4:15)—is perhaps best exemplified when one sees the life of Christ in the life of a fellow human being and desires it for himself or herself. This dynamic of transformative witness can be seen throughout the history of the church, for instance, in the many stories of the lives of the saints who have gone before us. This is why the sharing of autobiographical narratives was central to the life and energy of the small groups under the direction of the Wesleys. But this dynamic can also be seen in the products of our culture, even in those that are apparently designed primarily for entertainment.

Transformation in Community as Seen in *The Music Man*

In the classic of the American musical theater, *The Music Man*,[11] we see a town transformed by a charismatic man. His vision of a boys' band enlivens the small Iowa town of River City and puts a spring in the step of all those caught up in the vision. On first viewing, one might say that this film mocks the Christian vision of life. The protagonist, Harold Hill, with the gestures and inflections of a revivalist preacher, spends most of the play trying to sell the town instruments and uniforms for a boys' band that he has no intention of actually creating.

Here, we could see dramatized a Marxist critique of Christianity, which sees the church as mainly interested in the continuing financial support of the rank-and-file membership by spouting delusional stories of "pie in the sky, by and by." Some postmodernists would have Christianity portrayed primarily in terms of its financial and power relationships, symbolized by Harold Hill's desire to control and manipulate a town for the bottom line of power and material gain. *The Music Man*, however, provides a subtler analysis of human transformation in community that goes beyond such caricatures, for it is the change that takes place *in spite of* his desire to manipulate and control that is, finally, most compelling.

In the end, Harold Hill encounters the self-sacrificial love of Marian, who is willing to acknowledge his deceptive intentions but loves him nonetheless. The reason for this, in part at least, is the excitement that Hill's vision of the boys' band has brought about in Marian's little brother. Likewise, Harold Hill "got his foot caught in the door" by seeing genuine love shown toward him, a love that knows who he truly is yet seeks his best interest in spite of that knowledge. Even more amazingly, Harold Hill is caught up in his own (what he presumed to be totally fictive) vision of a boys' band. In the end, while handcuffed by the local police, he begins to conduct the band. And, uncertain and far from perfect, the band begins to play recognizable music.

Acts of faith and unconditional agape love do in fact bring about real transformation, but it is only when *all* of reality is acknowledged. Marian held up to Harold *both* a well-polished mirror *and* a vision of a new way of life. So it is with the church. When we are called to tell the truth to one another in love, we must remember both the true reality of our individual and corporate lives and the healing vision of forgiveness, hope, and love, which our tradition has handed to us.

At the end of *The Music Man*, the fascinating dialogue and interchange within a community is powerfully symbolized. From the beginning of the play, the theme music for Marian, "the librarian," (the guardian of the community's higher values, literally and figuratively, in her role as librarian) has been "Goodnight My Someone." This song is about a longing for an object for romantic love, a longing that is unfulfilled. Her mother says her longing was unfulfilled because Marian's vision of the love object was a combination of "St. Patrick, Paul Bunyan, and Noah Webster." In other words, Marian had overidealized the object for human love. Harold Hill, the sham "professor," is portrayed throughout the film with the theme song "Seventy-six Trombones" playing in the background. The booming bluster of the charismatic salesman blasting through to close the deal with all the subtlety of seventy-six trombones is a fittingly symbolic way of characterizing his attempts at manipulation. In the final scenes of the film, however, we see the realization of community shaping character through a surprising exchange of these theme songs.

Harold has caught a vision of a life quite different from that which his life of high pressure salesmanship has fostered, dominated as it was by manipulation and selfishness. This new vision is of a gentle, nonmanipulative love, exemplified in the witness of Marian's sacrifices for him. In an opposite way, Marian has decided to leave the realm of impossible ideals and to love a broken and sinful man, but a man through whom good things come. Through the dramatic medium of a duet between Harold and Marian, we see the evidence of this mutual transformation. With each in separate rooms of a house where they are preparing for a romantic encounter, Harold begins singing Marian's theme song, "Goodnight My Someone," while Marian begins singing Harold's theme song, "Seventy-six Trombones."

Marian has started to accommodate into her abstract and idealistic dreamy view of love the bold brassiness of human reality and sexuality, with her agreeing, finally, to meet the professor at the "footbridge," the neighborhood romantic rendezvous spot. By being real to each other and speaking frankly of the truths they know, while also being open to growing and transforming in areas they hadn't thought about, Harold and Marian offer imperfect, yet powerful, images of how spiritual growth can take place in community.

Christian "heart religion" is not about baptizing any state of one's "natural" or usual internal world and calling it "Christian." Being a Christian is dependent upon the congruency of one's deepest loves, fears, and joys, with the objects of those loves, fears, and joys that the Scriptures offer. And those who know us best can help us know where our hearts are truly centered. If it is truly God and our neighbor we love, if it is truly right relationship with God that gives us joy and peace, then we are leading a "grammatical" Christian life. If it is, instead, social prestige, a bank account, or fame that is the object of our heart's affections, then we have bought the lies and delusions of the world. The "world," in this sense, has not changed since the time of the prophets, even if these worldly invitations do come at the speed of light over the Internet and are virtually omnipresent through the miasma of advertising that we breathe in today. Our broken world needs voices both to proclaim the tradition and to name the truth of the world as it truly is in order to carry out Wesley's call to spread scriptural holiness throughout the land.

Keeping in Balance: A Pastoral Illustration

If we are to emphasize both forming in the truths of the tradition and listening to the truths that are unfolding in our contemporary communities, we need to be attentive to the challenge of keeping these elements in balance. In other words, we want to avoid looking *only* to the tradition or looking *only* to the contemporary community. The problem of holding these two realities in creative tension can be seen in some of the struggles about social issues in the contemporary United Methodist Church, specifically some of the struggles within local congregations. Covenant discipleship groups have their place in formation, and short-term, intense retreat experiences (such as the *Emmaus Walk* or the *Academy for Spiritual Formation* that the Board of Discipleship of The United Methodist Church sponsors) can be transformative. The community that I am writing about in this chapter, though, also must be realized, at least at times, in the larger worshiping community of the congregation.

As a senior pastor of a church of just under a thousand members in Waverly, Iowa, I was asked by several leaders in the congregation if we might have a series of presentations and discussions on a variety of social issues during our Lenten Wednesday night suppers. After some discussion and much prayer, I agreed, but only on the condition that they would be structured in a certain way. The discussions were not designed to lead to a particular consensus on any particular view of any particular social issue but were concerned with the tension between the truths of the tradition and the truths of the contemporary community.

While one week we would discuss abortion, and the next week homosexuality, and on through a litany of the typical issues that are discussed today, there was to be a common pattern to our gatherings. At the end of that Lenten season, there were no mass defections from the church or angry splits in the congregation, even though all of these divisive issues had in fact been talked about. I cannot claim absolute knowledge as to why the congregation came through that minefield unscathed, but it is my faith that the pattern in which these discussions were undertaken had something to do with it.

At the beginning of each week's deliberations, I asked all to stand and sing "The Church's One Foundation." We then discussed the issue of the week, often with representatives, so both "sides" spoke. And then at the end of the session, we again stood and sang "The Church's One Foundation." This embodied the truth that the basis for our community is not complete agreement on a list of issues that the present culture has presented to us. The basis for our community is Jesus Christ. We worship the God who Jesus revealed and embodied, we receive the forgiveness of sins that his death on the cross purchased for us, and we are called to a new life in the Holy Spirit, which came into the world in a special way after the resurrection of Jesus.

If I had refused to discuss these social issues and confined our Lenten topics only to creedal explications or to the retelling of biblical stories, I certainly would have been guilty of emphasizing the tradition alone, and the living tension would have died. Likewise, if we had had the discussions of contemporary issues without singing the hymn as a congregation (and thereby invoking all that the hymn proclaims), the tension between tradition's truths and the community's realities would also have died.

Choosing to live in that creative tension, where our freedom to respond to God's grace is seemingly reshaped from moment to moment by the realities of community, means living in both the excitement and challenge of ministry and, more generally, the Christian life. Living in that tension can sometimes feel like we are doing aerial acrobatics where the horizon is hard to find. But if we continue to check all of the "instruments" that the tradition and the community put before us, we will end up arriving where the well-formed heart longs to rest.

9

"SUBMITTING TO BE MORE VILE"

THE QUEST FOR HOLINESS AND ITS COST

Stephen A. Seamands

Whenever John Wesley was asked to describe the essence of Methodism and to explain why God had raised up the movement, his answer always revolved around one thing: holiness of heart and life. Consider the following representative statements. "The essence of it," Wesley wrote in his *Thoughts upon Methodism*, "is holiness of heart and life; the circumstantials all point to this."[1] In a letter to an inquiring friend, he explained:

> We set out upon two principles: (1) None go to heaven without holiness of heart and life; (2) whosoever follows after this (whatever his opinions be) is my "brother and sister and mother." And we have not swerved an hair's breadth from either one or the other of these to this day.[2]

In his *Minutes on Several Conversations*, Wesley provides a more lengthy description:

> Q. 3 What may we reasonably believe to be God's design in raising up the Preachers called Methodists?
>
> A. Not to form any new sect: but to reform the nation, particularly the Church; and to spread scriptural holiness over the land.

Q. 4 What was the rise of Methodism, so called?

A. In 1729, two young men, reading the Bible saw they could not be saved without holiness, followed after it, and incited others so to do. In 1737 they saw holiness comes by faith. They saw likewise, that men are justified before they are sanctified; but still holiness was their point. God then thrust them out, utterly against their will, to raise a holy people.[3]

Wesley and the early Methodists had a clear sense of identity and mission. They believed God had raised up the movement to promote holiness in every sphere of life—in the individual, the church, society, and the world. Holiness was Methodism's driving force and burning focus, the hub that held all the spokes of the wheel of the movement together. Indeed, all the major emphases of Wesley's theology and practice—prevenient grace, evangelism and the new birth, the means of grace, personal ethics, societies and class meetings, social justice, and Christian perfection—all flowed from his passion for holiness.

Later, this same passion propelled Methodism in America and was largely responsible for the church's remarkable growth, particularly in the first half of the nineteenth century. In an address delivered at the Methodist centenary celebration in 1866, John McClintock, first president of the newly established Drew Seminary, reiterated the centrality of holiness in Methodism and urged his church never to depart from it:

Knowing exactly what I say, and taking full responsibility for it, I repeat, we are the only church in history, from the apostles' time until now, that has put forward as its very elemental thought— the great central pervading idea of the whole book of God from the beginning to the end—the holiness of the human soul, heart, mind, and will. . . . Our work is moral work—that is to say, the work of making men holy. Our preaching is for that, our church agencies are for that, our schools, colleges, universities, and theological seminaries are for that. There is our mission—there is our glory—there is our power, and there shall be the ground of our triumph. God keep us true.[4]

Unfortunately, in the decades that followed, Methodism, by and large, drifted away from its original purpose and mission. As it moved into the twentieth century, its passion for holiness waned and was supplanted by other concerns. In a 1974 address, Albert C. Outler acknowledged the decline of Methodism's interest in holiness and lamented its consequences:

> The doctrine of holiness of heart and life that had been the keystone in the arch of Wesley's doctrine, by the turn of this century had become a pebble in the shoe of standard bred Methodists. And presently they took off the shoe, threw out the pebble, put the shoe back on and kept walking, with the same labels but without the same equipment. And this has been an uncomprehended and immense tragedy for all who claim John Wesley as their father in God.[5]

As a result, the average United Methodist today has little or no awareness of the church's original purpose and mission. Holiness of heart and life has become the lost treasure of Methodism.

As we look to the future, surely the recovery of this lost treasure ought to be a primary concern of every faithful heir of the Wesleys. But what are the keys to such a recovery? What must happen to rekindle a passion for holiness among us today? By considering John Wesley's own example, I want to maintain that restoring holiness in our church will not only involve the rediscovery of the neglected doctrine of holiness (education) and the rekindling of a passion for holiness (zeal), but it will also entail a willingness, in the pursuit of holiness, to face rejection and even hostility from others in our own religious community (opposition). Much has been written about the need for a recovery of a Wesleyan understanding and the rekindling of a zeal for holiness, but it is to this neglected element involving the relinquishment of religious respectability that I wish to pay particular attention.

Throughout his life and ministry, in his quest for holiness, Wesley was willing to engage in activities that caused scorn and criticism from his own Anglican religious community. Consider, for example, his embarrassing descent into field preaching on April 2, 1739, about ten months after his heartwarming experience at Aldersgate. Here is how he records the event in his journal: "Mon. 2. At four in the afternoon I submitted to 'be more vile', and proclaimed in the highways the glad tidings of salvation, speaking from a little eminence in a ground adjoining to the city, to about three thousand people."[6] Wesley had been a strict Oxford don who was concerned that things be done decently and in order. He had an aversion to commotion and disturbance, preferring the quiet of a university library to the noise of a large crowd. In the light of his personal preferences, no doubt field preaching for Wesley was submitting "to be more vile." Although he would continue to engage in it throughout his life, he never became fully comfortable with it. As late as 1772, he admitted that in many ways, field preaching was still a cross for him; but he continued in this work because the quest for holiness drew him forward.

But there was more to this vileness than immediately catches the eye. By engaging in this unconventional form of open-air evangelism, Wesley also subjected himself to the intense criticism of his beloved Church. Preaching was to be done inside churches, not outdoors. It was as simple as that. Many in the Church of England considered field preaching to be a flagrant violation of civil and canon law. Even Wesley's family members opposed his uncouth, unconventional practice. His elder brother, Samuel Jr., once wrote to their mother that he would rather see his brothers John and Charles "picking straws within the walls than preaching in the area of Moorfields."[7] Because of his passion to spread scriptural holiness over the land, however, Wesley continued to preach in the open air. For him, pursuing holiness and submitting to be more vile were strangely yet inextricably bound together.

Methodist Beginnings at Oxford

Wesley began his passionate pursuit of holiness in 1725, at the age of twenty-two, while he was a student at Oxford. In January of that year, he had written to his parents informing them of his decision to seek ordination as a priest in the Church of England. He had made this decision, however, not out of his passion for holiness, but because he wanted to pursue the life of a scholar as a Fellow and tutor at Oxford. Ordination was a necessary prerequisite for the position. To be sure, Wesley had been raised in an extremely devout Christian home and had continued to perform religious duties while he was away at school. But at the time, he was still a nominal Christian and was known at Oxford for his academic achievements, not his spiritual fervor.

His parents wrote back affirming him in his decision but also encouraging him to engage in serious self-examination as he prepared for ordination. Within a few weeks, it was apparent that Wesley had taken his parents' advice to heart. He began keeping a daily diary, which contained resolutions and reflections on his spiritual condition. And in the months that followed, he read the works of three great devotional writers. First, he read Jeremy Taylor's *Rules and Exercises of Holy Living and Dying.* Years later, he described the profound impact Taylor's book had upon him: "In reading several parts of this book, I was exceedingly affected; that part in particular which relates to purity of intention. Instantly I resolved to dedicate all my life to God, all my thoughts, and words, and actions."[8] Next, Wesley read Thomas à Kempis's classic, *The Imitation of Christ,* and was particularly impressed with its stress that true religion is essentially a matter of the heart. Shortly after he was ordained in September 1725, Wesley began reading the works of his contemporary, William Law, particularly *A Serious Call to a Devout and Holy Life* and *Christian Perfection.* "The light flowed in so mightily upon my soul," he later wrote, "that everything appeared in a new view. I cried to God for help and resolved not to prolong the time of obeying him as I had never done before."[9]

From this time on, Wesley was convinced that "none go to heaven without holiness of heart and life"[10] and was governed by an overarching desire for holiness. As a result, in 1729, Wesley joined the small group at Oxford that his brother, Charles, had recently started. The members pledged to be regular in private devotions, to receive Holy Communion at least once a week, and to carefully watch over their moral conduct. They also agreed to meet as a group from six to nine o'clock each evening for Bible study and discussion of other religious books. In the fall of 1730, the group widened its activities to include weekly visitation of the sick and of those in local prisons, as well as the poor, widows, and orphans. With Wesley's involvement and eventual leadership in the group, what had begun as his private quest for holiness now took on social dimensions.

This group's activities did not go unnoticed. In the 1730s, the spiritual climate at Oxford was orthodox, no doubt, but arid. A spiritual lethargy hung over the university. Students, schooled in the rationalistic principles of the Enlightenment, were encouraged to adhere to religious conventions and to avoid anything that smacked of fanaticism. The presence of this small group of diligent and pious students was a rare phenomenon on campus. They soon became the butt of campus jokes and acquired a wide variety of nicknames, such as "Sacramentarians," "Enthusiasts," "Supererogation Men," "The Reforming Club," "The Godly Club," "The Holy Club," and, of course, the one that eventually named the later movement: "Methodists."

"Methodist" was a pejorative label that had been pinned on other sect-like groups before.[11] It fit this group well because of its extremely strict, regimented, methodical involvement in religious activities. At first, it was only what Charles Wesley would call a "harmless nickname," a term of humorous derision. As time went on, however, opposition to the group increased and eventually turned to open hostility because of an incident involving John Wesley's student, Richard Morgan. He was a student at Lincoln College, Oxford, where Wesley served as a Fellow and a tutor. Because Richard's older brother, William, had been a member of the Methodist group, his father asked that Richard be assigned as Wesley's pupil. Richard, however, soon decided he did not want to follow in his brother's footsteps. In January 1734, he wrote to his father, begging that he request a different tutor for him:

> I am as much laughed at and despised by the whole town as any of them, and always shall be so while I am his pupil. The whole College makes a jest of me, and the Fellows themselves do not show me common civility, so great is their aversion to my tutor.... By becoming his pupil I am stigmatized with the name of a Methodist, the misfortune of which I cannot describe.... I think it incumbent upon me to inform you that it is my opinion that if I am continued with Mr. Wesley I shall be ruined.[12]

To Morgan, "Methodist" was a horrible, not a harmless, nickname. To be labeled a Methodist was anathema, the fulfillment of his worst nightmare.

To understand Morgan's extreme aversion for the term, we must turn the calendar back thirteen months. As a result of growing uneasiness and opposition toward the Oxford Methodists, an anonymous letter appeared in the December 9, 1732, issue of a

London newspaper, *Fog's Weekly Journal,* ridiculing this "sect called Methodists" on the grounds of their "absurd and perpetual melancholy," their "enthusiastic madness and superstitious scruples," and their "affinity to the Essenes among the Jews, as the pietists among the Christians in Switzerland." The unknown writer pinpointed the error into which he believed they had fallen:

> This proposition, that no action whatever is indifferent, is the chief hinge on which their whole scheme of religion turns. Hence they condemn several actions as bad which are not only allowed as innocent but laudable by the rest of mankind. They avoid as much as is possible every object that may affect them with any pleasant and grateful sensation.... They neglect and voluntarily afflict their bodies and practise several rigorous and superstitious customs which God never required of them: all Wednesdays and Fridays are strictly to be kept as fasts, and blood let once a fortnight to keep down the carnal man; at dinner they sigh for the time they are obliged to spend in eating; every morning to rise at four o'clock is supposed a duty, and to employ two hours a day in singing of psalms and hymns is judged as an indispensable duty requisite to the being of a Christian. In short, they practice every thing contrary to the judgment of other persons and allow none to have any but those of their own sect, which is the farthest from it.[13]

As a result of this published letter, the little group of Methodists began to attract considerable public attention at Oxford. On several occasions, Wesley noted in his diary that he found himself having to "talk about the Methodists" in his conversations with students, friends, and even university officials.

On January 1, three weeks after the letter appeared, Wesley mounted the steps of St. Mary's pulpit at Oxford to preach what would become one of his landmark sermons, "The Circumcision of the Heart," where he succinctly set forth the essentials of his doctrine of holiness. It was the earliest of his sermons to later be included in his Standard Sermons and one to which he would frequently point as summarizing what he had always taught about holiness. But on the day when he actually preached the sermon, if the congregation in the chapel was larger and more attentive than usual, it was only because of the heightened popular curiosity about the Methodists and the increased swirl of controversy around them fueled by the *Fog's Weekly Journal* letter.

And the controversy did not let up. In February, Wesley wrote to his father, wondering whether he could "stem the torrent" of criticism against the Methodists that was "rolling down from all sides."[14] This growing antagonism to the Oxford Methodists demonstrates how from the outset Wesley's understanding and passion for holiness was inseparable from his willingness to endure rejection, scorn, and even open hostility on account of it. The two seemed to be intricately bound together. Holiness as understood and practiced by Wesley was offensive to conventional Anglican sensibilities. As V. H. H. Green suggests, "The practical Christianity of the Holy Club impinged upon soft consciences and made uncomfortable the more negligent conformity with Christian principle which has always been, and probably always will be, the characteristic of the majority of those who call themselves Christian."[15] It demanded a degree of nonconformity that necessarily resulted in the loss of social status and reputation within the religious community.

The very name Methodist, which for Wesley was synonymous with holiness of heart and life, was originally a term of derision. Wesley would refer to the group later as the people who are "vulgarly" and "derisively" called Methodists. From the start, Methodism, holiness, and religious nonconformity were a threefold cord that could not be broken. Methodists pursued holiness, and this provoked hostility.

Mixing with the Moravians

Another example of Wesley's willingness to endure scorn and criticism from his own religious community and to sacrifice religious respectability in the pursuit of holiness can be seen in his involvement with the Moravians.

When he left Oxford in 1735, the Moravians played a crucial role in Wesley's ongoing spiritual journey. More than any other group, the Moravians helped him understand that justification by faith was the essential foundation of the holy life and helped him personally experience the full assurance of faith. Although they had roots going back to John Hus (c. 1372–1415), the Moravian society, under the leadership of Count Nicholas von Zinzendorf, was a fledgling movement in Wesley's day. Wesley first encountered them on board the *Simmonds* as he was sailing to Georgia to serve as a missionary. Twenty-six Moravians were on board the ship; they too were voyaging to Georgia to join a group of Moravian missionaries who were already there. Wesley was deeply impressed with their graciousness and humility and most of all, with the deep certainty of their faith in the face of death as raging Atlantic storms repeatedly threatened the ship.

Soon after his arrival in Savannah, Wesley became acquainted with August Spangenberg, the leader of the Moravian missionaries, through whom he learned more about Moravian beliefs and practices. Based on what Wesley had observed and learned, he concluded that the Moravians were certainly not a heretical sect but were, in fact, apostolic, orthodox Christians. Sensing the Moravians possessed something he lacked, Wesley requested counsel from Spangenberg about his own spiritual conduct. He was quite unprepared for the Moravian leader's response. As Wesley writes in his Journal:

> He said, "My brother, I must first ask you one or two questions. Have you the witness within yourself? Does the Spirit of God bear witness with your spirit that you are a child of God?" I was surprised, and knew not what to answer. He observed it, and asked, "Do you know Jesus Christ?" I paused, and said, "I know he is the Saviour of the world." "True", replied he, "but do you know he has saved you?" I answered, "I hope he has died to save me." He only added, "Do you know yourself?" I said, "I do." But I fear they were vain words.[16]

More than two years would pass before Wesley, having returned to England after his aborted mission to the colony of Georgia, received the faith and assurance he lacked during his heartwarming experience at Aldersgate. And it was Peter Böhler, a Moravian living in London, who in the months immediately preceding Aldersgate, was instrumental in conveying to Wesley the meaning of justification by faith.

Less than a month after Aldersgate, Wesley journeyed to Herrnhut, the Moravian settlement in Germany, in order to meet with Count Zinzendorf and other Moravian leaders: "I hoped the conversing with those holy men who were themselves living witnesses of the full power of faith, and yet able to bear with those that are weak, would be a means, under God, of so stablishing my soul, that I might 'go on from faith to faith, and from strength to strength.'"[17] Having spent time at Herrnhut and several other Pietist renewal centers on the Continent, Wesley returned to England, effusive about Moravian faith and piety. In fact, while he was at Herrnhut, he had written to his elder brother, Samuel, "I am with a church whose conversation is in heaven, in whom is the mind that was in Christ, and who so walks as he walked."[18] But he also returned home with several reservations about the Moravians. He was concerned about their quietism, their tendency toward spiritual complacency, and the personality cult revolving around Zinzendorf.

For the next two years as the Evangelical Revival emerged, Wesley stayed closely connected to the Moravians in England through his involvement in the Fetter Lane Society. This religious society had been cofounded by Wesley and Peter Böhler three weeks after Wesley's heartwarming in May 1738. Composed of Anglicans and Moravians, several former Oxford Methodists, and some who had been involved in other religious societies, the society quickly grew to about a hundred members. In the fall of 1739, however, while Wesley was away, Philipp Molther, a German Moravian, arrived in London and began advocating the doctrine of stillness (the notion that those who had not yet found justifying faith should be "still," refraining from all the means of grace including attendance at church services) at the Fetter Lane Society. The stillness doctrine also began to be strongly advocated by English Moravian leaders, such as John Bray, John Simpson, and Richard Bell. As a result, it was soon widely accepted at Fetter Lane.

Convinced that stillness spelled antinomianism and struck a blow at the root of holy living, Wesley tried to turn society members away from it, but to no avail. Finally, in July 1740, after several months of dissension and debate, Wesley removed himself from Fetter Lane and established a separate society at the nearby Foundery warehouse he had recently purchased. Although he continued to hold them in high affection and continued fellowship with Moravians throughout his life, this marked the end of his active involvement with them. From now on, Methodists and Moravians would go their separate ways. Yet during this five-year period (1735–1740), the Moravians, above all others, played a crucial role in both John and Charles Wesley's quests for holiness. Through the Moravian influence, they both came to understand that justifying faith and assurance provide the foundation of the holy life. The Moravians also afforded them models of Christian community, which they adapted and used in the Methodist societies. In fact, Moravian practices such as bands, love feasts, and watch night services soon became common in early Methodism.

Although everyone recognizes the significance of Wesley's involvement with the Moravians, little has been said about how it would have been looked upon by his fellow Anglicans, especially by the clergy. Despite the fact that the British Parliament finally granted legal status to the Moravian Church in England in 1749, during the previous decade when the Wesleys were actively involved with the Moravians, the group was generally perceived as a fanatical, enthusiastic sect. No self-respecting member of the Anglican clergy would have dared to associate with them or wanted to be perceived as a Moravian sympathizer.

We get a picture of the typical Anglican attitude toward the Moravians in Thomas Church's *Remarks on the Rev. Mr. John Wesley's Last Journal* published in 1744. By exposing the purported errors of Wesley and his growing number of Methodist followers, Church, a distinguished Church of England clergyman, hoped he could prevent others from making the same mistake they had made in getting mixed up with the Moravians: "One end of my making these extracts from the several parts of your journals, I own, is to give the most public warning I could to all sober serious persons, to all who have not totally cast off their regard for religion and virtue, that they be not deceived by any professions or pretences to think well of or mix with these *Moravians*."[19]

Having carefully read the account in Wesley's published *Journal* where he described what happened at Fetter Lane and how he had distanced himself from the Moravians, Church acknowledged that he couldn't simply lump Wesley in with the Moravians. Church wrote, "Do not mistake me. I by no means charge you with believing or teaching such pernicious tenets." But he can't understand why Wesley, while recognizing their errors, refrains from a wholesale condemnation of the Moravians. His unwillingness to condemn them only furthers their cause:

But have you not prepared the way for them? By unsettling the minds of weak people, and perplexing them with intricate points, very liable and easy to be mistaken—By countenancing and commending these *Moravians*, and being the occasion of so many of them coming over among us—By still speaking of them, and treating them, as if they were in the main the best Christians in the world, and only deluded or mistaken in a few points.[20]

In his extended reply to Thomas Church, Wesley refused to turn his back on the Moravians. Notwithstanding their faults, he is convinced they are sincere Christian believers with whom he longs to be reunited:

And I am in great earnest when I declare once more that I have a deep, abiding conviction by how many degrees the good which is among them overbalances the evil; that I cannot speak of them but with tender affection, were it only for the benefits I have received from them; and that at this hour I desire union with them (were those stumbling-blocks once put away which have hitherto made that desire ineffectual) above all things under heaven.[21]

Once again, Wesley's pursuit of holiness caused him to cast religious convention and respectability aside. As with his involvement with the Oxford Methodists, by mixing with the Moravians, he followed a path that led to hostility and opposition.

Other examples of this pattern abound. We could consider Wesley's openness to varieties of religious experience, which constantly caused the charge of enthusiasm, "the bugbear of decent and ordinary Anglicans"[22] to be leveled against him. We could also consider his persistent determined involvement with the poor, a topic already discussed at length in this volume by Rebekah Miles.[23] But the point has been sufficiently made. For Wesley, the pursuit of holiness meant forsaking religious respectability, thus provoking hostility from the standard-bred Anglicans of his day.

Contemporary Relevance

All this is particularly relevant with regard to the recovery of holiness today. By and large, Methodism at the beginning of this new millennium has developed attitudes similar to those of eighteenth-century Anglicans. The parallels are actually quite striking. A restoration of holiness of heart and life to the central place it originally held within our tradition may necessitate the same courage and perseverance we have witnessed in the Wesleys. Those who are committed to the quest for holiness of heart and life will need to count the cost. And, just perhaps, this is a perennial reality in the life of the church. It may be necessary for them, as was the case with the Wesleys, to forsake religious status and approval and to endure scorn and opposition within the very church they love and long to see renewed. The ultimate key to such revival within the hearts and minds of God's people, however, will most certainly be the Christlike spirit of those who seek to proclaim in their words and actions that God is love.

10

WORD AND TABLE

A WESLEYAN MODEL FOR BALANCED WORSHIP

Lester Ruth

The present is a tumultuous time for worship. Many churches feel as if they are in a tug-of-war. Consider the books on worship in any catalog. Materials suggesting truly different approaches to worship renewal sit uneasily next to each other. The time is tumultuous because it is unclear whether these differences will produce rupture or balance. Many congregations have experienced the former, fighting bitterly as worship wars erupted. But perhaps these same tensions can produce an era in which Methodist worship has new breadth. Perhaps being pulled in so many directions can lead, not simply to being pulled apart, but to being stretched.

If present tensions do lead to greater breadth in Methodist worship, it will be a recovery of John and Charles Wesley's example in holding together aspects of the Christian faith that others viewed as opposites. In the Wesleys' view certain polarities were necessary if Methodism was to reflect true Christianity. Their ability to hold things together created breadth. This breadth created balance. In this chapter, we will examine this balance using the categories of "Word" and "Table."[1] In the Wesleys' understanding, how do these terms, held together, reflect an appropriate balanced breadth for Methodist worship?

This classic Wesleyan emphasis on Word and Table can help contemporary Methodists hold together a solid approach to worship. It does so by offering Word and Table as a complementary balance in three particular areas: as a model for a worshiper's personal spirituality, as a model for congregational worship, and as a model for the church to engage the world. With respect to the first, Word and Table serves as a foundation for a Christian spirituality by providing a context for other experiences of God. As a model for congregational worship, Word and Table summarizes the breadth in the order of worship the Wesleys desired each Sunday. Finally, Word and Table reflects the distinctive way in which the Wesleys negotiated between aggressive evangelism, on the one hand, and accountable fellowship, on the other.

Word and Table as a Model for Worshipers' Spirituality

Early in John Wesley's ministry, a new teaching he heard troubled him. According to this teaching, people were to wait for grace by doing only that—waiting. Wesley was troubled because this teaching contradicted what had always been a crucial part of Methodist spirituality: methodical attendance to the ordinances of God, such as prayer, preaching, and participation in Holy Communion. Rejecting this new teaching, the Wesleys remained committed to the older approach: People wait for a deeper experience of grace by doing those things that God has commanded. Writing on the subject, John Wesley's tone is firm. Gospel ordinances are " 'means' ordained of God as the usual channels of his grace." These "means of grace" are "outward signs, words, or actions ordained of God, and appointed for this end—to be the *ordinary* channels" for how God conveys grace to people.[2] People should use these means not only because their use is commanded but also because normally through their use, God can be met.

The Wesleys elevated some ordinances as the "chief" means of grace. Three spiritual practices that often fell into this category were prayer, "searching the Scriptures," and receiving Communion. The Wesleys emphasized these particular means above others by assigning them a peculiar adjective related to their use. Their ideal was a "constant" practice of these gracious means. John included among his collection of Standard Sermons a sermonic essay entitled "The Duty of Constant Communion."[3] In many ways, constant prayer, Scripture, and Communion sum up a Wesleyan vision for spirituality. These means are not incidental to

Christian spirituality. They are the absolute bedrock. Of these three, the least likely to find constancy in the spirituality of the contemporary worshiper is the Lord's Supper. This disuse is antithetical to the Wesleys's teaching and their own spirituality.

John's statements on Communion were quite strong. The sacramental table is not only where we see a "figure" of our salvation by grace but also where God uses the sacrament as an "instrument" to convey grace. The opportunity is "not the bare *remembrance*" of the past but an invitation to partake of Christ's activity now, "to grace and mercy, still lasting, still *new*, still the same as when it was first offered for us." The sacramental points us forward to our Christian hope. It is a pledge of future glory "to assure us that when we are qualified for it, God will faithfully render to us the purchase" of heavenly communion. Moreover, the sacramental table proclaims the gospel in a multisensory manner. God's desire at the sacramental table is "to expose to all our senses, Christ's sufferings, as if they were present *now*." There "the sweet smell of the Offering still remains, the Blood is still warm, the Wounds still fresh, and the *Lamb* still *standing as slain*." The Table is the place where we can see and feel what God's grace in Christ is like.[4]

What John printed in prose, Charles expressed through poetry. At the sacrament, we "the mystic flesh of Jesus eat/Drink with the wine His healing blood/And feast on th'Incarnate God." There we taste "how glorious is the life above...That fulness of celestial love/That joy which shall for ever last!" For the Wesleys, the sacramental experience could be overwhelming: "A drop of heaven o'erflows our hearts/And deluges the house of clay." Such sentiments truly reflected their experience. Their journals constantly rang with the joy of grace experienced at the sacramental table.[5] It was a joy demonstrated in their frequent communing.

The Wesleyan emphasis on Word and Table provides balance for the contemporary worshiper. For one thing, the sacramental table expands our understanding and discourse about God's grace and our experience of it. It is not that the sacrament displaces the Word. Rather, the sacrament is a living sign of the same gospel, now in a tangible and visible form. In the same vein, an early theologian of the church described Communion as the "visible Word." "The end of the Holy Communion," John Wesley would say, "is to make us partakers of Christ in another manner than when we only hear the word."[6] The impact and potency of the Lord's Supper in John's life can be seen clearly in a typical comment from his journal: "I found much of the power of God in preaching, but far more at the Lord's Table."[7] Charles's testimony was similar. "The Lord gave us, under the word, to know the power of His resurrection," he once wrote, "but in the Sacrament, he carried us quite above ourselves and all earthly things."[8] The balancing of Word and Table also provides a context within which to interpret our other experiences of God. It serves as an anchor for revealing who this God is and what this God has done, apart from our feelings. Together, Scripture and Communion, to change the metaphor, provide a lens with which to more sharply focus God's identity and activity in our experience.

In their own time, the Wesleys were skeptical of any form of spirituality that separated the means of grace from their end, namely, love of God and neighbor. They frequently encountered Christians in their day who believed, for example, that the experience of God's presence was immediate and who thus felt no need for the means of grace. John Wesley believed that this was a dangerous presumption, subverting how people normally grow in grace. "Why are not we more holy? Why do not we live in eternity? Walk with God all the day long? Why are we not all devoted to God? Breathing the whole spirit of Missionaries?" he once asked. He answered: "Because we are enthusiasts; looking for the end, without using the means."[9] Although the Wesleys admitted that God can offer grace apart from the means that are ordained, they wanted to know why people thought God ordinarily would. They encouraged the use of the means of grace because these means truly identified God and revealed what God has done for all apart from feelings.[10]

This balance is important today. Worshipers are concerned about having a satisfying experience of God. Much worship renewal today stresses approaches that emphasize direct immediacy of God's presence. The role of music and feelings in the spirituality of worship is considered crucial. A Wesleyan emphasis on Word and Table does not contradict this trend but supplements it. The Wesleys' emphasis on the proclaimed Word and the Word made visible in the sacrament does not deny such satisfying experiences of God but roots them in a larger picture of who God is and what God has done. Using all the means of grace helps ensure that worshipers' religious experiences are not only satisfying but also true experiences of the God we have come to know in Jesus Christ.

Word and Table as a Model for Weekly Worship

Some Methodists told John Wesley that they were not going to worship at local churches. He had expected them not only to worship in his Methodist Societies but also to remain faithful to their local Church of England parish. He anticipated what they would argue: "Our own service (meaning Methodist worship in the Societies with their bands and classes) is public worship." Indeed, this Societal worship could be wonderful. There were love-feasts (testimonial services with bread and water), watch nights (extended vigil-type services), covenant services where Methodists laid their lives before God, preaching services as well as society, class, and band meetings. The fulfilling nature of these events made some think they had no need for other worship.

As good as this worship could be, however, it was not the Wesleys' design that it should compete with, or stand over against, the liturgical life of the Church of England. Throughout his lifetime, John never permitted the view that his services superseded the church service. This was not his design. He also noted that Methodist worship was essentially defective if it substituted for, rather than augmented, the services of the local church. Designed in particular for the exposition of the Word, early Methodist worship, on its own, lacked breadth, seldom having the four major aspects of public prayer (deprecation, petition, intercession, and thanksgiving) or the Lord's Supper. As personally satisfying as it might be, it was an unbalanced diet. Excitement was not to be the only criterion for assessing the worship life of the Wesleyan community.

After a lifetime of insisting that Methodism supplemented classic patterns of worship, John Wesley explicitly provided for that same breadth near the end of his life. For American Methodists, Wesley revised the worship resources of the Church of England in 1784, entitling this revision *The Sunday Service of the Methodists in North America*. It gave what he thought balanced worship should be on a weekly basis.[11] His vision included an approach to congregational worship with Word and Table as the linchpin. It was what he proposed his whole life: distinctive Methodist services supplementing, not displacing, classic worship patterns.

John's design for weekly congregational worship mirrored his lifelong practice. Sunday morning began with a prayer service including the acts of repentance, petition, intercession, and thanksgiving. The service also had a strong sense of formation since it provided for a systematic reading of the biblical text. If an elder was present, a Communion service followed, consisting of more Scripture with preaching and the administration of the Lord's Supper. If an elder was not present, a Methodist preaching service presumably concluded the morning worship. For the evening, Wesley provided another prayer service built on a full diet of prayer and Scripture, modeled after the Evening Prayer service of the *Book of Common Prayer*. His design provided for the weekly balance of prayer, Scripture, and sacrament. The retention of historical Methodist practices, which emphasized Christian fellowship and extemporaneous prayer, only increased the breadth of the design for congregational worship.

In one important sense, the Wesleys' ideal for weekly worship was radical in that it called for a norm of weekly Communion. That was the exception, not the rule, for their time. John stated his personal view succinctly in the cover letter for the Sunday service: "I also advise the elders to administer the supper of the Lord on every Lord's day."[12] The Wesleys' justification for this pattern was that it reflected both scriptural and historical norms. "The Christian Sacrifice was a constant part of the Lord's day's service," John once stated bluntly about the Lord's Supper, with regard to the first centuries of Christian history.[13] Charles argued the same sentiment in even stronger terms. For him, the loss of a weekly celebration of Communion represented nothing less than an abandonment of the historic faith and practice of the church. "From scripture as well as the tradition of the Church," he argued, "the Holy Communion ought necessarily to be administered every Lord's Day at the least."[14] For him, the matter was beyond dispute: "Both scripture and tradition do give plain evidence for the necessity of making at least a weekly oblation of the Christian sacrifice, and of honouring every Lord's Day with a solemn public celebration of the Lord's Supper."[15]

What would renewed commitment to a Wesleyan model of Word and Table look like for weekly worship? There would be no need to adopt the precise forms that Wesley prepared in 1784. What is more important than the form itself is the breadth and balance that the pattern suggests. One key rediscovery would be a wide and healthy diet of Scripture, read in some systematic way, that goes beyond the personal idiosyncracies of the preacher. The goal to be emulated would be a breadth of remembrance that looks at the wholeness of God and the person and work of Christ, in unity with the Holy Spirit. The model would also include the weekly celebration of the Lord's Supper. It would provide for a range of prayer, both in content and in form, and both extemporaneous and written. A Wesleyan model would also involve the full range of human emotions in worship. It would involve both evangelization and formation, proclamation and celebration, service in the sense of God's self-offering to humanity and the reciprocal human service to God and others. While the Wesleys were wise enough to realize that all of this could not be packed into a single service each week, they provided multiple worship practices that complemented each other and augmented the liturgical rhythms of the church.

Word and Table as a Model for the Church's Engagement with the World

John frequently described how he preached and then met the Society. This typical description, found pervasively throughout Wesley's journal, reflects two distinct ways in which the church should engage the world in worship. Saying that Wesley preached refers to his daily practice of opening Scripture for others through proclamation. The point of the Wesleyan preaching services was quite simply the communication of the gospel. "Word," in this sense, symbolizes "worship evangelism." Should worship be zealously evangelistic, concerned with those who are outside and do not know Christ? Yes, the Wesleys would answer without hesitation. But saying that he met the Society refers to the brothers' leadership over the closed meetings of those who had accepted the discipline of membership. The point of the Methodist Society was accountable discipleship and a form of Christian fellowship that nurtured its members. Nonmembers were admitted only on an exceptional basis. "Table," in this context, therefore, can be used as a symbol for "worship fellowship" leading to mission in the world. Should worship be an occasion for fellowship so intense that the members feel like their Lord is revealed in their midst and calls them into ministry? Yes, the Wesleys would answer again without hesitation. The phrase Word and Table thus serves as a remembrance of how the Wesleys not only envisaged their worship but also understood the church in relation to the world.

This model is an important one for the present time. There has been a recent resurgence of services targeted to those outside Christ and the church, and rightly so. But zeal turned into the direction of evangelism should not blind us to the importance of worship as an activity of God's gathered community. Sometimes proponents of evangelistic services argue that they are doing what the Wesleys did. They seem to ignore that evangelism was not the only purpose the Wesleys assigned to worship and that evangelistic preaching was not the only kind of worshipful activity in which they engaged. To truly do what the Wesleys did means to have a balance of different kinds of worship experiences, in which the interrelationship of church and world is expressed in different ways.

There is no doubt that the Wesleys were committed to aggressive outreach evangelism, taking the whole gospel to the whole world. Perhaps the best testimony to John's commitment to these ends was the encouragement he gave to his Methodist preachers in the work of field preaching. In addition to preaching services in meetinghouses, preaching in the streets and in the fields was encouraged by Wesley. In his *Minutes of Conversations* with his preachers, his rationale for field preaching was clear. Since the call was to save all that are lost, "we should go and seek them" because "we cannot expect such to seek us." The fact that many Methodist meetinghouses were large was no excuse. "The house may hold all that come to the house," claimed Wesley, "but not all that would come to the field." Even if the Methodists had a large meetinghouse on one side of town, he would encourage his preachers to "preach abroad" at the other side of town. Wesley's fear was clear: Unless the Methodist preachers carried the gospel out, the children of God who had not yet found their home would never be brought in. Field preaching, which in many ways signaled the birth of the Methodist movement, was essential to this evangelistic task in Wesley's day. "I do not find any great increase of the work of God," he once confided to his journal, "without it."[16] Evangelistic worship was an essential part of the church's engagement with the world.

But this was not the only way the Wesleys related church and world. If "Word" can refer to this centrifugal movement, "Table" can refer to the centripetal dimension of true fellowship in the community of believers. As important as evangelistic preaching was to early Methodism, so was the gathering of a worshiping fellowship apart from the world. In the Wesleyan vision, the church should be concerned not only with how effective it was in reaching the world with the Word but also in how proficient it was in nourishing those gathered around the table of worship fellowship who responded to God's liberating message in their lives.

In this regard, the Wesleys had several kinds of fellowship-centered meetings, to which access was restricted. There were the smaller groups of classes and bands. In any one locale, the entire membership could gather as a Society. Worship happened in both settings. John Wesley's language about the privacy of these meetings was quite strong. The meeting of a Society, he once explained, should be "inviolably private, not one stranger being admitted on any account or pretence whatsoever."[17] Methodist leaders closely monitored visitors to the meetings when visitors were permitted to attend. What this makes clear is that the early Methodists also had specific kinds of worship services open only to their fellowship. One such event was the covenant renewal service, in which Methodists met together to jointly lay their lives before God. The centerpiece of this service was a covenant to serve God with all one's heart and soul. Admission was restricted to members and to those who had received special permission to attend.[18] The conditions for admission to love-feasts were the same. Only members or those nonmembers who had received special permission could attend these periodic services that featured testimony and that used bread and water as signs of Christian unity. Doorkeepers stood ready to check for current quarterly membership tickets or permission notes from the preachers. Indeed, in the earliest days of Methodism, if a love-feast was to follow a preaching service, everyone left the space so that tickets could be checked for those returning for the sacred event.[19] The Lord's Supper, likewise, was a restricted kind of worship service, in which the same criteria for admission was applied. In fact, John Wesley criticized allowing spectators not receiving Communion to watch.[20]

The Wesleys had several reasons for holding these distinctive worship services privately. At one level, it was necessary for the fellowship to have the opportunity to watch over one another and to give advice and encouragement. Separate worship was necessary for the Society to build itself up. In some of the services, restricted access preserved the ability to testify freely. But there were also theological reasons for this practice. For the early Methodists, Christian fellowship provided the normal context for experiencing grace. Fellowship existed, not in abstract, but in reality when members gathered together in private worship. As one of Charles's love-feast hymns made clear, when Methodists assembled to build each other up, God would "meet in his appointed ways" and "nourish us with social grace."[21] God's grace is social grace. Having a Societal Table allowed Methodists to rehearse the relationships of the Kingdom of God. At the Societal Table, they showed God's love among themselves, which in turn empowered them to propel themselves back into the world, where such a show of God's love might mean a cross in return. The Table as private worship was what made the Word, as outreach to the world, a dynamic possibility.

It is not surprising that the Wesleys believed that private Table worship revealed the heart of what it means to be God's people. This aspect of their ecclesiology is perhaps most evident in their understanding of the Lord's Supper as a priestly sacrifice. Drawing on the work of a previous Anglican theologian, Daniel Brevint, the Wesleys based this notion on the unity of Christ and the people of God. Jesus Christ does nothing without his church. So close is their unity that sometimes they are represented as only one person. Christ acts and suffers for this Body as its Head; the church, in turn, imitates its Lord in the same way. It gives its life for the world. The Lord's Supper demonstrates this unity between Christ and the church in two important respects. First, the faithful are drawn into the priesthood of Christ. The interesting Wesleyan image is that we sit on the shoulders of Christ as he performs his priestly duties in heaven. Second, our sacrificial living in the world for the sake of the world is what the Pauline phrase, "participation in Christ," means. Since "Christ never designed to make a self-offering for the people, without the people...Jesus Christ and the whole Church do together make up that complete Sacrifice" at the Lord's Supper.[22] Our conformity to Christ's cross and our being joined to him at the Lord's Supper are really the making of just one sacramental offering to God. The Wesleys did not intend a merely ritualized, formal concept of sacrifice in the Lord's Supper. They intended that the Lord's Supper would show how we actually live by taking up the cross daily, dying to sin, denying ourselves, and enduring suffering that we might do good in the world. The Lord's Supper reveals that we are both priests and sacrifices like Christ is. This is the essence of what it means to be God's people.

This is the symbolic value of the Table. By this notion of the Lord's Supper as sacrifice, we see that worship is not only something that we receive—something directed to us—but also something that we do and something that we are. The church needs worship opportunities to express its basic character—who it is in Christ before God. The Wesleys' bifocal commitment to an evangelistic Word directed toward the world and to a gathered fellowship around the Table before God provides the proper balance.

Conclusion

With respect to worship, the Wesleys' legacy was the ability to hold things together. Whereas many Christian traditions—then and now—have been pulled apart by the competing polarities of preaching and sacrament, or evangelism and discipleship, the Wesleys demonstrated an ability to hold these important aspects of the Christian faith together. Unfortunately, few have chosen to follow the Wesleys' example; overemphasis in one direction or another is shattering many churches today.

For contemporary Methodists, the Wesleys offer a dynamic model of worship that is important in at least two ways. First, their model of worship shows that traditional tensions related to worship can, in fact, be held together. From their example, it is also possible for us to see the benefits of this approach. Their dynamic synthesis of Word and Table creates breadth in worship. It leads to the formation of deep Christians. They were able to see how each competing emphasis in worship had something significant to contribute to the upbuilding of the church. By embracing the biblical and historical patterns of worship, they gave equal emphasis to evangelistic zeal and accountable discipleship, to Christian nurture and social justice, to the church and mission in God's world. Moreover, their commitment to historic norms never precluded a concern for liturgical creativity and relevance, which are required in every age.

Specifically, with respect to contemporary tension points, the Wesleyan synthesis of Word and Table is particularly helpful. This balance provides a broad framework within which to appreciate and understand the personal dimensions of spirituality within the context of the biblical witness and the story of the communion of saints—God's people throughout human history. The balance of preaching and sacrament helps us find our place in God's unfolding story of redemption. God's identity is clarified, and God's activity becomes real in our lives as we remember who we are and who God is through the ongoing rhythm of Word and Table. Here is a balanced diet for a congregation's weekly worship—a way to encounter the Living Word in spoken and visible ways, to engage both head and heart, to employ our intellect and our senses, to expand our life of prayer, and to find our role in God's mission.

The phrase itself, "Word and Table," reminds us that we are called to offer the whole Christ to the whole world, on the one hand, and to be concerned about spiritual intimacy with Christ and with others in the family of God, on the other hand. We need opportunities to share the good news of God's love in Christ with a broken world; but we also need events that remind us we are a royal priesthood, a holy nation, God's own people conformed to the cross of Christ. Our challenge today is to rediscover this dynamic balance of Word and Table. It is the Wesleyan way. It is the biblical way. It is the means by which God forms us into a faithful community committed to love.

11

A FAITH THAT SINGS

THE RENEWING POWER OF LYRICAL THEOLOGY

Paul W. Chilcote

The Wesleyan tradition was born in song. Early Methodist people found their true identity as the children of God through singing, and the hymns of Charles Wesley, in particular, shaped their self-understanding and praxis. Certainly, the spiritual rediscoveries of the Wesleys put a song in the hearts of their followers who were liberated by the good news of God's love in Jesus Christ. But this lyrical heritage was not rooted in the simple joy of song; rather, the leaders of the nascent Revival recognized the potency of congregational singing as a legitimate medium of theology. The Wesleys understood, as an ancient writer once observed, that to sing is to pray twice, and as an African proverb maintains, if you can talk, you can sing. The singing of Christians is both prayer to God and speech about God. Hymns function as both a communal confession of faith and a common catechism for the faith.

This heritage of lyrical theology is to the Wesleyan tradition, therefore, what the *Institutes* of Calvin are to the Reformed, the Mass to a Roman Catholic, or the writings of the great Patristic theologians to the Christian of Eastern Orthodoxy. The hymns constituted, as John Wesley would suggest in his preface to the 1780 *Collection of Hymns for the Use of the People Called Methodists*, "a little body of experimental and practical divinity." So Methodists learned and practiced their theology by singing it. They were both formed and transformed by these texts of the faith put to music. When they sang the songs of Charles, in particular, they were singing scripture. The hymns, packed with the "oracles of God," as the Wesleys would say, exposed the singer and the community to the wide range of biblical image and story.

The singing of hymns was a characteristic practice of Wesleyan Christians at the outset of the Revival, and it has continued to be a hallmark of the tradition. The Methodist denomination is still known in many places around the world as the "singing church." While Charles Wesley stands out as the first and most formative of Methodism's lyrical theologians (and of the historic Christian community, for that matter), hymn writers have articulated faithfully and have continued to shape the tradition today. In this chapter, we will examine the role played by Charles Wesley's hymns in the renewal of Christianity during the age of the Wesleyan Revival. We also will explore the contributions of contemporary Methodist lyrical theologians, a global chorus of voices in a Methodist world parish. Finally, we will see how the singing of the Christian community can lead to the rediscovery of vital faith and abundant life in Christ.

The Lyrical Theology of Charles Wesley

Charles Wesley has finally come out from the shadow of his older brother, John.[1] Increasing attention is being given to the amazing contributions that Charles made to the birth, growth, and maturation of the Evangelical Revival. There is no question that Methodism was cofounded. It took both brothers, the preacher and the poet, as well as many others, to launch this great work of God, to give it direction, and to maintain its spiritual vitality over the course of the eighteenth century. Charles's hymns—not all nine thousand, but many of them—played a major role in this endeavor. His lyrical theology pointed to the centrality of grace in the Wesleyan understanding of salvation, encouraged accountable discipleship in such a way as to promote holiness of heart and life, and proclaimed the ultimate foundation of all things as God's unconditional love for us all in Christ Jesus. In relation to these primary themes, the early Methodist people sang and discovered their essential identity as children of God, learned how to integrate Christian faith and practice, and experienced the inclusivity of the community of faith through the very act of singing together. These salient rediscoveries are integral to renewal in any age.

The all-sufficiency of God's grace and our identification as the children of God

In the great hymn, "Jesus, Lover of My Soul," Charles proclaims of Jesus: "Thou art full of truth and grace./Plenteous grace with thee is found." Grace was the keynote of John's preaching, and for Charles, the "perfect pitch," around which everything else in life must be tuned. Both understood grace in a relational way as God's unexplained lovingkindness. It would be easy to characterize Charles's hymns using his own phrase, "so free, so infinite God's grace." His hymns are in many ways the poetic expression of his brother's sermon "Free Grace," in which John describes grace as God's free gift in all and for all.[2] John appended his brother's hymn "Universal Redemption" to that sermon, which includes the lines, "The glory of thy boundless grace,/Thy universal love," "Be justified by faith alone,/And freely saved by grace," and "Grace will I sing, through Jesu's name,/On all mankind bestowed." At the conclusion of no less than thirty-six stanzas extolling the grace of God, Charles pleads: "Come quickly, Lord, we wait thy grace,/We long to meet thee now."

The Wesleys had discovered the all-sufficiency of God's grace in their own lives. The God they had come to know in Jesus Christ was a God of grace and mercy and love. God's grace—the free, unmerited love and mercy of God flowing out to them at all times as an offer of restored relationship—was the central message that had changed their lives, led to their spiritual rebirth, and generated their movement of renewal in the life of the church. Charles had been particularly influenced by Matthew Henry's vision, described so vividly in his biblical commentary: "The springs of mercy are always full, the streams of mercy always flowing. There is mercy enough in God, enough for all, enough for each, enough for ever."[3] In his hymn "The Woman of Canaan," he ends the last several stanzas with the repeated "Thy grace is free for all," and then concludes the hymn:

> If thy grace for all is free,
>   Thy call now let me hear;
> Show this token upon me,
>   And bring salvation near.
> Now the gracious word repeat,

The word of healing to my soul:
Canaanite, thy faith is great!
Thy faith hath made thee whole.[4]

Each of the four stanzas of one of Charles's "Recovery" hymns ends with the plea, "Keep me, keep me, gracious Lord,/And never let me go."[5] Here is the bedrock of the Wesleyan tradition, namely, the discovery that God is characterized by grace and promise and will not let us go. The early Methodist singers understood themselves to be God's children, therefore saved by grace and embraced by God. They viewed the Christian life as a life of gratitude founded upon the kind of transformation that is possible only through grace. In the hymn that Charles likely penned when he was in the throes of his own evangelical conversion in May of 1738, "Where shall my wond'ring soul begin?" he sings:

O how shall I the goodness tell,
    Father, which thou to me hast showed?
That I, a child of wrath and hell,
    I should be called a child of God!
Should know, should feel my sins forgiven,
Blest with this antepast of heaven![6]

Methodism was a profound movement of spiritual renewal because it pointed to the all-sufficiency of God's grace and gave its followers a new identity, that of the children of God. It should be no surprise that nearly every hymnal of the Methodist tradition opens with the most famous four lines that Charles Wesley ever wrote:

O for a thousand tongues to sing
My great Redeemer's praise,
The glories of my God and king,
The triumphs of his grace!

Holiness of heart and life and our integration of Christian faith with practice

There is no question that the Wesley brothers believed salvation by grace through faith is the only proper foundation for the whole of the Christian life if, in fact, grace is the key to all of life itself. In other words, faith is the essential response to God's prior offer of an unconditional, loving relationship. But they also maintained that the purpose of a life reclaimed by faith alone is the restoration of God's image, namely, love, in the life of the believer. In other words, holiness of heart and life is the goal toward which the Christian life moves. Faith is a means to love's end. Faith working by love leading to holiness of heart and life is the very essence of the gospel proclamation of free grace. Faith without activated love, on the one hand, and works founded upon anything other than God's grace, on the other, are equally deficient visions of the Christian life.

This integral theology of faith and works, heart and life, found potent expression in Charles's hymns. One of the most explicit statements about these syntheses he articulates in one of the love-feast hymns:

> Let us join ('tis God commands),
> Let us join our hearts and hands;
> Help to gain our calling's hope,
> Build we each the other up.
> God his blessing shall dispense,
> God shall crown his ordinance,
> Meet in his appointed ways,
> Nourish us with social grace.
>
> Plead we thus for faith alone,
> Faith which by our works is shown;
> God it is who justifies,
> Only faith the grace applies,
> Active faith that lives within,
> Conquers earth, and hell, and sin,
> Sanctifies, and makes us whole,
> Forms the Saviour in the soul.
>
> Let us for this faith contend,
> Sure salvation is its end;
> Heaven already is begun,
> Everlasting life is won.

> Only let us persevere
> Till we see our Lord appear;
> Never from the rock remove,
> Saved by faith which works by love.[7]

The Wesleys were not only concerned that people experience forgiveness for the brokenness in their lives, but also wanted them to move toward wholeness and healing as well. The goal of spiritual maturity is love of God (a vertical dimension) and love of neighbor (a horizontal dimension). The important thing to the Wesleys was the simple fact that in this concept of the Christian life, faith leads to love, and to be loving or holy is to be truly happy. Holiness as happiness is a key to the renewal of the church.

The proclamation of God's love and the inclusivity of Christian community

One of Charles's most popular hymns, "Love divine, all loves excelling," reveals God's unconditional love. "Jesu, thou art all compassion," he sings, "Pure, unbounded love thou art." There is most certainly a mystical spirit in many of these texts, a concept of the Christian life that could be encapsulated in the closing line of this same hymn, "Lost in wonder, love, and praise."[8] For the Wesleys, love is the goal toward which everything else in life moves. Nothing fueled the Wesleyan Revival more than the simple discovery of God's essential nature revealed in Jesus Christ, namely, love. Charles fervently and eloquently expresses this fundamental understanding in a definitive hymn, "O for a heart to praise my God," which concludes:

> Thy nature, gracious Lord, impart;
> Come quickly from above;
> Write thy new name upon my heart,
> Thy new, best name of love![9]

It was amazing, indeed, to discover that God's "name is love," but all the more critical to come to the conclusion that this love is universal. Love is not only the nature and name of God but also the very life of God offered to everyone, without exception. It is, perhaps, for this very reason that Isaac Watts once described Charles's hymn "Wrestling Jacob" as the single poem worth all the verse he himself had ever written. Wesley uses the ancient narrative of Jacob at Peniel to illustrate his own struggle to find God. This hymn is not only autobiographical but also reflects the quest of every soul. In one of the most powerful descriptions of the Christian experience of God in English literature, the light breaks through, and the most important discovery of life is made:

> Yield to me now—for I am weak,
>> But confident in self-despair!
> Speak to my heart, in blessings speak,
>> Be conquered by my instant prayer:
> Speak, or thou never hence shalt move,
> . And tell me if thy name is LOVE.
>
> 'Tis Love! 'Tis Love! Thou diedst for me;
>> I hear thy whisper in my heart.
> The morning breaks, the shadows flee,
>> Pure Universal Love thou art:
> To me, to all, thy [mercies] move—
> Thy nature, and thy name, is LOVE.[10]

"Without the use of the ordinary technique of the theologian," Rattenbury observed in his reflections on this hymn, "it tells how sinful man, self-condemned, when his pride is broken and when in the presence of God he despairs utterly of himself, can achieve the vision and receive the power of God. Thus faith is born and faith penetrates into the mystery of God and discovers the secret that He is: PURE UNIVERSAL LOVE."[11]

The result of this discovery in the Wesleyan Revival was the creation of inclusive communities of people that shared this experience of the good news and sought to live it out in their lives with the help of small groups, in which they were held accountable to one another. These communities were the substance of which true renewal is made.

Charles Wesley was so prolific that his hymns, and his alone, almost filled the Methodist chapels of the next century. Before turning our attention to the contemporary scene, it will be worth remembering two important voices and hymn writers. It was not until the close of the nineteenth century and the birth of the "gospel hymn" that a new, and equally prolific, voice was heard within the tradition. Fanny Crosby is the only hymn writer in the history of the church to challenge Charles Wesley's nine thousand hymns.[12] She probably wrote just as many. Written in a popular style that spoke to the emotions, the hymn that epitomizes her lyrical ethos is, without question, "Blessed Assurance" (1873):

> Blessed assurance, Jesus is mine!
>   O what a foretaste of glory divine!
> Heir of salvation, purchase of God,
>   Born of his Spirit, washed in his blood.

This was her story and her song.

The other great hymn writer of the tradition who stands between Wesley and the contemporary church is Charles Albert Tindley.[13] Born of slave parents in Maryland, this self-educated preacher attracted so many people to his Philadelphia church by means of street preaching and community activities that a new sanctuary seating three thousand had to be constructed. He preached to packed congregations in his church, later named Tindley Temple in his honor. And at one point, he boasted the largest Methodist church in the world, with over twelve thousand members. Tindley also wrote hymns. His lyrical theology revolved around his experiences as an African American and the way God had sustained him through difficult times. No single hymn characterizes his life and work better than "Stand By Me" (1906):

> When the storms of life are raging, stand by me;
> When the storms of life are raging, stand by me.
> When the world is tossing me, like a ship upon the sea,
> Thou who rulest wind and water, stand by me.

Other hymn writers have emerged from time to time, such as Frank Mason North, who promoted the social gospel through his hymns, and Georgia Harkness, who renewed a global vision for the Methodist family. But no era has witnessed the rebirth of Christian song quite like our own.

The Contemporary Global Chorus of Voices

There is today a global chorus of voices that is giving renewed expression to the Wesleyan vision of the Christian life through song. In 1739, John Wesley proclaimed prophetically, "I look upon all the world as my parish."[14] He never could have imagined in his own day just how far reaching his movement of renewal would become one day. One of the most encouraging aspects of the renewal of the Wesleyan tradition in our time is the amazing diversity of forms and expressions of the faith that we share. Several Methodist hymn writers, in particular, help us appreciate the central themes of jubilation, journey, justice, and joy that are part and parcel of the renewing influence of Christian song in the Wesleyan spirit.

Jubilation

Erik Routley, an important historian of the Christian hymn, described Fred Pratt Green as the greatest Methodist hymn writer since Charles Wesley. There is no doubt that Green now reigns as the most significant pastor/poet of the twentieth century. His contribution to the writing of hymns has been immense and unique, and decidedly Wesleyan.[15] In 1975, he offered this patently Methodist vision of his craft as a hymn writer:

> He is a servant of the Church. It is the Church which asks him to write hymns and provides opportunities—such glorious opportunities!—for them to be sung. The hymn writer exists to enrich the Church's worship, to express the wide range of Christian devotion, to offer salvation, to teach doctrine, and to guide our feet into the way of scriptural holiness.[16]

No single word, I think, better characterizes his hymns than jubilation.

The Christian community is jubilant in its adoration of God, jubilant in accepting redemption through Christ, jubilant in asking the Spirit to lead, jubilant in addressing the needs of the poor, jubilant in answering God's call to mission in the world. The jubilant band of Christ's followers we encounter in Green's hymns is thankful and thoughtful, hope-filled and helpful. The hymns are uplifting and inspiring. One hymn in particular, "The Caring Church," actually addresses the central theme of this volume, the renewal of the church:

> The church of Christ in every age
> Beset by change but Spirit led,
> Must claim and test its heritage
> And keep on rising from the dead.
>
> Then let the servant Church arise,
> A caring Church that longs to be
> A partner in Christ's sacrifice,
> And clothed in Christ's humanity.[17]

Fred Pratt Green's signature hymn, "Let the People Sing!" closes with this exultant stanza:

> Let every instrument be tuned for praise!
> Let all rejoice who have a voice to raise!
> And may God give us faith to sing always:
> Alleluia![18]

Journey

Simei Monteiro taught at the Methodist School of Theology (Faculdade de Teologia de Igreja Metodista) in São Paulo, Brazil. Showing her fascination of the relationship between liturgical song and theology, a theme that she explores in *O Cântico da Vida* (The Song of Life, 1991), her compositions appear in collections throughout the Latin world. A consistent theme, drawn from both her native Guarani culture and her Christian experience, is that of a pilgrimage or journey.

In her hymn "Tua Palavra na vida" (Your Word in Our Lives), having described the Word of God, for example, as the "seed of the Kingdom," "food for the least," and "the mirror where we see," she concludes this powerful litany by singing:

> Your word in our lives, eternal,
>> Is light that shines on the long road,
>
> That leads us to the horizon,
>> And the bright Kingdom of God.[19]

At a conference on mission evangelism in 1995, Monteiro described in vivid detail how her people walk, or journey. "We see our peoples moving from one place to another," she explained, "going and coming from one part of the country to another, looking for jobs, a better life, dignity, food, nurture....Their song sounds in the way, telling us about the long, long journey."[20] Her hymn "Canção da caminhada" (If Walking Is Our Vocation), reminds us of this central Wesleyan theme. We are renewed when we journey together!

> If the journey is what is needful, we shall take to the road
>   together,
>   and our feet, our arms, will sustain our steps.
> We will be no more a mob without choice, nor voice, nor
>   history
>   but a church that moves out in a hope that unites.
>
> If the journey is what awaits us, we shall walk with all eyes
>   on one vision,
>   and the Kingdom of God shall we have, as horizon for
>   our life.
> We'll share the pains, and the sufferings and hardships,
>   as we are spreading the power of love in this hope that
>   unites.
>
> If the journey is what is given us, we shall walk, pilgrims,
>   together,
>   and our voice in the desert will make to spring forth new
>   fountains.
> And the new life on earth will be foreseen in our frolics and
>   joy.
> . . . God, who is among us in the hope that forever unites.[21]

These hymns reveal the important truth that the Christian life is a journey, often characterized by struggle, but moving toward God's vision of shalom.

Justice

I-to Loh has become well known in the Western world through his editorial work on Asian and ecumenical collections of hymns. A musician and specialist in the tribal melodies of his native Taiwan, he has edited hymn collections that carry titles such as *Christ the Light to Bali* and *The Love of God Sets Us Free*. He is noted primarily for his own musical compositions, for his artful paraphrasing of the Psalms, and for his masterful translation of other Asian hymn writers, and some of his most impressive work can be found in the Christian Conference of Asia Hymnal (1990) entitled *Sound the Bamboo*. In this amazing collection, his particular contributions, as in his other publications, sound the note of justice.

To a particularly powerful Malasian hymn, "God of All Gods," he adds a characteristic verse: "Good news for poor folk, light in the darkness, see, the redeemer lives./Pardon for hatred, new life to sinners, freedom from chains he gives."[22] The gifted Japanese poet Ko Yuki and I-to Loh, the musician/translator, collaborate in "On the Shore of Galilee":

> Through the days of pain and trial,
>   And the nights of fearful cries,
> Christ our Savior's ever near;
>   He shall overcome our fears.
> . . . .
>
> Lord, when will you hear our prayers,
>   Bring your kingdom down to earth?
> When shall oppression, hate disappear,
>   Peace and love forever prevail?[23]

In the hymn "Lord, We Thank You for This Food," one of the few hymns for which he composes both the musical and the lyrical texts, I-to sings: "Lord, we thank you for this food, help us share with all in need;/body, soul refresh anew to live the Gospel,/Serve your people, give your people love."[24] His hymns remind us of the Wesleyan call to be God's agents of justice in the world.

Joy

To be in the presence of Patrick Matsikenyiri, Zimbabwean composer and choral director, is to find oneself caught up in joy. He has been instrumental in the introduction and growth of African church music within the global community, and the amazing body of African song that he has composed and arranged is now receiving widespread attention. Perhaps none of his compositions is more widely known than "Jesu, Tawa Pano" (Jesus We Are Here), which has now been sung on every continent. He has been particularly concerned in adapting traditional Shona music for use in the church, and he has often given credit to women within the life of the church for the indigenization of Christian song. He explains exactly how this actually happened:

> Africans were forced to live two lives at once. When they were in church they had to sing like missionaries and when they got home they were free to sing with liberty of movement in the accompaniment of the drum, the shaker, and the rattle.... Innovative women in the church, and in the United Methodist Church in particular, started to improvise tunes for some of the translated texts which were in the hymn books....They would start to sing *Ndindindi ndindi, ndindi vanamai imi* ("Oh, oh, oh you mothers") with movement and ululation in the process. The women's faces would light up with joy and expression.[25]

The keynote of this African Methodist contribution to global Wesleyan praise is joy. In virtually every one of Patrick's compositions, the rhythmic melodies and dancing schemes communicate a contagious spirit of rejoicing. From "Tino tenda Jesu" (Thank you Jesus, amen! Alleluia, amen!) and "Sana, Sananina" (Praise God) to "The Dream," which he composed for the official opening of Africa University, his hymns plant joy in the hearts of all who sing and hear. Joyous Christians renew the church.

Singing Our Way into a New Millennium

What can we learn about the renewal of the church today from the lyrical theology of our tradition as Wesleyan Christians? First, Christian song is a powerful tool in God's process of reviving the community of faith. From the very beginning, Methodist people have learned and practiced their faith by singing it. Christian hymns and songs have the amazing capacity to engage the whole person—thinking, feeling, and acting—and thereby form and transform in lasting ways. Moreover, since hymns are written for singing congregations, they draw us immediately into community and enable us to experience the power of solidarity in Christ. Nothing could be more Wesleyan.

Second, the hymn as theology is important. We have seen how the Wesleys communicated a theology rooted in grace and love to their followers and to their spiritual progeny through the hymns they created. These lyrical creations exhibit a theology that is deep and broad, richly textured, and thoroughly biblical in its orientation. In an age that is essentially biblically illiterate and bereft of the images and stories that have shaped God's people throughout history, the sung story may be one of the most appealing means of communicating God's love in the many cultures today. We need to make sure, therefore, that the theology we sing is sound and that the singing in which we engage is Wesleyan, that is to say, rooted in God's unexplained lovingkindness.

Third, lyrical theology brings together the text and the context in such a way as to make the story of God's love come alive with relevance and potency. This is perhaps the most important quality of the Christian hymn. In our multicultural world today, we have much to learn from the global Methodist family. Perhaps a crucial aspect of our renewal will be related to the rediscovery of the Wesleyan message of God's unconditional love as it is filtered through the life and experience of those from outside our own culture and set to the rhythms and tones of worlds distant from our own. Perhaps we have something to learn from songs that speak a word of hope even though hammered out on the anvil of oppression, or from the exuberant melodies of Methodists who have learned to dance as they sing in the face of poverty and AIDS. Certainly, the renewal of our global family will come only through the sharing of our giftedness with one another. Rest assured, global praise has within it every potential to revive a global people in God.

It is most fitting, certainly, to close this discussion of lyrical theology and renewal with one of Charles Wesley's hymns:

Since the Son hath made me free,
Let me taste my liberty;
Thee behold with open face,
Triumph in thy saving grace,
Thy great will delight to prove,
Glory in thy perfect love.

Abba, Father! hear thy child,
Late in Jesus reconciled;
Hear, and all the graces shower,
All the joy, and peace, and power,
All my Saviour asks above,
All the life and heaven of love.[26]

Could anyone devise a more potent catalyst for renewal in the life of the church than this portrait of a true child of God? And when children who have been renewed by God begin to sing, God is surely there.

12

OFFER THEM CHRIST

CHARACTERISTICS OF A WESLEYAN PARADIGM FOR EVANGELISM

Laceye C. Warner

Wesley's highly organized, methodical, and theologically comprehensive mission within the eighteenth-century Church of England was intensely evangelistic. While other denominational traditions often trace their roots to disagreements regarding confessional or theological points, the Wesleyan tradition emerged from an evangelistic and missional imperative.[1] This Wesleyan evangelistic imperative and its embodiments in the Wesleyan tradition contribute to the foundations of our heritage and can offer hope and guidance for the future. The mission statement of The United Methodist Church, adopted at the 1996 General Conference, continues to demonstrate the characteristically Wesleyan evangelistic imperative: "The mission of the Church is to make disciples of Jesus Christ. Local churches provide the most significant arena through which disciple-making occurs."[2] Although Wesley referred to Methodist itinerant preachers as "evangelists," he did not use contemporary language in his discourse regarding evangelism.[3] By discerning the primary characteristics of Wesley's evangelistic imperative, I hope to articulate a Wesleyan paradigm for evangelism that will be useful for the life of the church and the world today.

Characteristics of a Wesleyan paradigm for evangelism include a scripturally based, theologically comprehensive, balanced, and compassionate approach to ministry addressing the needs of the whole person. Important to the recovery of a Wesleyan paradigm of evangelism is an emphasis upon the interdependent relationships of evangelistic ministries such as preaching, small groups, and mission outreach that are shaped by Wesley's holistic vision. The rediscovery of a Wesleyan model of evangelistic ministry offers essential guidance to the Wesleyan tradition and to its practice of evangelism for the integrity of ministry into the twenty-first century.

Characteristics of a Wesleyan Evangelism

Defining the concept of evangelism can be an elusive task. Essential to any definition of evangelism are scriptural roots and examples regarding the content and methodology of sharing "the good news." For the purpose of this discussion, the language of "evangelism" will refer to those ministry activities that facilitate an individual's introduction to the gospel of Jesus Christ and initiation into the kingdom of God.[4] Such ministry activities usually imply but are not limited to the office of kerygma, or preaching, since often the process of Christian initiation and belief may also necessitate ministries of koinonia, or fellowship, and diakonia, referring to service.[5] Several pervasive characteristics shape the Wesleyan model of evangelism. Ideally, they should never stand alone as exclusive sources or methods of evangelism. Instead, these characteristics should work together as interrelated activities pertinent to the various contexts and circumstances encountered in a process of Christian initiation.

The following characteristics inherent to a Wesleyan evangelism emerge from, and are woven together within, the story of the people called Methodists and from John Wesley's role within the Evangelical Revival. Each of the characteristics may be found in the Wesleyan tradition beginning with John Wesley's ministry, leadership, and theological reflection as well as in evangelistic activities found later in the Wesleyan tradition. These distinctive characteristics include: (1) the centrality of scripture and the gospel of Jesus Christ, (2) comprehensive theological reflection, (3) dialectic tension maintaining a holistic balance between distinct emphases of Christian doctrines, and (4) the consistent challenging of socially prescribed boundaries such as class and gender. In the following pages, these characteristics of Wesleyan evangelism will be examined in the context of three examples, namely, preaching, religious societies, and missions, that offer paradigmatic guidance for our consideration of the future of evangelism in the Wesleyan tradition.

Scripture

The most significant characteristic of Christian evangelism in most traditions is the presence of scriptural foundations. All evangelistic ministries find their impetus in scripture and culminate in the gospel of Jesus Christ. According to John Wesley, in his sermon "The Scripture Way of Salvation," the words "faith" and "salvation" include the substance of the entire Bible. Scripture provides examples of the proclamation of God's message of salvation, the good news. For the Wesleyan tradition, Scripture is the source of Christian doctrine and the norm for Christian behavior.[6] Scripture not only provides the message of salvation, its urgency and relevance but also shapes the methodology of its communication in both verbal proclamation and practice. Wesley believed that Scripture was a cohesive whole inspired by God, especially with regard to the understanding of salvation. For him, Scripture was the primary, though not exclusive, source of Christian authority.

Theological reflection

John Wesley is not considered a systematic theologian. His theological reflection was strongly influenced by his and others' spiritual and life experiences. John Wesley's scholarly approach to ministry included continual study and theological discourse in conversation with fellow scholars, ministers, and believers regarding issues of faith and doctrine. The intense theological integration pursued by John Wesley provides a useful model for a contemporary consideration of evangelism. According to William Abraham, a steady decline in theological aptitude has occurred in the last two centuries among those interested in evangelistic ministries. John Wesley and Jonathan Edwards are both considered great scholars and practitioners of evangelistic theology and ministry of their generations. However, the beginnings of a major shift may be detected during the nineteenth century, shifting toward a growing apathy for the classical traditions and a lacking interest in theological discourse by those related to evangelistic thought and practice.[7] For evangelistic ministries to be effective and maintain integrity with regard to Scripture, they must emerge from the integration of not only contextual relevance but also theological reflection. Evidence of shifting perspectives toward a thoughtful approach to doctrine and practice related to mission and evangelism continues to grow. A recovery of Wesleyan roots can contribute to this positive shift.

Dialectic

A strong theme throughout the Wesleyan heritage, fostered by John Wesley's ministry, is the continuous effort to maintain dialectic tension between seemingly opposing yet complementary emphases of Christian doctrine. Wesley seems to labor for the maintenance of such dialectics in order to strengthen the theology and ministry of the people called Methodists. He skillfully articulated the significance of doctrines, such as justification and sanctification, faith as event and process, as well as the importance of works of piety and mercy representing individual spiritual discipline and social responsibility. The importance of the general dialectic of grace and mission in his theology and ministry demonstrates the wholeness that characterized the early Wesleyan heritage. Wesley encouraged those who professed the Christian faith to witness to that faith through its demonstration in both words and actions. Albert C. Outler argues that Wesley's understanding of faith was personal and inward, as well as public and social. This is evident in Wesley's *General Rules* written for use in the Societies. The *General Rules* consist of three basic instructions that Wesley then elaborated upon in significant detail. The three basic instructions include:

> *First*: By doing no harm, by avoiding evil of every kind. . . .
> *Secondly*: By doing good; by being in every kind merciful after their power; as they have opportunity, doing good of every possible, sort, and, as far as possible to all.... *Thirdly*: By attending upon all the ordinances of God.[8]

According to Outler, therefore, authentic evangelism within the church is possible through the recovery of a characteristically Wesleyan evangelism that demonstrates these dialectical tensions.[9]

Challenging boundaries

Wesley's practical theology and ministry challenged contemporary societal and ecclesiastic boundaries in both subtle and direct ways for the purpose of spreading scriptural holiness. For example, Wesley's reluctant following of George Whitefield's encouragement to engage in field preaching challenged ecclesiastic boundaries of acceptable behavior as we have seen in Stephen A. Seamand's contribution to this volume. Wesley also cultivated avenues for women's participation in activities, which blurred acceptable boundaries for their work in the church as exhorters and preachers as well as class leaders, stewards, and even advisors to Wesley himself.[10] Inherent in Wesley's challenging of socially and ecclesiastically prescribed boundaries is his emphasis upon living out one's Christianity not only as an inward but also as an outward experience. The social implications of Wesley's vision of holiness resulted in his interest and sensitivity to human rights, including violence, poverty, and slavery.[11] Wesley's sensitivity was not limited to awareness, but included his active participation in working against social and economic injustices. A Wesleyan evangelism for the twenty-first century that considers the contextual needs and oppression of individuals and communities will be able to offer Christ in more effective ways.

Embodiments of a Wesleyan Evangelism

Three significant characteristics of evangelism were manifest in the ministries of the Wesleyan tradition. They worked together within the contextual circumstances and by means of an evangelistic methodology to create a characteristically Wesleyan paradigm for evangelism. The first example of evangelistic ministry encouraged by John Wesley was preaching—the activity perhaps most often associated with evangelistic ministry. The effectiveness of the Wesleyan movement in the eighteenth century benefited from two specific forms of preaching, namely, open-air and lay preaching. The second aspect of Wesleyan evangelism that complemented preaching was Christian nurture and discipleship in the Societies, band, and class meetings. The third embodiment of a characteristically Wesleyan evangelism was the centrality of mission in the Methodist movement. Preaching, accountable discipleship, and mission in the early Methodist movement should not be viewed as independent features of evangelism, but rather as interdependent aspects of the Wesleyan paradigm. An analysis of these salient features reveals both the complexity and the wholeness of John Wesley's evangelistic vision.

Preaching

There is no question that open-air preaching was one of the most definitive characteristics of the Evangelical Revival. Possibly the most definitive characteristic of this transatlantic movement was preaching in general, and in particular, preaching in the open air. Wesley, as mentioned earlier, began his practice of field preaching in 1739. The preaching of the Wesleyan Revival resulted in thousands of conversions and new members for Methodists, as well as for Baptists, Presbyterians, and Independents.[12] Through the method of open-air preaching, Wesley and other Methodist itinerant preachers were able to address a wider audience than ever before, including the poor and working classes. By preaching in fields, marketplaces, and even public hangings, they effectively carried the gospel of grace to the people, rather than waiting for the people to come to them. Preaching in the open air contributed to Wesley's greater accessibility to, and effectiveness among, the lower class persons who, because of rigid class boundaries, would never have attended worship or darkened the doors of the churches of their day.

Although the preaching of figures like Whitefield and Wesley is well documented for its evangelistic impact upon British as well as North American Christianity, preaching did not stand alone as a method of effective evangelism. Wesley, in particular, worked tirelessly to expand the roles of laity, including the roles of laywomen, within the church by cultivating avenues for their participation in a variety of ministries including preaching. Relatively early in the Methodist movement, Wesley accepted lay preaching unlike his intolerant brother, Charles. John later referred to these laymen as "sons in the gospel."[13] Lay preaching, in addition to open-air preaching, was not considered an acceptable practice within the Church of England. The office and role of preaching was reserved and protected as an appropriate role for the ordained clergy, an office open only to men in that tradition until 1994. Germane to John Wesley's challenge of the existing boundaries was his cautious encouragement of women to fulfill relatively nontraditional roles, including leading mixed meetings, exhorting, and at times preaching. Among those women groomed and respected by Wesley for their ministries as leaders, educators, practitioners in evangelistic work, and on specific occasions, as preachers were Sarah Crosby, Mary Bosanquet Fletcher, and Sarah Mallet.[14]

Preaching within the Wesleyan tradition, particularly John Wesley's own sermons, was firmly based upon Scripture with numerous biblical quotations and references. He also appealed to a variety of other sources for his sermons, including classical literature, Christian antiquity, medieval Christianity, the English Reformation, the Anglican and Puritan traditions, and his own contemporary culture.[15] His favorite New Testament preaching text was Mark 1:15, a strongly evangelistic text often described as a summary of Jesus' commission to the disciples in Mark.[16] In this verse, Jesus proclaims: "The time is fulfilled, and the kingdom of God has come near; repent, and believe in the good news." One specific example of Wesley's theological reflection in the context of an evangelistic purpose is the sermon, "The Scripture Way of Salvation." This sermon, which represents Wesley's mature theology and soteriology, demonstrates both his critical theological reflection and his dialectic emphasis upon grace and good works in the Christian life.[17]

Preaching remained a significant characteristic of Wesleyan evangelism into the nineteenth century with subsequent revivals including the Second Great Awakening and the emergence of camp meetings in both the British Isles and North America. However, camp meetings and open-air preaching were not consistently accepted within the British Wesleyan tradition. One group in particular suffered expulsion from Wesleyan Methodism on the grounds that it engaged in camp meetings as well as open-air preaching. It subsequently formed the Primitive Methodist

Church. This intolerance of open-air preaching in Wesleyan Methodism was later reversed in the last decades of the nineteenth century.[18] In addition to the controversy around open-air preaching following John Wesley's death in 1791, severe limitations were placed upon women within the increasingly respectable Wesleyan Methodist tradition. Although nineteenth-century revivalism at times held together the dialectic of grace and mission characteristic of eighteenth-century Wesleyan evangelism, the separation of this balanced tension occurred more frequently throughout the nineteenth century as a result of the impending fundamentalist modernist controversy.[19] A consequence of this controversy, which culminated in the early twentieth century, is demonstrated in the tendency to isolate the spiritual from the material, grace from mission, evangelism from social action, creating a truncated understanding of evangelistic ministries in the Wesleyan and other traditions.[20]

Societies, classes, and bands

The definitive organism of the early Wesleyan tradition was the small group meeting. The purpose of these classes and bands within the larger Society structure was a form of Christian nurturing that provided a foundation from which to engage in missional and evangelistic ministries. These gathered groups were originally inspired most directly by Anglican religious societies made up predominantly of laity, specifically those associated with the Society for Promoting Christian Knowledge.[21] Groups such as the SPCK tended to focus on nurture rather than conversion. Their agenda was to reform society one individual at a time instead of pursuing a larger program to execute widespread social reform. Band meetings emerged initially as individuals voluntarily banded together to encourage one another in their quests for holiness of heart and life. The membership of the bands did not constitute the whole Society, but the bands were composed of the more spiritually mature, although penitential bands also emerged for those struggling against backsliding. Class meetings arose initially as a method of fund-raising but quickly evolved into structured systems of pastoral care. Typically larger than bands, consisting of approximately twelve members, classes encompassed the entire membership of a

local Society and provided a means for the practice and maintenance of disciplinary standards, such as examination with regard to
one's readiness for admission to the Lord's Supper.

In the context of bands and classes, individuals encouraged one
another in their Christian journeys through public and private
prayer, study of Scripture, confession, and fasting, as well as praise
and worship. Discussed in an earlier chapter by Steve Harper, these
activities, also known as works of piety, were means of grace,
through which individuals might come to know faith in Jesus Christ.
In addition to works of piety, members of Societies, classes, and
bands also engaged in works of mercy, also discussed by Rebekah
Miles. Whereas works of piety emphasized individual spiritual
growth, works of mercy included feeding the hungry, clothing the
naked, and visiting the imprisoned, sick, and afflicted. The bands
and class meetings served as organizational means, by which members of the Wesleyan Societies might provide not only pastoral care
and economic support to its membership but also spiritual and economic outreach to the poor, infirm, and aged in their communities.
The small group structure thereby helped to facilitate organized missional efforts through the means of their works of mercy.

John Wesley chose trustworthy individuals as leaders of the
bands and class meetings. Those chosen for these important roles
were often lay members. Class leaders carried an important function as pastoral links between the thousands of members within
local religious societies and John Wesley. Band and class leaders
became spiritual overseers of those in the Methodist movement,
enabling Wesley to manage the leadership as his delegates. Roles
of substantial responsibility, including band and class leaders,
with few exceptions, were not only entrusted to lay members by
John Wesley but also often filled by women.

During the nineteenth century, class meetings in British and
North American Methodism steadily declined as a result of several
cultural and ecclesiological dynamics.[22] Within the Wesleyan tradition in North America, the waning of circuit structures and class
meetings was caused by larger gatherings in the context of camp
meetings, and later by the construction of impressive centenary
church facilities. Religious education, particularly Sunday schools
predominantly for children and youth, received growing attention
toward the end of the nineteenth century, most likely at the expense

of adult discipleship in the context of class meetings. In the second half of the nineteenth century, however, women's organizations within Methodism, such as the Deaconesses, proliferated. This encouraged the organization and continuance of class meetings, particularly in rural and poor urban areas. The recovery of Wesleyan small groups in recent decades is a promising development toward a Wesleyan evangelism for the twenty-first century.

Methodist missions

The complexity of a Wesleyan paradigm for evangelism includes the significance of mission outreach inspired by the proclamation of Scripture and its implications worked out in the context of small groups. This discussion of characteristics and embodiments of a Wesleyan paradigm for evangelism would be incomplete without reference to Methodist mission and outreach ministries organized by John Wesley. Formed and influenced by his devotional and exegetical study of scripture, Wesley worked diligently to commit the whole of his life, thought, action, and financial resources to the spreading of scriptural holiness and to the offering of Jesus Christ to the world. "Wesley's parish was not only without boundaries and his congregation without pedigree," Richard P. Heitzenrater has observed, "but his concept of ministry was without limits so long as the activities fit into his vision of scriptural Christianity by helping a person receive the wholeness that God's salvation could bring to humanity."[23]

Through the financial support of Wesley's followers in Bristol, the New Room,[24] the oldest Methodist building in the world, was opened for use in 1739. The New Room became the hub of a dynamic and systematic mission to the poor through a variety of ministries, including the distribution of food and medical services. In this way, the New Room, as well as the Foundery in London, served as a center not only for fellowship, worship, and the proclamation of the gospel but also for the demonstration of scriptural holiness and mission.

This mission included working with impoverished and orphaned children, addressing the pathetic state of educational opportunities for the powerless. Among Wesley's efforts in the Bristol area was the establishment of a school for the poor children of laborers in

Kingswood. An economic support service was also managed through the Foundery and funded by Wesley and the Methodists to assist promising entrepreneurs lacking in financial resources. Similar to these missional centers in Bristol and London, the preaching house in Newcastle was called the Orphan-house and housed several services, including an orphanage, a school, and an infirmary.

Wesley's missional paradigm held evangelism, discipleship, and social service in dynamic unity. This, in fact, was the genius of his movement of renewal within the life of the Church of England.

This holistic vision to meet the needs of the whole person provided an impetus and example for subsequent generations within the Wesleyan tradition. Thomas Coke, for example, more concerned with "foreign missions" than Wesley, organized missionary efforts before the end of the eighteenth century, setting a precedent for the historic emphasis on foreign mission and outreach. Methodist women have also maintained Wesley's imperative for mission in foreign and domestic contexts. The work of eighteenth-century sick visitors encouraged by Wesley inspired the ministry of a number of middle- and late-nineteenth-century women's organizations. The ministries of the Ladies and Pastors' Christian Union, the Woman's Home and Foreign Missionary Societies, and several Deaconess orders demonstrate the responsibility and desire of the faithful to share the love of Jesus Christ with their neighbors through visitation. The ministry of Methodist women, beginning with the sick visitors organized by John Wesley, ministered to both the souls and the bodies of the afflicted. The ministry of Wesleyan women's organizations in both Great Britain and North America, and the church at large, help remind contemporary Christians of the complexity of our call as believers and followers of Jesus Christ. Christian vocation in the Wesleyan tradition not only revolves around spiritual matters but also embraces profound social and economic implications.

Conclusion

In this chapter, I offer a paradigmatic guide for the recovery and reappropriation of Wesleyan evangelism in our time. By examining the characteristics of Wesleyan evangelistic ministries, particularly related to the life and witness of John Wesley, models for the practice of a Wesleyan evangelism in our own contexts emerge. One profound lesson to learn from Wesley's experience is that the complexity of interwoven themes and dialectics that finds its foundation in Scripture can lead to a holistic ministry to and for all people. Wesley was keenly aware of his contemporary context, including the social, economic, and political circumstances that shaped the lives of the people around him. He was attentive to their conditions. But he also listened closely to the perennial message of liberation and love contained in God's Word. He worked tirelessly to relate scriptural values and norms to the context of the people he felt God had called him to serve.

Any future paradigm of evangelism that seeks to be authentically Wesleyan will have *preaching* at its center. Our own context may call for different forms of proclamation than the age of Wesley in which open-air and itinerant preaching opened God's message of love to thousands. Whatever the form or medium, the kerygmatic proclamation of the death and resurrection of Jesus Christ as God's good news to humanity will be the core of Wesleyan evangelism. Grace will be its keynote, and love will be its end. An authentic Wesleyan paradigm will also make sure that *accountable discipleship* is both understood and practiced in the life of the church. Christian nurture and discipleship will be viewed, not as consequences of evangelistic activity, but as part and parcel to the evangelistic task. The great success of programs such as Disciple Bible Study and Covenant Discipleship Groups is a sign of hope in this regard. Finally, the authentic Wesleyan evangelist—and that means all Methodist Christians—will find their essential vocation in *mission*. "To serve the present age," sang Charles Wesley, "my calling to fulfil."[25] For the Wesleyan tradition, it is not so much that the church has mission as a programmatic aspect of its life; rather, the church is mission. When Methodist churches begin to write mission into their statements of purpose, a Wesleyan authenticity will begin to percolate among the rank and file. Mission is contagious; evangelism is its heart.

The gospel of grace proclaimed to all, care for one another within the family of God, solidarity with the least, the last, and the lost—these are the hallmarks of a Wesleyan paradigm of evangelism. When viewed with excitement as the whole gospel for whole persons, and as energized by the Spirit of God, this vision will surely renew the church, to the glory of God and to the salvation of many.

13

"THE LAW OF LOVE"

REPENTANCE AND THE RESTORATION OF LOVE

Amy Laura Hall

Faith, then, was originally designed of God to re-establish the law of love.... It is the grand means of restoring that holy love wherein man was originally created.[1]

There is great reason to fear that it will hereafter be said of most of you who are here present that this Scripture [1 Cor. 13:3], as well as all those you have heard before, profited you nothing. Some, perhaps, are not serious enough to attend to it; some who do attend will not believe it. Some who do believe it will yet think it a hard saying, and so forget it as soon as they can.[2]

Either therefore you must consent to give up your *principles*, or your fond hope of pleasing men.[3]

Introduction

According to Wesley, a person's life of faith must bear the fruits of love. A church experiencing a Wesleyan renewal should therefore bear the fruits of a loving community. But this is no simple task. As Wesley explains in the sermons quoted above, the law of love that is to guide us in discipleship and discernment is "hard," not in that it is unduly complex, but in that it is quite strenuous. And the scripture readings on love too often "profit us nothing" because we so creatively eschew their difficult import for our lives. John Wesley, following in the Christian tradition, maintained that this perpetual avoidance of the "hard sayings" of love is universal. After the Fall, we avoid faithful love as a rule. According to Wesley, Christians must therefore constantly, perpetually avail ourselves of the means of grace. In order to live sanctified, loving lives, we must sincerely repent, avoid sin, and actively seek to grow in the grace that makes us ever more loving. His elaboration of this strenuous Christian life led his contemporaries to describe his followers thus: "You are grown so precise and *singular*, so monstrously *strict*, beyond all sense and reason, that you *scruple* so many harmless things, and fancy you are *obliged* to do so many others which you need not."[4]

Although, according to Wesley, our sinful avoidance of real Christianity is universal, he describes occasions for sin that are particular to context. In his sermons, he describes the contours of our falsehood as varying according to setting and opportunity. Reading several key sermons, we may discover that we have particular cultural incentives to avoid Wesley's hard interpretation of holy love. Affluent and middle-class Americans are, by both geographic and temporal comparison, a remarkably prideful, self-centered, pleasure-seeking people. Not coincidentally, Americans by and large want faith with a small "f" and spirituality with a small "s." Preaching a Wesleyan "Faith" that truly transforms our present lives and a "Spirituality" that issues in holy love is increasingly counterintuitive in our cultural context. This poses for us a problem. As evangelicals (and I count myself among them) seek "church growth," we will be sorely tempted to cater to the shallow, selfish "loves" of a people whose desires are shaped by shopping malls and television. When we do so cater, Christian love becomes little more than sentimental fellow feeling for those similarly trapped in the American way of pride and the pursuit of pleasure. As a blessedly rude colleague has put it, being Methodist becomes synonymous with being blandly, nonthreateningly "nice." We thus often chuckle uncomfortably at the Wesleyan call for perfection, in part because we cannot envision what perfect lives would look like in such a mediocre setting.[5]

In order to restore love, we must retrieve Wesley's emphasis on individual and social holiness, recover the means of grace, and foster the radical expectation that our lives will be transformed. For according to Wesley, receiving faith means also receiving, increasingly, the gift of holy love. And that holy, self-giving love should change the very way we live in this relatively lust-driven and prideful nation. In order to do any of this, however, we must take a radically courageous step. We must be willing to offend and even repel the very middle-class, upwardly mobile seekers and choosers we otherwise hope to attract. We must be willing to require prospective (and present) members to turn away from their false loves before the church can be reestablished in God's law of love. After first describing more fully our current, problematic context, I will turn to Wesley's compelling indictment of a setting wherein love cannot flourish. Finally, I will anticipate the ways that our lives may become more truly loving as we make Wesley's vision our own.

The Temptation of Easy Evangelism

> If Christ be risen, ye ought then to die unto the world, and to live wholly unto God. A hard saying this to the "natural man" who is alive unto the world, and dead unto God, and one that he will not readily be persuaded to receive as the truth of God, unless it be so qualified in the interpretation as to have neither use nor significancy left.[6]

Two hundred years ago, Methodists experimented, for three years, with an innovative, informal method of evangelism. Given that the world was in desperate need of the gospel, and given that the teeming masses were neither comfortable with nor welcomed to traditional worship, we tried a new way. The Methodist Conference of 1745 decided to try broad-reaching evangelism in every possible venue, even in places where corresponding societies to foster discipleship did not exist. As William Abraham observes, Methodists very wisely overturned this decision three years later.[7] Our Methodist grandparents discerned early on that true faith requires real catechesis, prayer, and hard, grace-filled work. They decided that hearing the gospel and responding in faith is only the first step, and that the subsequent steps depend on Christian community. To employ another metaphor, without mutual accountability, prayer, study, and repentance, the seeds of evangelism would bear neither stalk (real faith) nor fruit (holy love).

The Christian community today faces a similar temptation. In a society hostile or indifferent to the church, we are tempted to try new forms of accessible, marketable evangelism. We can reach more unchurched people if we cast a wide net in culturally acceptable venues, gathering folks into sports arenas, shopping malls, and by way of the computer. We can persuade them to come to weekly services if we offer them entertaining worship and stadium-style seating. And, more important, we can keep them coming back on Sunday if we require little of them in return. This can look temporarily successful, in the shallow terms set by church growth experts. But such evangelism makes a mockery of the saying "Each One Disciple One" because, in truth, real discipleship does not occur. Participants may glimpse faith in the passing spectacle, but they do not become "reestablished in the law of love." As our Methodist grandparents discerned so many years ago, such reestablishing requires hard, grace-filled work.

We presently face a temptation particular to our time and setting. Whereas in 1745, Methodists were tempted to practice irresponsible evangelism in order more broadly to reach the poor gathered in new, industrial centers, we now practice irresponsible evangelism in order to attract the relatively privileged middle class. Rightly perceiving that many potential members have little interest in living a life of self-giving love, we too often fashion the church into an unholy center of self help, entertainment, child care, and career networking. We too often fashion a church that meets the needs of a people whose very needs are distorted and sinful rather than a church that seeks to redefine for the people what their real needs should be. To put the problem a bit differently, we are tempted to forget that we cannot grow a real church if we focus only on the number of people who join in a year. From a Wesleyan perspective, true church growth requires that Christians truly grow in faith. And for Wesley, this means being reestablished in the law of love. For eighteenth-century Methodists, this crucial emphasis on the life of holy love meant refusing to evangelize in areas where they could not sustain discipleship. For Methodists in the twenty-first century, this requires our willingness potentially to repel the average "seeker." We have to be open to the scriptural reality that, in particularly vicious settings, God's word may be so counterintuitive as to be repulsive.

Blessedly, not all congregations, pastors, and bishops have given in to this temptation. There are churches of every size and shape, across the country, that work faithfully through sustained scriptural studies, that form Sunday school classes that actually practice mutual accountability, that worship God in joy and gratitude, and that practice temperance in all things material. But there are too many other churches that have jettisoned Wesley's emphasis on loving discipleship in order to increase church attendance. In an effort to retain and gain members, some bishops subtly or overtly encourage pastors to preach easy, reassuring sermons, to keep their services short, simple, and specialized, and, in general, to give the people what they want. We spend too much time thinking about materially attracting unchurched "seekers" and the growing number of people who are disillusioned with their denomination of origin, a group I call "choosers." Some writers acknowledge the tension between remaining true to the gospel, on one hand, and attracting those who might otherwise be repelled by church, on the other.[8] But too often we, as Methodists, have loosened this tension. And inasmuch as we try to make our message more comfortable and comforting, we mislead prospective members about the strenuous, antimaterialistic, self-giving love to which we are called. We invite such members under false pretenses, forgetting that the one who preceded Jesus shouted: "You brood of vipers! . . . Bear fruits worthy of repentance!" (Luke 3:7).

This temptation is not new to Methodists, but the manifestation of our temptation is specific to America. Because our present culture is quite intent on appearances, success, and ease, we are continually tempted to pitch our evangelism in ways that are attractive, easy, and efficient. Consider a few examples. One church recently decided to spend a significant amount of its outreach budget to have Starbucks cater its preworship coffee hour. Correctly perceiving that the most "attractive" seekers and choosers appreciate good coffee, the church decided to experiment with this tool for evangelism. Another church included in its building plan an extravagant floor-to-ceiling aquarium. This beautiful addition to the new building would, its advocates explained, draw in visitors who would then overhear the gospel.

While these may be extreme examples, allow me to mention one that is, to many of us, all too familiar. Consider how many congregations are determined to end their worship service precisely on the hour. Some laity determine whether to join or to remain in a church by this criterion alone. And worship committees consequently worry over ways to make services even shorter, hoping to attract churchgoers and seekers alike who are increasingly unwilling to spend more than one hour a week worshiping the one who died for their sakes.

Another example in which American culture has taken over evangelism is in the push for stadium seating and/or large screens. The argument goes something like this: "Seekers like the movies. They are comfortable in movie theaters. They are uncomfortable in churches. If we make church look more like a movie theater, these people will come to church." In this way, we hospitably meet people "where they are," so to speak. But here is the crucial point: Note that "where they are" is a culture that encourages (1) the passive reception of pleasing or exciting images and then (2) the subsequent appraisal of such images by the shallow criteria of individual enjoyment. When seekers or choosers arrive at a church that meets their expectations, they easily bring these expectations with them. They sit, they receive, they may stand up, tap their feet, or wave their hands, but they are still in the mode of pursuing happiness. Was the service "good"? Was it worth their time? The answer they give is likely to be on the basis of whether they enjoyed themselves, whether the show deserved one or two thumbs up. Rather than transforming their expectations, we attempt to meet them. Those of us who are offering the gospel thus become confused about what it is we are offering. Propelled by a false, numerical standard of "growth," we forget what it is that we should offer. In some ways, a small, unattractive sanctuary, uncomfortable pews, or "gloomy" Gothic architecture might be more apt. These signals warn the choosers and seekers who walk through our doors that Christian worship will not meet their present expectations, hopes, or dreams. Aesthetically odd or awkward sanctuaries may serve to notify those who enter that church is a place where our expectations, hopes, and dreams are transformed. Church is a place where we are conformed to a totally new way of loving.

Heeding Wesley

> Cutting off both the lust of the flesh, the lust of the eye, and the pride of life, engaging the whole man, body, soul, and spirit, in the ardent pursuit of that one object, is so essential to a child of God that "without it whosoever liveth is counted dead before him."[9]

> How exceedingly strange must this sound in the ears of those who are, by the courtesy of England, called Christians![10]

In two sermons, "The Circumcision of the Heart" and "On Charity," John Wesley takes up Saint Paul's juxtaposition of worldly and Christian love. Worldliness, Wesley explains in the quote above, is a problem both of lust and of pride, and our hearts must be cured of both. Wesley often depicts the *un*circumcised heart as one that pursues ardently the goods of the flesh (lust) and worldly success for oneself (pride). Wesley, with Paul, assumes that the pursuits of lust and pride combine to make the default way of the world. A faithful Christian must therefore repent and turn away from the life of false love encouraged in the world. Preaching, prayer, and fraternal accountability are all means for the continuation of the grace that enables repentance. Through these means, God pulls us further away from false love and closer toward Godself as the rightful focus of our love. Inasmuch as Christians take away the "strangeness" of this life, inasmuch as we transform the description of discipleship to fit the pursuit of lust and pride, we thwart God's will and leave lives bereft of holy love. Wesley points out the irony of this mistake in the second quote above. By the supposed "courtesy" of England, people whose lives have not been transformed consider themselves faithful. On the contrary, Wesley insists, true discipleship does not occur until one's heart is circumcised in love. True discipleship requires hearing the discourteous call to repent, to turn from the false loves of the world.

In the first sermon, Wesley explicitly identifies the circumcision of our hearts with the graced virtue of love. His metaphor of circumcision is apt, given Wesley's strong emphasis on humility as a mark of love. The wound that marks us also chastens the pride that seeks its own. Through grace, God pulls us to Godself, altering our tendency to rely on ourselves, and we come to cling ever more fervently to God. Through grace, our hearts are thus

181

circumcised, altered, so that our desire is for God. We are turned outward, toward God and neighbor, rather than inward, toward the abyss that is our selfishness. Wesley contrasts this transforming love with "the pride of life" that concentrates on worldly gain. The graced virtue of love is, for Wesley, linked intrinsically with our turning away from gain as the world would have it. Otherwise, our supposedly "faithful" actions are counterfeit. As he words it provocatively in his sermon "On Charity," "The brightest talent, either for preaching or prayer, if it was not joined with humble, meek, and patient resignation, might sink me the deeper into hell, but will not bring me one step nearer heaven."[11] In the sermon, Wesley follows with other examples of counterfeit talents—counterfeit because they are not truly loving. If love is, as Wesley believes, the highest fruit of faith, humility is a mark of this fruit. Our obsession with ourselves is both deadly and damning, according to Wesley. Faithful Christians, he insists, will be those who lose themselves for the sake of their love for God. They will be "humble, meek, and resigned," turned toward God's will.

If pride goes before our fall, "lust of the flesh and eye"[12] travels closely with pride. Wesley often closely links lust and pride as manifestations of love's opposite. Rather than contrasting the sins of greed and pride, he suggests that they are intertwined in a self-centered person. He warns that the uncircumcised heart seeks novelty, greatness, or beauty, focusing outward on the world with the consequence of missing God. "The seeking happiness in what gratifies" these false desires, Wesley explains, "is the distinguishing mark of those who will not have him reign over them."[13] This contrast is significant here, as well as in other sermons. The graced virtue of love draws Christians away from self-centered desire, humbling us and chastening us to find God always at the center of our movement. This brings Christians closer to one another, in the true love that propels a community of discipleship. A false love of the world instead keeps our desires self-centered and sends us to seek that which will satisfy our longing for pleasure and for approval of those from whom we can gain. This alternative, idolatrous cycle draws us toward one another in a system of false applause and admiration. By seeking pomp, grandeur, and power, whether in petty backwater cesspools or oceanic whirlpools, we exist in systems of sin rather than of grace. The circumcision of our heart, in faith, is to issue forth in a new life and a new love, with God as our focus and our guide.

While Wesley knows that vice can spring forth in paltry soil, riches provide the most fertile opportunities for pride and lust. To put this differently, wealth of goods and of power is itself an occasion for the sins that hinder love. A group of people whose foundation is power and wealth will form a twisted combination of rotten vines, bearing deadly fruits. In the sermon "On Riches," Wesley makes this point clearly. Interpreting Mark 10:23, he explains that "it is easier for a camel to go through the eye of a needle than for those that *have riches* not to *trust* in them."[14] Riches become, for the wealthy, the foundation for an alternative faith. Wesley tackles a desperate problem of his (and our) time: the false gods of success and pleasure. The uncircumcised heart, in a setting of wealth, has ample opportunity to remain falsely secure in pride and dangerously enamored with lust. In this sermon, Wesley suggests a vicious setting wherein the rich are cut off from grace. Encouraged by their success to rely upon themselves, the rich become ever more prideful. Enabled by their success to purchase their satisfaction, they become ever more lustful. Riches, Wesley explains, both "hinder humility," inasmuch as they encourage us to have faith in ourselves, and foster "temptation," inasmuch as we become ever more intent on our own satisfaction.

We may be tempted to pass too quickly over Wesley's condemnation of what he calls "the lust of the eye." Wesley elaborates at length on the vicious collaboration of riches and this sort of lust:

> Now how numerous are the temptations to this kind of idolatry which naturally spring from riches! How strongly and continually are they solicited to seek happiness (if not in grand, yet) in beautiful houses, in elegant furniture, in curious pictures, in delightful gardens!... Yea, in every new thing, little or great, which fashion, the mistress of fools, recommends?[15]

Wesley so well narrates the individual and social dimension to this form of sin. First, allowed the means with which to satisfy her desires, a wealthy person becomes ever more desirous. Second, a person of wealth becomes ever more privy to the luring solicitations of "fashion." Wesley beautifully meets his middle-class hearers in his illustrations, noting that "fashion" may not encourage gaudy excess but instead encourages the constant satiation of seemingly "little" desires. By seeking the latest "curiosity," cultivating small but lovely gardens, and finely appointing a modest house, we participate in an alternative faith: faith in the pleasure of our own self-centered happiness. As we become more successful, as we begin to enjoy the "little and great" things of life, and as we gain the means to keep up with what "fashion" dictates, we become ever more ensnared in the idolatrous system of unfaith.

This alternative faith pulls us away from our love of God and, consequently, from our love of neighbor. As we become the center of our own acquisitive, attractive universe, we resist God's pull toward our neighbor. Losing God as our focus and our center, we lose the capacity for "pure, disinterested goodwill to every child of man." As Wesley continues to explain, such love "can only spring from the love of God, which [a wealthy person's] great possessions expelled from his soul."[16] Having replaced God with the things we have or wish to acquire, we are not moved to love God's children. We go about our world seeking that which will make us more lovely, new, interesting, or comfortable, moving out from our selfish center. This works in clear opposition to a love with God as our center, whereby we move outward toward all of God's children as the recipients of our self-giving love. Again, Wesley does not write this sermon to admonish merely the English aristocracy. He clearly has in mind as well the more modest but insidious middle-class pursuit of what is novel and pleasurable. To pursue society in this way prohibits a life of love.

Wesley indicts wealth as an enemy to such love most bluntly in his sermon "On Dress." Here, he insists that "the wearing costly array is directly opposite to the being 'adorned with good works.'"[17] Clothing becomes, in this sermon, a powerful metaphor for our reliance on worldly goods rather than on the faith that leads to love. Beautifully employing Paul's baptismal imagery, he insists that, inasmuch as we "put on" the attractive clothes of the world, we fail to "put on Christ." As we pursue this alternative clothing, we fail to seek, in love, the good of our neighbor. He states: "Nothing can be more evident than this; for the more you lay out on your own apparel, the less you have left to clothe the naked, to feed the hungry, to lodge the strangers."[18] Characteristically, Wesley shines light on the real, material connection between faith and love. Self-reliance and greed not only make us less faithful. They also make us less loving, less capable of concrete good works. In one of his most searing lines from this sermon, Wesley tells us, "every shilling which you needlessly spend on your apparel is in effect stolen from God and the poor."[19] And lest we think that this vice is localized, neglecting only the poor immediately around us, Wesley elaborates on the expanse of this sin's influence. By spending money on "gay or costly apparel," you "poison both yourself and others, as far as your example spreads."[20] When we spend unnecessarily on our clothing (or on our SUVs, our children's private schools, our golf clubs, or our vacations), we encourage others to do so as well. And the cycle, to which Wesley refers in his sermon "On Riches," continues as the society whirls downward away from love and toward material success, lust for more, fashion's enticements, the encouragement of envy, lust for more, and the neglect of the poor.

But I have yet to name the most menacing (and, for our purposes, important) feature of this vicious cycle that Wesley describes. Wealth discourages repentance. The admonition that leads to real repentance, the very antidote by which the viciously wealthy and pleasure-seeking society might be cured, is squelched by the illness itself. Success and the pursuit of happiness, intertwined, build a self-enclosed system of vice. In the sermon "On Riches," Wesley explains that wealth prohibits "that freedom of conversation whereby [the wealthy] might be made sensible of their defects, and come to a true knowledge of themselves."[21] The wealthy are cut off from fraternal admonition, from real preaching, and thus from real repentance because everyone who might otherwise speak the truth to them wishes instead to curry their favor: "O how pitiable is your condition! And who is able to help you? You need more plain dealing than any men in the world. And you meet with less."[22] A successful and pleasurable society is spiritually disastrous because it cuts us off from the truth that can bring about our transformation. Wealth, Wesley implies, brings with it the damning temptation of false preaching.

Love Transformed

If you walk by this rule, continually endeavoring to know, and love, and resemble, and obey the great God and Father of our

Lord Jesus Christ, as the God of love, of pardoning mercy; if from this principle of loving, obedient faith, you carefully abstain from all evil, and labour, as you have opportunity, to do good to all men, friends or enemies; if, lastly, you unite together to encourage and help each other in thus working out your salvation, and for that end watch over one another in love—you are they whom I mean by Methodists.[23]

There are United Methodist Women circles that meet weekly to conform their lives to this image set forth in Wesley's "advice" to us. They pray together, not only for God to heal their infirmities, but also for God to sanctify their daily lives. They gather their widows' mites in order to give to the poor. In small and substantial ways, they partake of and live on the means of grace. They come to weekly communion, knowing that they desperately need it. They spend weeks learning about the Children of Africa Initiative, and then they give real gifts to the cause. They support one another in the faith, knowing that such support requires sororal admonition as well as encouragement. I knew such a circle in Connecticut. "The Ruth Circle" was made up of faithful women in their seventies and eighties. In the middle of an extravagantly wealthy town, these women knew that they needed to repent continually, to avail themselves of God's grace and to enact the works of mercy. Lest I overly romanticize the group, I must acknowledge that it, too, had faults. All such circles do, of course, bear the marks of sin. But these women were on their way to perfection.

We cannot submit to the circumcision of our hearts unless we recognize that our hearts are currently in need of transformation. The church cannot become more loving unless we recognize that we must first repent. UMW circles, at their best, represent one way that Methodism continues our forefathers' decision long ago to refuse evangelism without transformation. But in a trend indicative of our present problems, UMW groups are on the wane. It is increasingly difficult to convince young women to make the time and effort to pursue holiness on a daily basis. (When younger groups do meet, they too often discuss the latest tips in *Good Housekeeping* or in *Living Simple*, depending on their income.) This is not even to mention the fact that even the more active United Methodist Men groups meet only once a month, with a generous showing once a year at the Mother's Day pancake breakfast. How many of us are willing to require our potential members to become members of a group that actually actively pursues personal and social holiness? If we are to preach Wesleyan faith, a faith that leads to love renewed, we will have to require such participation. To put the point provocatively, if evangelical Methodists are going to take seriously Wesley's understanding of love, we will require that seekers become much more like octogenarian widows than self-interested yuppies.

Wesley well perceived the disincentives for such preaching and such requirements. When the most "attractive" young adults in a society become entrenched in the pursuit of success and pleasure, it is tempting to curry their favor. This is why Wesley's depiction of the dangers of wealth is apt for the church in America at this time. It is painful to realize that many of our congregations have been built on the false foundations of success, wealth, and the pursuit of an increasingly shallow happiness. And now, as we see our membership declining, it is so tempting to shed any remaining traces of our holiness heritage. It is tempting to eschew our responsibility to speak the truth in a greedy and shallow land. In particular, it is tempting to throw off Wesley's emphasis on the dangers of wealth and pleasure, to fashion a church that offers Starbucks before the service, a floor-to-ceiling aquarium in the foyer, theater seats in the sanctuary, and an entertaining worship that lasts under an hour. To the extent that we then offer opportunities for more intimate Christian gatherings, we are tempted to tolerate coffee and doughnuts rather than to encourage the hard work of discipleship. And if we allow the needs of our most "prospective" members to dictate our evangelistic outreach, we will be tempted to offer aerobics rather than a bilingual after-school program. As I suggested in the introduction, we thus become "nice" rather than truly, faithfully loving. Rather than lovingly call our brothers and sisters to task for our individual and collective pride and greed, we remain blandly complacent in a sinful, untruthful system.

My assignment for this volume was to write about Wesley, the mission of Methodism, and love. Wesley's description of Christian love is, as we know, uncomplicated and straightforwardly scriptural. Through grace, we come to love God humbly, with our whole being, and we come continually closer to loving our neighbors and even our enemies. Similarly, his prescription for receiving the gift of Christian love is clear and straightforwardly traditional. We are to pray daily, fast weekly, partake of constant communion, read scripture alone and together, form small groups for the purpose of spiritual encouragement and admonition, and practice healthy living.[24] And by partaking of these means of grace, we may grow in our capacity to practice the acts of merciful love. Love is thus the fruit of a humble faith and constant discipline. Both Wesley's description and prescription are clear and relatively undisputed. The question posed to the church is: Will we grow in this Wesleyan grace and love even if we might thereby shrink? Are we willing to preach the truth in love, to wealth, lust, and power, even if it means offending the members we have managed to keep, even if we repel the seekers we are told to pursue? It is my hope and prayer that we will receive from God the courage to do so.

NOTES

1. The Wesleyan Tradition

1. The Wesleyan tradition as a movement of renewal in the church continues to invite thoughtful studies. Some of the more recent works that touch upon this theme include Ted A. Campbell, *John Wesley and Christian Antiquity: Religious Vision and Cultural Change* (Nashville: Kingswood Books, 1991); Richard P. Heitzenrater, *Wesley and the People Called Methodists* (Nashville: Abingdon Press, 1995); Leon O. Hynson, *To Reform the Nation: Theological Foundations of Wesley's Ethics* (Grand Rapids: Francis Asbury Press, 1984); and especially, Howard A. Snyder, *Signs of the Spirit: How God Reshapes the Church* (Grand Rapids: Academie Books, 1989) and his earlier work, *The Radical Wesley and Patterns for Church Renewal* (Downers Grove, Ill.: InterVarsity Press, 1980). On the life of John Wesley, see the recent biographies of Henry D. Rack, *Reasonable Enthusiast: John Wesley and the Rise of Methodism* (Nashville: Abingdon Press, 1993) and Kenneth J. Collins, *A Real Christian: The Life of John Wesley* (Nashville: Abingdon Press, 1999). The most reliable recent theological writing on John Wesley is Randy L. Maddox, *Responsible Grace: John Wesley's Practical Theology* (Nashville: Kingswood Books, 1994). On Charles, the best study available today is S T Kimbrough Jr., ed., *Charles Wesley: Poet and Theologian* (Nashville: Kingswood Books, 1992). John Wesley's writings are being published in a new 35-volume edition, *The Works of John Wesley*, 14 volumes of which have been published to date.

2. "On a Single Eye," *Works* 4:121.

3. W. A. Visser 't Hooft, *The Renewal of the Church* (London: SCM Press, 1956), 67.

4. There are many different approaches to the matter of renewal, revival, or reform within the life of the church. In the study *Signs of the Spirit*, Howard A. Snyder describes seven perspectives or frameworks within which to understand the phenomenon of renewal. They include the *Ecclesiola in Ecclesia* Model, Sect/ Church Typologies, Believers' Church Theories, Revivalism Theories, Revitalization Movements, Modality/Sodality Typology, and Catholic/Anabaptist Typology (pp. 35-61). My approach to these issues is much more modest and focuses on the descriptive as opposed to the analytical dimensions of renewal. My primary question is what does renewal look like? What are its primary characteristics?

5. Roland H. Bainton, *Here I Stand: A Life of Martin Luther* (Nashville: Abingdon Press, 1950), 65.

6. See Edmund Colledge, *Mediaevel Netherlands Religious Literature* (Leydon: E. J. Brill, 1965); cf. Fiona Bowie, ed., *Beguine Spirituality: Mystical Writings of*

Mechthild of Magdeburg, Beatrice of Nazareth, and Hadewijch of Brabant (New York: Crossroad Publishing, 1990), which highlights some of the more noteworthy Beguines of the thirteenth century, whose mystical writings have been rediscovered in our time.

7. Visser 't Hooft, *Renewal of the Church*, 71-72.

8. Dietrich Bonhoeffer, *Letters and Papers from Prison*, enlarged ed., ed. Eberhard Bethge (New York: Macmillan, 1972), 381-82.

9. "Causes of the Inefficacy of Christianity," *Works* 4:93. For a discussion of Wesley's view of scripture, see Scott J. Jones, *John Wesley's Conception and Use of Scripture* (Nashville: Kingswood Books, 1995). For further discussion of the dynamic Wesleyan conception of biblical authority, consult W. Stephen Gunter et al., *Wesley and the Quadrilateral: Renewing the Conversation* (Nashville: Abingdon Press, 1997).

10. *Works* 19:158.

11. Ibid. 7:186.

12. Hester Ann Rogers, *An Account of the Experience of Hester Ann Rogers* (New York: T. Mason and G. Lane, 1837), 129.

13. *Works* 7:323.

14. For a helpful discussion of these distinctions, see Geoffrey Wainwright, *Doxology: A Systematic Theology* (New York: Oxford University Press, 1980), 4, 9-10.

15. From the Homily of the Church of England entitled "Of True Christian Faith," in Albert C. Outler, *John Wesley* (New York: Oxford University Press, 1964), 130.

16. William Bennet, *Memoirs of Mrs. Grace Bennet* (Macclesfield: Printed and sold by E. Bayley, 1803), 83.

17. "The Important Question," *Works* 3:191.

18. See the pioneering work in this area by David Lowes Watson, *Accountable Discipleship: Handbook for Covenant Discipleship Groups in the Congregation* (Nashville: Discipleship Resources, 1984) and *The Early Methodist Class Meeting: Its Origins and Significance* (Nashville: Discipleship Resources, 1985).

19. *Works* (Jackson) 14:321. This issue is so critical to Wesley that he devotes nearly the entirety of a sermon on the point. In the fourth of his thirteen expositions on the Sermon on the Mount he discusses the danger of viewing Christianity simply as an "inward religion of the heart" to the neglect of its "severely ethical" orientation. Religion that is purely inward, he claims, is a subtle device of Satan; cf. *Works* 1:531-49. It is noteworthy that "social holiness" does not connote "social service or action" for Wesley; rather, it means essentially Christian fellowship.

20. *Works* 7:677.

21. Thomas Jackson, ed., *The Journal of Charles Wesley* (London: John Mason, 1849), 1:450.

22. S T Kimbrough Jr., *Lost in Wonder: Charles Wesley, the Meaning of His Hymns Today* (Nashville: Upper Room Books, 1987), 11-12.

23. Sarah Colston, Manuscript Account of Religious Experience (Methodist Archives and Research Centre, Manchester, England), 4; the original language of the manuscript has been modernized here.

24. See Rupert E. Davies's important discussion of these issues in *Works* 9:2-6.

25. *Works* 7:465.

26. S T Kimbrough Jr., ed., *Songs for the Poor* (New York: General Board of Global Ministries, 1997), Hymn 1.

27. The best introduction to this ministry is Michael Slaughter's book, *Spiritual Entrepreneurs: 6 Principles for Risking Renewal*, ed. Herb Miller (Nashville: Abingdon Press, 1995).

2. Scripture in the Church

1. John Wesley, "Preface to *Sermons on Several Occasions*," *Works* (Jackson), 5:3.

2. Scott J. Jones, *John Wesley's Conception and Use of Scripture* (Nashville: Kingswood Books, 1995).

3. Mack B. Stokes, *The Bible in the Wesleyan Heritage* (Nashville: Abingdon Press, 1979), 15.

4. This last point is documented in Jones, *John Wesley's Conception and Use of Scripture*.

5. This is true even outside of United Methodism, where Wesley's theological method—and by extension, that of Methodists—is presumed to be represented in the so-called Wesleyan Quadrilateral; cf. e.g., Donald G. Bloesch, *A Theology of Word and Spirit: Authority and Method in Theology* (Downers Grove: InterVarsity Press, 1992), 208-11 and H. Darrell Lance, "Response to 'The Bible and Human Sexuality,'" *American Baptist Quarterly* 12 (1993): 323-28.

6. See, e.g., W. Stephen Gunter et al., *Wesley and the Quadrilateral: Renewing the Conversation* (Nashville: Abingdon Press, 1997).

7. Robert Wuthnow, *Acts of Compassion: Caring for Others and Helping Ourselves* (Princeton, N.J.: Princeton University Press, 1991), chap. 6.

8. See the helpful essay by Robert N. Bellah, "The Recovery of Biblical Language in American Life," *Radix Magazine* 18, no. 4 (1988): 4-7, 29-31.

9. J. I. Packer, "Infallibility and Inerrancy of the Bible," in *New Dictionary of Theology*, ed. Sinclair B. Ferguson and David F. Wright (Downers Grove, Ill.: InterVarsity Press, 1988), 337-39. For greater nuance, see Robert K. Johnston, *Evangelicals at an Impasse: Biblical Authority in Practice* (Atlanta: John Knox Press, 1979), 15-47.

10. Cf. John Goldingay, *Models for Scripture* (Grand Rapids: William B. Eerdmans, 1994), 194-96.

11. Francis Watson, "The Task of a Confessing Biblical Scholarship," *Catalyst* 23, no. 2 (1997): 1. See further, Joel B. Green, "Scripture and Theology: Uniting the Two So Long Divided," in *Between Two Horizons: Spanning New Testament Studies and Systematic Theology*, ed. Joel B. Green and Max Turner (Grand Rapids: William B. Eerdmans, 2000), 23-43.

12. Robert Morgan with John Barton, *Biblical Interpretation* (New York: Oxford University Press, 1988), chap. 1.

13. Charles Taylor, *Sources of the Self: The Making of the Modern Identity* (Cambridge: Harvard University Press, 1989).

14. Goldingay, *Models for Scriptures*, 121.

15. Trevor Hart, *Faith Thinking: The Dynamics of Christian Theology* (Downers Grove, Ill.: InterVarsity Press, 1996), 143.

16. Ibid., 161-62.

3. Living in the Reign

1. For a more detailed treatment of this section of this essay, see my book *Jesus, Paul, and the End of the World: A Comparative Study in New Testament Eschatology* (Downers Grove, Ill.: InterVarsity Press, 1992), 51-72.

2. The complete list is as follows: 1 Thess. 2:11-12; 2 Thess. 1:5-12; Gal. 5:21; 1 Cor. 4:20-21, 6:9-10, 15:50; Rom. 14:17; and Col. 4:10-11.

3. See my essay "*Praeparatio Evangelii*: The Theological Roots of Wesley's View of Evangelism," in *Theology and Evangelism in the Wesleyan Heritage*, ed. James C. Logan (Nashville: Abingdon Press, 1994), 51-80.

4. *Works* 2:485-99.

5. "The General Spread of the Gospel," *Works* 2:499.

6. See, for example, the very late sermon "The Signs of the Times," *Works* 2:521-33.

7. *Works* 4:215-23.

8. Ibid., 4:219.

9. Ibid., 4:220.

10. *Works*, 1:217-32.

11. Ibid., 1:218.

12. Ibid., 1:218-19.

13. Ibid., 1:224.

14. Ibid., 1:232.

15. *Notes on the New Testament* (New York: T. Mason and G. Lane, 1839), 188.

16. Ibid., 442.

17. This material appears in a somewhat different form in my book *The Realm of the Reign: Reflections on the Dominion of God* (Nashville: Discipleship Resources, 1999), 83-93.

4. Salvation by Grace Through Faith

1. Robert McAfee Brown, *The Spirit of Protestantism* (New York: Oxford University Press, 1961).

2. On the Wesleyan Revival, see Richard P. Heitzenrater, *Wesley and the People Called Methodists* (Nashville: Abingdon Press, 1995), chaps. 3-6. On justification by grace through faith, see Kenneth J. Collins, *The Scripture Way of Salvation: The Heart of John Wesley's Theology* (Nashville: Abingdon Press, 1997), chap. 3. See also two of Wesley's sermons: "The Scripture Way of Salvation," *Works* 2:153-69 and "The Lord Our Righteousness," *Works* 1:444-65.

3. See Eldon R. Fuhrman, "The Concept of Grace in the Theology of John Wesley" (Ph.D. dissertation, State University of Iowa, 1963).

4. "The Scripture Way of Salvation," *Works* 2:153-69.

5. "The Lord Our Righteousness," *Works* 1:444-65.

6. Albert C. Outler, ed., *John Wesley* (New York: Oxford University Press, 1964), 128.

7. *Works* 1:194.

8. Paul W. Chilcote, "Sanctification as Lived by Women in Early Methodism," *Methodist History* 34, no. 2 (January 1996): 92.

9. There are two key words that get into the meaning of "foundation": redemption and sacrifice of atonement (propitiation). The Greek word *hilasmos* can mean (1) redemption: ransom or by payment or liberation in meaning (cf. Matt. 20:28; 1 Cor. 6:20, 7:23; 1 Tim. 2:6,); or (2) propitiation: sacrifice of atonement is in essence the payment of atonement (cf. Heb. 9:5).

10. Initiation of redemption lies in God alone. Grace is the act of God in Jesus Christ. See Romans 1:13, 3:25, and Ephesians 1:9.

11. The calling language (Rom. 4:17; 8:30; 9:12, 24; 1 Cor. 1:9; 7:15, 17; 1 Thess. 2:12; 4:7; 5:24; etc.) recalls the privilege and mission of the elect and stresses the calling act of God (cf. Gal. 1:15) in the gracious act of Christ (cf. Gal. 2:9).

12. The word *ergo* ("works") is a key word in Galatians; see 2:16; 3:2, 5, 10; 5:19; 6:4.

13. The word *nomos* ("Law") is a key word in Galatians; see 2:16, 19, 21; 3:2, 5, 10-13, 17-19, 21, 23, 24; 4:4, 5, 21; 5:3, 4, 14, 18, 23; 6:2, 13.

14. The word *pistis* ("faith") is a key word in Galatians; see 2:16, 20; 3:2, 5, 7-9, 11, 12, 14, 22-26; 5:5, 6, 22; 6:10.

15. *En chariti* ("in the grace") could be translated "by grace" (instrumental dative), but the use of *en* points to the *en Christo* reality of grace.

16. "Being justified" appears three times with the same root word in Greek in Galatians 2:16; the verb "being justified" has the same root word as the noun "righteousness" in Greek. Therefore, despite linguistic clumsiness, for consistency, it would be better to translate the verb as "being made righteous," "being rightwise." See C. H. Cosgrove, "Justification in Paul: A Linguistic and Theological Reflection," *Journal of Biblical Literature* 106 (1987): 653-70.

17. T. D. Gordon, "The Problem at Galatia," *Interpretation* 41 (1987): 42-43.

18. Cosgrove, "Justification in Paul," 661-62.

19. Consult the usage of this word *dikaioun* in Galatians 2:16, 17; 3:8, 11, 24; 5:4 and in Romans 2:13; 3:4, 20, 24, 26, 28, 30; 4:2, 5; 5:1, 9; 6:7; 8:30, 33.

20. James Dunn is right in asserting that, "in this verse (2:16) faith in Jesus Messiah begins to emerge not simply as a narrower definition of the elect of God, but as an alternative definition of the elect of God. . . . Faith in Jesus as Christ becomes the primary identity marker which renders the others (law and circumcision) superfluous." (J. D. G. Dunn, "Paul and 'Covenantal Nomism'," *The Parting of the Ways Between Christianity and Judaism and Their Significance for the Character of Christianity* [London/Philadelphia: SCM/Trinity Press International, 1991], 112).

21. The proper connotation of this phrase is not that "Paul lived by faith in the Son of God"; rather, he is talking about how "he lived by the faithfulness of God's Son." "By" is understood in the sense of "through," or participation in the faith or faithfulness of God's Son.

22. See Romans 1:4; 5:10; 8:3, 29, 32; 1 Corinthians 1:9; 15:28; Galatians 1:16; 2:20; 4:4; and 1 Thessalonians 1:10.

23. *En nomou* can mean "in the Law" or "by/through the Law." The locative sense, rather than the instrumental sense, is probably meant here because Paul has been contrasting realm or sphere in which the Galatian Christians are living. Verse 6 has "in Christ Jesus," which speaks of the realm in Christ, in contrast to "in the Law."

24. The word *katargein* ("to cut off") is used by Paul twenty-five out of the twenty-seven times it is used in the New Testament. It is used in Galatians 3:17; 5:4, 11. The verb *katargein* is aorist tense, indicating an action that is decisive.

5. The Way of Salvation

1. "A Farther Appeal to Men of Reason and Religion, Part II," III:1, "How much more sensible must you be of this if you do not rest on the surface, but inquire into the bottom of religion, the religion of the heart?" *Works* 1:250.

2. *Works* 18:220, n. 25.

3. I have explored these movements and their complex relationships to each other in my study *The Religion of the Heart: A Study of European Religious Life in the Seventeenth and Eighteenth Centuries* (Columbia: University of South Carolina Press, 1991).

4. "The Great Privilege of Those that are Born of God," III:4, *Works* 1:442-43.

5. Charles Wesley, *Select Hymns, with Tunes Annext* (1761), Hymn No. 55; with slight variations from *The United Methodist Hymnal* (Nashville: The United Methodist Publishing House, 1989), Hymn No. 410.

6. Works of Piety as Spiritual Formation

1. "The Means of Grace," *Works* 1:380.

2. For those readers for whom the term "means of grace" is new, let me simply refer you to the more common phrase in use today: "the spiritual disciplines." While the contemporary list of disciplines sometimes differs from those Wesley included in the means of grace, the idea is the same. The means of grace are those disciplines that we practice in order to appropriate God's grace and thus to become more conformable to the image of Christ.

3. *Works* 1:377.

4. Ibid., 1:381.

5. In the sermon "The Means of Grace," Wesley deals with only three of the instituted means (prayer, searching the scriptures, and the Lord's Supper), but in a later list, he added fasting and Christian conference. See *Works* (Jackson) 8:322-23.

6. Henry H. Knight III, *The Presence of God in the Christian Life: John Wesley and the Means of Grace* (Metuchen, N.J.: Scarecrow Press, 1992). Dr. Knight explores the context of Wesley's use of the means of grace in detail, which will carry you beyond the brief survey that I offer in this chapter.

7. This is Knight's central thesis, and it is one with which I agree. A theology of God's historicity and Jesus' incarnation places the notion of "presence" at the center of faith. Without the ontological reality of God's presence and our response to it, the Christian life is robbed of its intended meaning.

8. *Letters* (Telford) 4:90.

9. In his diary, Wesley used symbols to evaluate the temper of his prayers, ranging from "warm and effectual" to "cold and indifferent."

10. Wesley's three words actually incorporate the more traditional terminology of *lectio divina*: *oratio, lectio, meditatio,* and *contemplatio.* For more on Wesley's use of the scripture in spiritual formation, see M. Robert Mulholland Jr., *Shaped by the Word: The Power of Scripture in Spiritual Formation* (Nashville: Upper Room Books, 1985).

11. *Works* 1:106.

12. John Wesley, *Explanatory Notes Upon the Old Testament* (Bristol: William Pine, 1765; Salem, Ohio: Schmul, 1975) 1:viii.

13. In a chapter like this one, it is impossible to sound the depths of Wesleyan hermeneutics. But we must note that Wesley was never a "Bible only" Christian. He integrated tradition, reason, and experience into the process of searching the scriptures. Thomas C. Oden has provided a detailed and documented look at Wesley's theological method in his book, *John Wesley's Scriptural Christianity: A Plain Exposition of His Teaching on Christian Doctrine* (Grand Rapids: Zondervan, 1994), 55-99.

14. *Works* (Jackson) 7:148.

15. Knight, *Presence of God*, 130-48.

16. Colin W. Williams, *John Wesley's Theology Today* (New York: Abingdon Press, 1960), 134.

17. *Works* (Jackson) 3:144.

18. "The Means of Grace," *Works* 1:396.

19. Again, it is not possible to chronicle all the evidence for the resurgence of interest in the spiritual life. We can note, for example, the work of Richard Foster in the Renovare ministry and the writings of such persons as Henri Nouwen. We also observe the renewal of interest in historic liturgies such as the Daily Office through communities like Taizé and Iona.

20. Gregory S. Clapper, *As If the Heart Mattered: A Wesleyan Spirituality* (Nashville: Upper Room Books, 1997), 17-24.

21. I remind you again that *Shaped by the Word*, by M. Robert Mulholland Jr., is an excellent resource for going further in both knowledge and appreciation for the role of biblical Christianity in our formation.

22. Here again it is impossible to point to all the ways the "classical" element is being renewed today. I would remind you of the Paulist Press series, *The Classics of Western Spirituality* and alert you to be on the lookout for a growing number of publishers that are both reprinting and bringing out new translations of the devotional classics. For example, at the time of this writing, Upper Room Books is in the process of producing a series entitled *Upper Room Spiritual Classics*, which excerpt materials from a variety of authors and traditions.

23. "Sermon on the Mount, I," *Works* 1:481.

7. Works of Mercy as Spiritual Formation

1. For studies of Wesley's ethic, see Manfred Marquardt, *John Wesley's Social Ethics: Praxis and Principles,* trans. John E. Steely and W. Stephen Gunter

(Nashville, Abingdon Press, 1992); Ronald Stone, *John Wesley's Life and Ethics* (Nashville: Abingdon Press, 2001); Leon O. Hynson, *To Reform the Nation: Theological Foundations of Wesley's Ethics* (Grand Rapids: Francis Asbury Press, 1984); and Theodore Weber, *Politics and the Order of Salvation: Transforming Wesleyan Political Ethics* (Nashville: Kingswood Books, 2001).

2. Wesley's (and Wesleyan) views on economic matters such as wealth, poverty, and work are the subject of many studies. In addition to discussions of economic ethics in the books listed above, see also Theodore W. Jennings, *Good News to the Poor: John Wesley's Evangelical Economics* (Nashville: Abingdon Press, 1990); John McEllhenney, "Two Critiques of Wealth: John Wesley and Samuel Johnson Assess the Machinations of Mammon," *Methodist History* 32 (April 1994): 147-59; John Tyson, "Why Did John Wesley 'Fail': A Reappraisal of Wesley's Evangelical Economics," *Methodist History* 35 (April 1997): 176-87; M. Donald Meeks, ed. *The Portion of the Poor: Good News to the Poor in the Wesleyan Tradition* (Nashville: Kingswood Books, 1995); Richard P. Heitzenrater, ed., *The Poor and the People Called Methodists* (Nashville: Kingswood Books, forthcoming). It is interesting to note that while much of the most recent work on Wesley and economics centers on his relationship to the poor, the great majority of his writings on money are about the rich. Wesley is desperate because he fears that money will harden the hearts of the rich and weaken their love.

3. "On Visiting the Sick," §1, *Works* 3:385.

4. For Wesley's writings on works of mercy, see, for example, "On Visiting the Sick," *Works* 3:384-97 and "On Zeal," *Works* 3:308-21.

5. *Works* 1:573, I.1.

6. Ibid.

7. Details of early Methodist social activities are widely available. See, for example, Marquardt, *John Wesley's Social Ethics*, 19-34, and Richard P. Heitzenrater, *Wesley and the People Called Methodists* (Nashville: Abingdon Press, 1995).

8. *Works* 3:313, II.5.

9. Ibid., 3:385-86, §2.

10. Ibid., 3:385 §1.

11. Wesley's views on money and wealth run throughout his writings. See, for example, "The Use of Money," *Works* 2:263-80; "The Danger of Riches," *Works* 3:227-46; "The Danger of Increasing Riches," *Works* 4:177-86; and "The Good Steward," *Works* 2:281-98.

12. Wesley's best-known advice on money (Make all you can. Save all you can. Give all you can.) is found in his famous sermon "The Use of Money," *Works* 2:263-80, as well as in "The Danger of Riches," II.5-9, *Works* 3:237-40, and "Causes of the Inefficacy of Christianity," 8, *Works* 4:90-91.

13. *Works* 4:91, §8.

14. Ibid., 3:240, II.9.

15. Ibid., 3:258, §22.

16. Ibid., 4:181-82, I.8.

17. Ibid., 4:91, §9.

18. Ibid., 4:185-86, I.16.

19. Monday, November 26, 1753, *Works* 20:482.

20. "An Earnest Appeal to Men of Reason and Religion," §96, *Works* 11:87-88.

21. *Works* 2:268, §2.

22. Ibid., 4:11, II.1.

23. Ibid., 2:281-98.

24. Ibid., 2:286, I.7.

25. Ibid., 3:528, II.11-12.

26. See, for example, his sermon "On Dress," §14, *Works* 3:254.

27. *Works* 3:254, §15.

28. Ibid., 3:234, I.11.

29. Ibid., 3:236, I.18.

30. "On Dress," §27, *Works* 3:260.

31. "On Visiting the Sick," §1, *Works* 3:385.

32. *Works*, III.6.

33. See the conclusion of Wesley's sermon "On Riches," §12, *Works* 3:528.

34. *Works* 3:242, II.13.

35. Ibid., 3:236, I.19.

36. "Dives and Lazarus," *Works* 4:11, II.1.

37. *Works* 4:185, II.15.

38. For more on American patterns of spending and debt, see Juliet Schor's *Overspent American: Why We Want What We Don't Need* (New York: HarperPerennial, 1999). For a religious perspective on these issues, see Robert Wuthnow, *God and Mammon in America* (New York: Free Press, 1994).

39. *Works*, 3:240, II.9.

8. Making Disciples in Community

1. For a detailed understanding of what Wesley meant by the "religious affections" and "heart religion," see my *John Wesley on Religious Affections: His Views on Experience and Emotion and Their Role in the Christian Life and Theology* (Metuchen, N.J.: Scarecrow Press, 1989). For a recent discussion of the subtle interplay between the supposedly "inner," and the more communal "outer," dimensions of spirituality, see Owen C. Thomas's "Interiority and Christian Spirituality," *Journal of Religion* 80, no. 1 (January 2000): 41-60. I will briefly address Wesley's views of "assurance" below.

2. For the history of the small covenant groups as Wesley started them, see David Lowes Watson, *The Early Methodist Class Meeting: Its Origins and Significance* (Nashville: Discipleship Resources, 1985). For a look at a contemporary attempt to revive these practices, see Watson's book *Covenant Discipleship: Christian Formation Through Mutual Accountability* (Nashville: Discipleship Resources, 1991).

3. See the section entitled "Repentance as 'Self-Knowledge'" in my book *As If the Heart Mattered: A Wesleyan Spirituality* (Nashville: Upper Room Books, 1997), 30-32.

4. For an overview of this issue of canon, see the article by Daniel J. Harrington, S.J. "Introduction to the Canon," in *The New Interpreter's Bible*

(Nashville: Abingdon Press, 1994), 1:7-21. We can certainly acknowledge the human role in the process of canon formation at the same time as we say that the final form did take shape under the inspiration of the Holy Spirit. This is parallel to biblical scholars acknowledging the different emphases of, for instance, the four Gospels, as at least partly being a reflection of the different human writers, while the Spirit-inspired truths about God and Christ shine in, with, and under the particular different emphases.

5. See, for example, Justo L. González's discussion of the Arian controversy in *The Story of Christianity* (San Francisco: Harper & Row, 1984), where he says "From its very beginning, the church had worshiped Jesus Christ, and Arius' proposal would now force it either to cease such worship, or to declare that it was worshiping a creature. Both alternatives being unacceptable, Arius was proven wrong" (1:161).

6. See Geoffrey Wainwright's *Doxology: A Systematic Theology* (New York: Oxford University Press, 1980), especially chaps. 7 and 8 ("Lex Orandi" and "Lex Credendi") and Don E. Saliers, *Worship as Theology: Foretaste of Glory Divine* (Nashville: Abingdon Press, 1994).

7. See his later works, especially *Philosophical Investigations: The English Text of the Third Edition*, trans. G. E. M. Anscombe (New York: Prentice Hall, 1999).

8. See George A. Lindbeck, *The Nature of Doctrine: Religion and Theology in a Postliberal Age* (Philadelphia: Westminster Press, 1984) and Wayne Proudfoot, *Religious Experience* (Berkeley: University of California Press, 1985) for further reflections on this distinction.

9. *Works* 1:295, IV.8.

10. Preface to his *Hymns and Sacred Poems*, published in 1739.

11. I have chosen *The Music Man*, even though it is almost 50 years old, to illustrate the role of community in formation for two reasons. First, it is regarded as one of the most popular and engaging musicals of all time, often staged in high schools and community theaters, and it is currently being brought back in a revival on Broadway. (I have been surprised at the number of college students who are familiar with it because of their own high school productions.) Second, the film version is available on video should anyone want to study on his or her own how this play illustrates these dynamics.

9. "Submitting to Be More Vile"

1. *Works* 9:529.

2. *Letters* (Telford) 6:61.

3. *Works* (Jackson) 8:299-300.

4. Olin Curtis, *The Christian Faith* (New York: Eaton & Mains, 1905), 372.

5. Albert C. Outler, "Whither Wesleyan Theology," a lecture delivered at Asbury Theological Seminary, Wilmore, Ky., March 14, 1974.

6. *Works* 19:46.

7. A. Skevington Wood, *The Burning Heart* (Grand Rapids: William B. Eerdmans, 1967), 95.

8. *Works* (Jackson) 11:366.

9. *Works* 18:244.

10. *Works* (Jackson) 8:299-300.

11. See Martin Schmidt, *John Wesley: A Theological Biography*, trans. Norman P. Goldhawk (Nashville: Abingdon Press, 1962), 1:102.

12. V. H. H. Green, *The Young Mr. Wesley: A Study of John Wesley and Oxford* (New York: St. Martin's Press, 1961), 198-99.

13. The full text of this letter can be found in Richard P. Heitzenrater, *The Elusive Mr. Wesley* (Nashville: Abingdon Press, 1984), 2:29-31.

14. Heitzenrater, *The Elusive Mr. Wesley*, 2:31.

15. Green, *The Young Mr. Wesley*, 199.

16. *Works* 18:146.

17. Ibid., 18:254.

18. Herbert McGonigle, *John Wesley and the Moravians* (Derbys, England: Moorley's Bookshop, 1993), 13.

19. Heitzenrater, *The Elusive Mr. Wesley*, 2:94.

20. Ibid., 2:95.

21. *Letters* (Telford) 2:186.

22. Henry D. Rack, *Reasonable Enthusiast: John Wesley and the Rise of Methodism* (Nashville: Abingdon Press, 1993), 275.

23. Cf. Theodore W. Jennings Jr., *Good News to the Poor: John Wesley's Evangelical Economics* (Nashville: Abingdon Press, 1990).

10. Word and Table

1. See Karen B. Westerfield Tucker, "Form and Freedom: John Wesley's Legacy for Methodist Worship," in *The Sunday Service of the Methodists: Twentieth-Century Worship in Worldwide Methodism*, ed. Karen B. Westerfield Tucker (Nashville: Kingswood Books, 1996), 17-30.

2. *Works* 1:378, 381. From Wesley's sermon "The Means of Grace." See Henry H. Knight III, *The Presence of God in the Christian Life: John Wesley and the Means of Grace* (Metuchen, N.J.: Scarecrow Press, 1992) for a fuller discussion of this central theme.

3. See *Works* 3:427-39. Here is the fullest possible expression of John and Charles Wesley's eucharistic spirituality.

4. See J. Ernest Rattenbury, *The Eucharistic Hymns of John and Charles Wesley*, 2nd American ed. (Cleveland: Order of St. Luke Publications, 1990), 146-54. Here is the fullest possible expression of Charles Wesley's eucharistic spirituality—a theology in hymns.

5. For passages about their experience, see John C. Bowmer, *The Sacrament of the Lord's Supper in Early Methodism* (Westminster: Dacre Press, 1951), 189ff.

6. Rattenbury, *Eucharistic Hymns*, 151.

7. *Works* 21:438.

8. Charles Wesley, *The Journal of the Rev. Charles Wesley, M.A.*, ed. Thomas Jackson (Grand Rapids: Baker Book House, 1980) 1:450.

9. *Minutes of the Methodist Conferences, From the First, Held in London, by The Late Rev. John Wesley, A.M., In the Year 1744* (London: John Mason, 1862) 1:69.

10. See Knight, *The Presence of God*, 127ff.

11. James F. White, introduction to *John Wesley's Prayer Book: The Sunday Service of the Methodists in North America*, by John Wesley (Akron, Ohio: OSL Publications, 1991).

12. Wesley, *Prayer Book*, 32 (p. ii). For a fuller discussion of this instruction in context, see Lester Ruth, "A Reconsideration of the Frequency of the Eucharist in Early American Methodism," *Methodist History* 34, no. 1 (October 1995): 51-54.

13. Wesley, "The Duty of Constant Communion," *Works* 3:430.

14. Charles's argument is found in Bowmer, *The Sacrament of the Lord's Supper in Early Methodism*, 227.

15. Ibid., 231-32.

16. *Works* 21:473.

17. "John Bennet's Copy of the Minutes of the Conferences of 1744, 1745, 1747, and 1748; with Wesley's Copy of Those for 1746," *Proceedings of the Wesley Historical Society* (1896) 52-53, entry for Thursday, 2/3 June 1748.

18. See David H. Tripp, *The Renewal of the Covenant in the Methodist Tradition* (London: Epworth Press, 1969), 16-35.

19. Frank Baker, *Methodism and the Love-Feast* (New York: Macmillan Press, 1957), 36.

20. See *Works* 21:181. Recent concern about open communion and the sacrament as a "converting ordinance" should not obscure that the Wesleys did not grant wide-open access to the sacrament.

21. Hymn 507, "The Love-feast Part III," §1, *Works* 7:698.

22. Rattenbury, *Eucharistic Hymns*, 158-59.

11. A Faith That Sings

1. See the work of S T Kimbrough Jr., founder of the Charles Wesley Society, who has devoted considerable energy to the rediscovery of the younger brother; in particular, his edited volume, *Charles Wesley: Poet and Theologian* (Nashville: Kingswood Books, 1992) and *A Heart to Praise My God: Wesley Hymns for Today* (Nashville: Abingdon Press, 1996); cf. Teresa Berger, *Theology in Hymns? A Study of the Relationship of Doxology and Theology*, trans. Timothy E. Kimbrough (Nashville: Kingswood Books, 1995); and John R. Tyson, ed., *Charles Wesley: A Reader* (New York: Oxford University Press, 1989).

2. See *Works* 3:542-63.

3. Ibid., 7:383.

4. Ibid., 7:278-79.

5. Ibid., 7:305-6.

6. Ibid., 7:116.

7. Ibid., 7:698-99.

8. Ibid., 7:545, 547.

9. Ibid., 7:490-91.

10. Ibid., 7:251.

11. J. Ernest Rattenbury, *The Evangelical Doctrines of Charles Wesley's Hymns* (London: Epworth Press, 1941), 98-99.

12. See Bernard Ruffin, *Fanny Crosby* (Philadelphia: United Church Press, 1976).

13. See Ralph H. Jones, *Charles Albert Tindley: Prince of Preachers* (Nashville: Abingdon Press, 1982).

14. *Works* 19:67.

15. See the two-volume collection of his works, Fred Pratt Green, *The Hymns and Ballads of Fred Pratt Green* (Carol Stream, Ill.: Hope Publishing, 1982) and *Later Hymns and Ballads and Fifty Poems* (Carol Stream, Ill.: Hope Publishing and London: Stainer & Bell Ltd., 1989).

16. Fred Pratt Green, "Poet and Hymn Writer," *Worship* 49, no. 4 (April 1975): 192-93.

17. Green, *The Hymns and Ballads*, 17.

18. Ibid., 52.

19. S T Kimbrough, gen. ed., *Global Praise 1* (New York: GBGMusik, 1996), Hymn 65.

20. Simei Monteiro, "Evangelization and Music in a Latin American Context from a Wesleyan Perspective, " in *Evangelization, The Heart of Mission: A Wesleyan Perspective*, ed. S T Kimbrough Jr. (New York: GBGMusik, 1995), 134.

21. English translation from the original Portuguese has been provided by J. Parke Renshaw.

22. *Sound the Bamboo: CCA Hymnal 1990* (Quezon City, Philippines: The Christian Conference of Asia and The Asian Institute for Liturgy and Music, 1990), Hymn 139.

23. *Banquet of Praise* (New York: Bread for the World, 1990), Hymn 205. Reprinted with permission from Bread for the World.

24. *Sound the Bamboo*, Hymn 163.

25. Paul W. Chilcote with Katheru Gichara and Patrick Matsikenyiri, "A Singing and Dancing Church: Methodist Worship in Kenya and Zimbabwe," in *The Sunday Service of the Methodists: Twentieth-Century Worship in Worldwide Methodism*, ed. Karen B. Westerfield Tucker (Nashville: Kingswood Books, 1996), 243.

26. *Works* 7:552.

12. Offer Them Christ

1. James C. Logan, "The Evangelical Imperative: A Wesleyan Perspective," in *Theology and Evangelism in the Wesleyan Heritage*, ed. James C. Logan (Nashville: Kingswood Books, 1994), 16.

2. *The Book of Discipline of The United Methodist Church* (Nashville: The United Methodist Publishing House, 1996), 114.

3. James Logan, "Offering Christ: Wesleyan Evangelism Today," in *Rethinking Wesley's Theology for Contemporary Methodism*, ed. Randy L. Maddox (Nashville: Kingswood Books, 1998), 118. According to Logan, "Wesley never employed the term 'evangelism' itself. This noun was simply not in currency in his day, though he did speak of his itinerant lay preachers as 'evangelists,' denoting their sole responsibility to preach."

4. See William Abraham, *The Logic of Evangelism* (Grand Rapids: William B. Eerdmans, 1989).

5. See Walter Klaiber, *Call and Response: Biblical Foundations of a Theology of Evangelism* (Nashville: Abingdon Press, 1997).

6. Scott J. Jones, "The Rule of Scripture," in *Wesley and the Quadrilateral: Renewing the Conversation*, ed. W. Stephen Gunter et al. (Nashville: Abingdon Press, 1997), 47.

7. Abraham, *Logic of Evangelism*, 9.

8. *The Book of Discipline of the United Methodist Church*, 69-72.

9. Albert C. Outler, *Evangelism in the Wesleyan Spirit* (Nashville: Tidings, 1971), 33. According to Outler, "It is the Wesleyan *spirit* that we must pray and hope for once again: that strange miracle that turned a censorious zealot into a herald of grace, that fusion of mind and heart and muscle in joyful service, that moved from passion to *com*passion, that linkage of revival *and* reform, that stress on *local initiative* within a connexional system—that actual willingness to live in and to be led by the Spirit of God in faith and hope and love."

10. See Earl Kent Brown, *Women of Mr. Wesley's Methodism* (New York: Edwin Mellen Press, 1983) and Paul W. Chilcote, *John Wesley and the Women Preachers of Early Methodism* (Metuchen, N.J.: Scarecrow Press, 1991).

11. Theodore Runyon, *The New Creation: John Wesley's Theology Today* (Nashville: Abingdon Press, 1998), chap. 6.

12. David Bebbington, *Evangelicalism in Modern Britain: A History from the 1730s to the 1980s* (London: Routledge, 1989), 21.

13. Richard P. Heitzenrater, *Wesley and the People Called Methodists* (Nashville: Abingdon Press, 1995), 115. See his discussion of the Thomas Maxfield incident that occurred in 1739 and of Susanna Wesley's role in shaping John's later attitude.

14. See Chilcote, *John Wesley and the Women Preachers of Early Methodism*. Mary Bosanquet Fletcher is also well known for her comprehensive defense of women's preaching addressed to John Wesley, which argued for the legitimacy of the "extraordinary call."

15. Albert C. Outler, *John Wesley's Sermons: An Introduction* (Nashville: Abingdon Press, 1991), chap. 5.

16. Outler, *John Wesley's Sermons*, 78; cf. Mortimer Arias and Alan Johnson, *The Great Commission: Biblical Models for Evangelism* (Nashville: Abingdon Press, 1992), chap. 2 in particular.

17. Heitzenrater, *Wesley and the People Called Methodists*, 220ff.

18. See Laceye C. Warner, *Methodist Episcopal and Wesleyan Methodist Deaconesses in the Late Nineteenth and Early Twentieth Centuries: A Paradigm for Evangelism* (unpublished dissertation, Trinity College, University of Bristol, 2000), chap. 7.

19. Logan, "Offering Christ," 116. Logan discusses the implications of nineteenth-century revivalism and camp meetings within the context of the Second Great Awakening upon the increasingly truncated evangelistic understanding within the Wesleyan tradition.

20. The fundamentalist/modernist split, however, does not seem to have influenced Methodist women's organizations or historically African Methodists as extensively. See Jean Miller Schmidt, *Souls or the Social Order: The Two-party System in American Protestantism* (Brooklyn: Carlson Publishing, 1991).

21. Heitzenrater, *Wesley and the People Called Methodists*, 21. The Society for Promoting Christian Knowledge has its roots in the religious societies founded by Anthony Horneck in the 1670s, the English counterparts to the *collegia pietatis* organized by Jacob Spener.

22. Logan, "Offering Christ," 124. See also David Lowes Watson, *Covenant Discipleship: Christian Formation Through Mutual Accountability* (Nashville: Discipleship Resources, 1989) and *Class Leaders: Recovering a Tradition* (Nashville: Discipleship Resources, 1991).

23. Heitzenrater, *Wesley and the People Called Methodists*, 106.

24. Ibid., 170. The New Room was later registered under the Act of Toleration in 1748.

25. *Works* 7:465.

13. *"The Law of Love"*

1. "The Law Established by Faith," in *John Wesley*, ed. Albert C. Outler (New York: Oxford University Press, 1964), 228-29. Wesley continues: "It follows, that although faith is of no value in itself (as neither is any other means whatsoever), yet as it leads to that end—the establishing anew the law of love in our hearts . . . it is on that account an unspeakable blessing to man and of unspeakable value before God."

2. "On Love," *Works* 4:380.

3. "Advice to the People called Methodists," *Works* 9:128.

4. Ibid., 9:127-28.

5. I find that many members of my generation—"Generation X"—resonate with this dire assessment of our church. We know painfully well that the young adults whom growing churches yearn for are, by and large, a shallow, greedy lot. Our desires have been so thoroughly shaped by *Seventeen*, *MTV*, football, and shopping malls that our lives beg for real transformation.

6. "The Circumcision of the Heart," *Works* 1:401-2.

7. William Abraham, *The Logic of Evangelism* (Grand Rapids: William B. Eerdmans, 1989), 54-55.

8. See, for example, Marva Dawn, *A Royal Waste of Time* (Grand Rapids: William B. Eerdmans, 1999).

9. "The Circumcision of the Heart," *Works* 1:413.

10. "On Charity," *Works* 3:305.

11. Ibid., *Works* 3:301, III.1.

12. *Works* 1:408-9.

13. "The Circumcision of the Heart," *Works* 1:408, §I.13.

14. *Works* 3:520, §3.

15. "On Riches," *Works* 3:524-25, §II.2.

16. Ibid., *Works* 3:522, §I.3.

17. *Works* 3:254, §14.

18. Ibid.

19. Ibid.

20. Ibid., *Works* 3:260, §27.

21. "On Riches," *Works* 3:522, §I.3.

22. Ibid., *Works* 3:528, §II.11.

23. "Advice to the People called Methodists," *Works* 9:125.

24. See Wesley's sermon "The Means of Grace," *Works* 1:376-97.

SELECT BIBLIOGRAPHY

JOHN WESLEY SCHOLARS PUBLICATIONS

Albin, Thomas R. *Teach Me to Pray*. Nashville: United Methodist Publishing House, 1985.

Albin, Thomas R., and Oliver A. Beckerlegge, eds. *Charles Wesley's Earliest Evangelical Sermons: Six Manuscript Shorthand Sermons Hitherto Unpublished*. London: Wesley Historical Society, 1987.

Bell, Daniel M. *Liberation Theology After the End of History: The Refusal to Cease Suffering*. New York: Routledge, 2001.

Campbell, Ted A. *Christian Confessions: A Historical Introduction*. Louisville: Westminster John Knox Press, 1996.

———. *John Wesley and Christian Antiquity: Religious Vision and Cultural Change*. Nashville: Kingswood Books, 1991.

———. *Methodist Doctrine: The Essentials*. Nashville: Abingdon Press, 1999.

———. *The Religion of the Heart: A Study of European Religious Life in the Seventeenth and Eighteenth Centuries*. Columbia: University of South Carolina Press, 1991.

Cartwright, Michael G. *The Gospel in Black and White: Theological Resources for Racial Reconciliation*. Downers Grove, Ill.: InterVarsity Press, 1997.

———, ed. *The Royal Priesthood: Essays Ecclesiological and Ecumenical by John Yoder*. Grand Rapids: William B. Eerdmans, 1994.

Cartwright, Michael, and John Berkman, eds. *The Hauerwas Reader*. Durham, N. C.: Duke University Press, 2001.

Chilcote, Paul W. *An African Journal of Hope*. New York: General Board of Global Ministries, 1998.

———. *Her Own Story: Autobiographical Portraits of Early Methodist Women*. Nashville: Kingswood Books, 2001.

———. *John Wesley and the Women Preachers of Early Methodism*. Metuchen, N.J.: Scarecrow Press, 1991.

———. *Praying in the Wesleyan Spirit: 52 Prayers for Today*. Nashville: Upper Room Books, 2001.

———. *She Offered Them Christ: The Legacy of Women Preachers in Early Methodism*. Nashville: Abingdon Press, 1993.

———. *Wesley Speaks on Christian Vocation*. Nashville: Discipleship Resources, 1986.

Christensen, Michael J. *Children of Chernobyl: Raising Hope from the Ashes*. Minneapolis: Augsburg Press, 1993.

———. *City Streets, City People: A Call for Compassion*. Nashville: Abingdon Press, 1988.

————. *C. S. Lewis on Scripture: His Thoughts on the Nature of Biblical Inspiration, the Role of Revelation, and the Question of Inerrancy*. Nashville: Abingdon Press, 1989.

————. *The Samaritan's Imperative: A Compassionate Ministry to People Living with AIDS*. Nashville: Abingdon Press, 1991.

————. *The World After Chernobyl*. New York: Crossroad Press, 1997.

————, ed. *Equipping the Saints: Mobilizing Laity for Ministry*. Nashville: Abingdon Press, 2000.

Clapper, Gregory S. *As If the Heart Mattered: A Wesleyan Spirituality*. Nashville: Upper Room Books, 1997.

————. *John Wesley on Religious Affections: His Views on Experience and Emotion and Their Role in the Christian Life and Theology*. Metuchen, N.J.: Scarecrow Press, 1989.

————. *When the World Breaks Your Heart: Spiritual Ways to Live with Tragedy*. Nashville: Upper Room Books, 1999.

Colyer, Elmer M., *How to Read T. F. Torrance: Understanding His Trinitarian and Scientific Theology*. Downers Grove, Ill.: InterVarsity Press, 2001.

————, ed. *Evangelical Theology in Transition: Theologians in Dialogue with Donald Bloesch*. Downers Grove, Ill.: InterVarsity Press, 1999.

————, ed. *The Promise of Trinitarian Theology: Theologians in Dialogue with T. F. Torrance*. Lanham, Md.: Rowman & Littlefield Publishers, 2001.

Dean, Kenda Creasy, and Ron Foster. *The Godbearing Life: The Art of Soul Tending for Youth Ministry*. Nashville: Upper Room Books, 1998.

Dodd, Brian J. *Paul's Pardigmatic "I": Personal Example as Literary Strategy*. Sheffield: Sheffield Academic Press, 1999.

————. *The Problem with Paul*. Downers Grove, Ill.: InterVarsity Press, 1996.

————. *Praying Jesus' Way: A Guide for Beginners and Veterans*. Downers Grove, Ill.: InterVarsity Press, 1997.

Dodd, Brian J., and Ralph P. Martin, eds. *Where Christology Began: Essays on Philippians 2*. Louisville: Westminster/John Knox Press, 1998.

Green, Joel B. *Beginning with Jesus: Christ in Scripture, the Church, and Discipleship*. Nashville: The United Methodist Publishing House, 2000.

————. *The Death of Jesus: Tradition and Interpretation in the Passion Narrative*. Wissenschaftliche Untersuchungen zum Neuen Testament II, 33. Tübingen: J.C.B. Mohr, 1988.

————. *The Gospel of Luke*. New International Commentary on the New Testament. Grand Rapids: William B. Eerdmans, 1997.

————. *How to Read the Gospels and Acts*. Downers Grove, Ill.: InterVarsity Press, 1987.

————. *How to Read Prophecy*. Downers Grove, Ill.: InterVarsity Press, 1984.

————. *The Kingdom of God: Its Meaning and Mandate*. Wilmore, Ky.: Bristol Books, 1989.

————. *The Theology of the Gospel of Luke*. New Testament Theology 3. Cambridge: Cambridge University Press, 1995.

————. *The Way of the Cross: Following Jesus in the Gospel of Mark*. Nashville: Discipleship Resources, 1991.

————, ed. *Hearing the New Testament: Strategies for Interpretation*. Grand Rapids: William B. Eerdmans, 1995.

Green, Joel B., and Mark D. Baker. *Recovering the Scandal of the Cross: Atonement in New Testament and Contemporary Contexts.* Downers Grove, Ill.: InterVarsity Press, 2000.

Green, Joel B., and John T. Carroll. *The Death of Jesus in Early Christianity.* Peabody, Mass.: Hendrickson Publishers, 1995.

Green, Joel B., and Michael C. McKeever. *Luke-Acts and New Testament Historiography.* Grand Rapids: Baker Books, 1994.

Green, Joel B., and Scot McKnight, gen. eds. *Dictionary of Jesus and the Gospels.* Downers Grove, Ill.: InterVarsity Press, 1992.

Green, Joel B., and Max Turner, eds. *Between Two Horizons: Spanning New Testament Studies and Systematic Theology.* Grand Rapids: William B. Eerdmans, 2000.

Green, Joel B., and Max Turner, eds. *Jesus of Nazareth: Lord and Christ. Essays on the Historical Jesus and New Testament Christology.* Grand Rapids: William B. Eerdmans, 1994.

Green, Joel B., and Max Turner, eds. *The Two Horizons Commentary on the New Testament Series.* 20 vols. Grand Rapids: William B. Eerdmans, launched in 1995.

Green, Joel B., Paul J. Achtemeier, and Marianne Meye Thompson. *The New Testament: Its Literature and Theology.* Grand Rapids: William B. Eerdmans, 2001.

Harper, Steve. *Devotional Life in the Wesleyan Tradition. A Workbook.* Nashville: Upper Room Books, 1983.

———. *Embrace the Spirit.* Wheaton, Ill.: Victor Books, 1987.

———. *A Fresh Start: A Devotional Study of the Gospel of John.* Elgin, Ill.: D. C. Cook Publishing, 1979.

———. *God's Call to Excellence.* Wilmore, Ky.: Bristol Books, 1989.

———. *John Wesley's Message for Today.* Grand Rapids: Zondervan, 1983.

———. *Prayer and Devotional Life of United Methodists.* Nashville: Abingdon Press, 1999.

———. *Prayer Ministry in the Local Church.* Grand Rapids: Baker Books, 1976.

———. *Praying Through the Lord's Prayer.* Nashville: Upper Room Books, 1992.

———. *Reflecting God.* Kansas City, Mo.: Beacon Hill Press, 2000.

Harper, Steve, and Robert L. Wilson. *Faith and Form: A Unity of Theology and Polity in the United Methodist Tradition.* Grand Rapids: Francis Asbury Press, 1988.

Hawk, Dan. *Every Promise Fulfilled: Contesting Plots in Joshua.* Literary Currents in Biblical Interpretation. Louisville: Westminster/John Knox Press, 1991.

———. *Joshua.* Berit Olam: Studies in Hebrew Narrative & Poetry. Collegeville, Minn.: Liturgical Press, 2000.

Hays, Richard B. *Echoes of Scripture in the Letters of Paul.* New Haven and London: Yale University Press, 1989.

———. *The Faith of Jesus Christ: An Investigation of the Narrative Substructure of Galatians 3:1–4:11.* SBL Dissertation Series 56. Chico, Calif.: Scholars Press, 1983.

———. *First Corinthians.* Interpretation Commentaries. Louisville: Westminster/John Knox Press, 1997.

———. "The Letter to the Galatians." *The New Interpreter's Bible*, vol. 11. Nashville: Abingdon Press, 2000.

———. *The Moral Vision of the New Testament: Community, Cross, New Creation.* San Francisco: HarperSanFrancisco, 1996.

———. *New Testament Ethics: The Story Retold.* The 1997 J. J. Thiessen Lectures. Winnipeg: CMBC Publications, 1998.

Heath, Elaine R. *More Light on the Path: Daily Scripture Readings in Hebrew and Greek.* Grand Rapids: Baker Books, 1998.

Hill, Craig C. *Hellenists and Hebrews: Reappraising Division Within the Earliest Church.* Minneapolis: Fortress Press, 1992.

———. *The Last Days.* Nashville: Abingdon Press, 2001.

———. *Romans.* Oxford Bible Commentary. Oxford: Oxford University Press, 2001.

Hunt, Allen R. *The Inspired Body: Paul, the Corinthians, and Divine Inspiration.* Macon, Ga.: Mercer University Press, 1996.

Johnson, Daniel G. *From Chaos to Restoration: An Integrative Reading of Isaiah 24–27.* Sheffield, England: JSOT Press, 1988.

———. *Neglected Treasure: Rediscovering the Old Testament.* Wilmore, Ky.: Bristol Books, 1989.

Jones, L. Gregory. *Embodying Forgiveness: A Theological Analysis.* Grand Rapids: William B. Eerdmans, 1995.

———. *Transformed Judgment: Toward a Trinitarian Account of the Moral Life.* Notre Dame, Ind.: University of Notre Dame Press, 1990.

Jones, L. Gregory, and Stephen E. Fowl. *Reading in Communion: Scripture and Ethics in Christian Life.* Grand Rapids: William B. Eerdmans, 1991.

Jones, L. Gregory, and Stanley Hauerwas, *Why Narrative? Readings in Narrative Theology.* Grand Rapids: William B. Eerdmans, 1989.

Jones, L. Gregory, and James J. Buckley, eds. *Spirituality and Social Embodiment.* Malden, Mass.: Blackwell Publishers, 1997.

Jones, L. Gregory, and James J. Buckley, eds. *Theology and Scriptural Imagination.* Oxford and Malden, Mass.: Blackwell Publishers, 1998.

Jones, L. Gregory, Robert K. Johnston, and Jonathan R. Wilson, eds. *Grace upon Grace: Essays in Honor of Thomas A. Langford.* Nashville: Abingdon Press, 1999.

Jones, Scott J. *Gathered into One: The World Methodist Conference Speaks.* Nashville: Discipleship Resources, 1982.

———. *John Wesley's Conception and Use of Scripture.* Nashville: Kingswood Books, 1995.

Khiok-khng, Yeo. *Ancestor Worship: Rhetorical and Cross-Cultural Hermeneutical Response* (Chinese). Hong Kong: Chinese Christian Literature Council, 1996.

———. *Between Female and Male: Feminist Theology and Hermeneutic* (Chinese). Hong Kong: Alliance Seminary, 1995.

———. *A Biblical Reflection on Spirituality* (Chinese). Malaysia: Bridge, 1996.

———. *Cross-Cultural Rhetorical Hermeneutics* (Chinese). Jian Dao Supplement, Bible and Hermeneutics 1. Hong Kong: Alliance Seminary, 1995.

———. *Eschatology and Hope: First and Second Epistles to the Thessalonians* (Chinese). Hong Kong: Renewal Resources, 2001.

———. *Pauline Parallels* (Chinese). Hong Kong: International Bible Society, 1997.

———. *Probing into Spirituality* (Chinese). Hong Kong: Chinese Christian Literature Council, 2000.

————. *Rhetorical Interaction in 1 Corinthians 8 and 10: A Formal Analysis with Implications for a Cross-Cultural, Chinese Hermeneutic*. Leiden: E. J. Brill, 1995.

————. *Truth and Life* (Chinese). Kuala Lumpur: Bridge, 1995.

————. *Unveil the Hyprocrisy: Reflection on the Word of God* (Chinese). Hong Kong: Renewal Resources, 2001.

————. *What Has Jerusalem to Do with Beijing? Biblical Interpretation from a Chinese Perspective*. Harrisburg, Pa.: Trinity Press International, 1998.

————, ed. *Lucan Wisdom: A Literary and Theological Reading of Luke* (Chinese) Hong Kong: Excellence, 1995.

————, trans. *Nag Hammadi Library: Codices 1-2* (Chinese). Edited by James M. Robinson and Richard Smith. Hong Kong: Institute of Sino-Christian Studies, 2000.

Kristiansen, Roald E. *Kontekstuell teologi: Bidrag til en nordnorsk kulturteologi* (Contextual theology: Contributions to a north Norwegian cultural theology). Norges Forskningsråd: KULTs skriftserie nr. 49, 1996.

————. *Økoteologi: Religiøsitet og Naturforståelse* (Ecotheology: Religion and the conception of "Nature"). Frederiksberg, Danmark: Anis Forlag, 1993.

Kristiansen, Roald E., and Sölve Anderzén, eds. *Ecology of Spirit. Conference: Cultural Plurality and Religious Identity in the Barents Region*. Umeå: Album Religionum Umense 6, 1998.

Kristiansen, Roald E., and Peter W. Bøckman, eds. *Redaktør av Context: Essays in Honour of Peder Borgen*. Trondheim: Universitetsforlaget Tapir, 1988.

Kristiansen, Roald E, and Nikolay M. Terebikhin, eds. *Religion, Church, and Education in the Barents Region*. Arkhangelsk: Pomoruniversitetet, 1997.

Long, D. Stephen. *The Divine Economy: Theology and the Market*. Radical Orthodoxy Series. London: Routledge, 2000.

————. *The Goodness of God: Theology, Church and the Social Order*. Grand Rapids: Brazos Press, 2001.

————. *Living the Discipline: United Methodist Theological Reflections on War, Civilization, and Holiness*. Grand Rapids: William. B. Eerdmans, 1992.

————. *Tragedy, Tradition, Transformism: The Ethics of Paul Ramsey*. Boulder, Colo: Westview Press, 1993.

Longden, Leicester R., and Thomas C. Oden, eds. *The Wesleyan Theological Heritage: Essays of Albert C. Outler*. Grand Rapids: Zondervan, 1991.

Meade, David G. *Pseudonymity and Canon: An Investigation into the Relationship of Authorship and Authority in Jewish and Early Christian Tradition*. WUNT 39. Tübingen: J.C.B. Mohr (Paul Siebeck), 1986. American edition: Grand Rapids: William B. Eerdmans, 1987.

Miles, Rebekah. *The Bonds of Freedom: Feminist Theology and Christian Realism*. Oxford: Oxford University Press, 2001.

————. *The Pastor as Moral Guide*. Minneapolis: Fortress Press, 1999.

Moore, Steven G. W. *Campus Ministry: The Church at the Frontlines of the Culture*. Seattle: Ivy Jungle Press, 1996.

————. *An Experiment in Prayer*. Seattle: Vision Press, 1995.

————, ed. *The University Through the Eyes of Faith*. Indianapolis: Light and Life Communications, 1998.

Padgett, Alan G. *God, Eternity and the Nature of Time.* Library of Philosophy and Religion, ed. John Hick. New York: St. Martin's Press, 1992.

————, ed. *The Mission of the Church in Methodist Perspective: The World Is My Parish.* Studies in the History of Missions, 10. Lewiston, N.Y.: Edwin Mellen Press, 1992.

————, ed. *Reason and the Christian Religion: Essays in Honour of Richard Swinburne.* Oxford: Oxford University Press, 1994.

Padgett, Alan G., and Steve Wilkens. *Christianity and Western Thought.* Vol. 2: *Faith and Reason in the Nineteenth Century.* Downers Grove: InterVarsity Press, 2000.

————, et al. *God and Time: Four Views.* Downers Grove: InterVarsity Press, 2001.

Paschal, R. Wade, Jr. *Vital Adult Learning.* Nashville: Abingdon Press, 1994.

————. *Serving with Christ: A Study of Jesus' Farewell Commission to His Disciples.* Nashville: Discipleship Resources, 1998.

Pope-Levison, Priscilla. *Evangelization from a Liberation Perspective.* American University Studies, series 7, Theology and Religion, vol. 69. New York: Peter Lang Publishing, 1991.

Pope-Levison, Priscilla., and John R. Levison. *Jesus in Global Contexts.* Louisville: Westminster/ John Knox Press, 1992.

Pope-Levison, Priscilla., and John R. Levison, eds. *Return to Babel: Global Perspectives on the Bible.* Louisville: Westminster/John Knox Press, 1999.

Ruth, Lester. *Accompanying the Journey: A Handbook for Sponsors.* Nashville: Discipleship Resources, 1997.

————. *A Little Heaven Below: Worship at Early Methodist Quarterly Meetings.* Nashville: Kingswood Books, 2000.

Seamands, Stephen A. *Christology and Transition in the Theology of Edwin Lewis.* Lanham, Md.: University Press of America, 1987.

————. *A Conversation with Jesus* Wheaton, Ill.: Victor Books, 1994.

————. *Holiness of Heart and Life.* Nashville: Abingdon Press, 1990.

Simmons, Michael B. *Arnobius of Sicca: Religious Conflict and Competition in the Age of Diocletian.* New York: Oxford University Press, 1995.

Strong, Douglas M. *Perfectionist Politics: Abolitionism and the Religious Tensions of American Democracy.* Syracuse, N.Y.: Syracuse University Press, 1999.

————. *They Walked in the Spirit: Personal Faith and Social Action in America.* Louisville: Westminster/John Knox Press, 1997.

Strong, Douglas M., and J. Philip Wogaman. *Readings in Christian Ethics: A Historical Sourcebook.* Louisville: Westminster/John Knox Press, 1996.

Tyson, John R. *Charles Wesley on Sanctification: A Biographical and Theological Study.* Grand Rapids: Francis Asbury Press, 1986.

————. *In the Midst of Early Methodism: Lady Huntingdon and Her Correspondents.* 2 vols. Metuchen, N. J.: Scarecrow Press, 2001.

————, ed. *Charles Wesley: A Reader,* 2nd ed. New York: Oxford University Press, 1999.

————, ed. *Invitation to Christian Spirituality: An Ecumenical Anthology.* New York: Oxford University Press, 1999.

Wagner, J. Ross. *Heralds of the Good News: Paul and Isaiah "In Concert" in the Letter to the Romans.* Leiden: E. J. Brill, 2000.

Walls, Jerry, *Hell: The Logic of Damnation*. Notre Dame, Ind.: University of Notre Dame Press, 1992.

———. *The Problem of Pluralism: Recovering United Methodist Identity*. Wilmore, Ky.: Good News Books, 1986.

Walls, Jerry L., and Scott R. Burson. *C. S. Lewis and Francis Schaeffer: Lessons for a New Century from the Most Influential Apologists of Our Time*. Downers Grove, Ill.: InterVarsity Press, 1998.

Walters, John R. *Perfection in New Testament Theology: Ethics and Eschatology in Relational Dynamic*. Lewiston, N.Y.: Edwin Mellen Press, 1995.

Watson, Duane F. *Invention, Arrangement, and Style: Rhetorical Criticism of Jude and 2 Peter*. Society of Biblical Literature Dissertation Series 104. Atlanta: Scholars Press, 1988.

———. "The Letter of Jude." *The New Interpreter's Bible*, vol. 12. Nashville: Abingdon Press, 1998.

———. "The Second Letter of Peter." *The New Interpreter's Bible*, vol. 12. Nashville: Abingdon Press, 1998.

———, ed. *Persuasive Artistry: Studies in New Testament Rhetoric in Honor of George A. Kennedy*. Journal for the Study of the New Testament Supplement Series 50. Sheffield, England: Sheffield Academic Press, 1991.

Watson, Duane F., and Alan J. Hauser. *Rhetorical Criticism of the Bible: A Comprehensive Bibliography with Notes on History and Method*. Biblical Interpretation Series 4. Leiden: E. J. Brill, 1994.

Wimmer, John R. *No Pain, No Gain: Hope for Those Who Struggle*. New York: Ballantine Books, 1985.

———. *Torrents of Grace*. New York: Epiphany Books, n.d.

Witherington, Ben, III. *The Acts of the Apostles: A Socio-Rhetorical Commentary*. Grand Rapids: William B. Eerdmans, 1998.

———. *The Christology of Jesus*. Minneapolis: Fortress Press, 1990.

———. *Conflict and Community in Corinth: A Socio-Rhetorical Commentary on 1 and 2 Corinthians*. Grand Rapids: William B. Eerdmans, 1995.

———. *Friendship and Finances in Philippi: The Letter of Paul to the Philippians*. Valley Forge, Pa.: Trinity Press International, 1994.

———. *Grace in Galatia: A Commentary on St. Paul's Letter to the Galatians*. Grand Rapids: William B. Eerdmans, 1998.

———. *Jesus, Paul, and the End of the World: A Comparative Study in New Testament Eschatology*. Downers Grove, Ill.: InterVarsity Press, 1992.

———. *The Jesus Quest: The Third Search for the Jew of Nazareth*. Downers Grove, Ill.: InterVarsity Press, 1995.

———. *Jesus the Sage: The Pilgrimage of Wisdom*. Minneapolis: Fortress Press, 1994.

———. *Jesus the Seer: The Progress of Prophecy*. Peabody, Mass.: Hendrickson Publishers, 1999.

———. *John's Wisdom: A Commentary on the Fourth Gospel*. Louisville: Westminster/John Knox Press, 1995.

———. *The Many Faces of the Christ: The Christologies of the New Testament and Beyond*. New York: Crossroad Publishing, 1998.

———. *The Paul Quest: The Renewed Search for the Jew of Tarsus.* Downers Grove, Ill.: InterVarsity Press, 1998.

———. *Paul's Narrative Thought World: The Tapestry of Tragedy and Triumph* Louisville: Westminster/John Knox Press, 1994.

———. *The Realm of the Reign: Reflections on the Dominion of God.* Nashville: Discipleship Resources, 1999.

———. *Women in the Earliest Churches.* Cambridge: Cambridge University Press, 1988.

———. *Women and the Genesis of Christianity.* Cambridge: Cambridge University Press, 1990.

———. *Women in the Ministry of Jesus: A Study of Jesus' Attitudes to Women and Their Roles as Reflected in His Early Life.* Cambridge: Cambridge University Press, 1984.

———, ed. *History, Literature, and Society in the Book of Acts.* Cambridge: Cambridge University Press, 1996.

ABBREVIATIONS

Letters (Telford)   *The Letters of the Rev. John Wesley, A. M.* Edited by John Telford. 8 vols. London: Epworth Press, 1931.

Works   *The Bicentennial Edition of the Works of John Wesley.* Edited by Frank Baker and Richard P. Heitzenrater. 35 volumes projected. Nashville: Abingdon Press, 1984ff. (Volumes 7, 11, 25, and 26 originally appeared as the *Oxford Edition of the Works of John Wesley.* Oxford: Clarendon Press, 1975–83).

Works (Jackson)   *The Works of John Wesley.* Edited by Thomas Jackson. 14 vols. 3rd edition. London: Wesleyan Methodist Book Room, 1872; reprint edition Grand Rapids: Baker, 1979.

INDEX OF SUBJECTS
AND NAMES

INDEX OF SCRIPTURE REFERENCES